INITIATED

*UAP, Dreams, Depression, Delusions,
Shadow People, Psychosis, Sleep Paralysis, and Pandemics*

MATTHEW ROBERTS

Initiated: UAP, Dreams, Depression, Delusions, Shadow People, Psychosis, Sleep Paralysis, and Pandemics

Copyright © 2020 by Matthew Roberts

All rights reserved. No part of this book may be reproduced or transmitted in any form or by any means, electronic or mechanical, including photocopying, recording, or by any information storage and retrieval system without the written permission of the author, except where permitted by law.

Edited by George Verongos and Katarina Castillo.

Cover Produced by Matt Lacasse.

ISBN: 978-0-578-79658-1

The passage of this book to those ready for the instruction will attract the attention of such as are prepared to receive the Teaching. And, likewise, when the pupil is ready to receive the truth, then will this little book come to him, or her. Such is The Law.
–The Kybalion

There are many who are called, but few who become bacchoi.
–Plato

TABLE OF CONTENTS

FOREWORD i
NOTE TO THE READER ix
THE CALL TO ADVENTURE AND REFUSAL OF THE CALL 1
SUPERNATURAL AID 53
PASSING THE THRESHOLD INTO THE BELLY OF THE BEAST ... 79
CHALLENGES AND TEMPTATIONS; ABYSS DEATH AND REBIRTH 105
TRANSFORMATION AND ATONEMENT 125
RETURN 171
THE PSYCHOLOGY OF TRANSFORMATION 189
MODERN AND ANCIENT EVIDENCE 263
    Book of Revelation 284
    Ancient Evidence/Greek Mythology and the Homeric Hymns . 299
    The Renaissance 308
    Reddit 318
SUBTLE MANIFESTATIONS OF CONSCIOUSNESS 331
    Modern Myth 343
    Elias Hicks 353
ACCIDENTS, BELIEFS, AND SUPERSTITIONS 359
SELECTED BIBLIOGRAPHY 413

FOREWORD

I was honored when Matthew first contacted me in 2018. After he read my book, *Incident at Devils Den*, he concluded that we had many shared experiences and parallels in our pasts. He wanted to discuss and compare our stories. Like me, Matt recognized the differences, commonalities, and parallel aspects of our experiences. At times in our lives we both faced being under the control of otherworldly forces.

Like so many others who have contacted me over the years, what Matthew truly sought was validation. Confirmation that he was not losing his grip on reality. Because of the sensitive nature of his duties in the USN, Matthew's ability to discuss his encounters candidly with a friend or colleague were limited. My career in the legal world and position as a public servant made it impossible to tell my story openly for 40 years.

We had so many things in common. I understood him immediately. It's an odd thing when one experiencer meets another and discovers that common ground. The stories are not identical, but the experience of being manipulated and physically controlled by these entities, ETs, interdimensional beings, or demons… whatever you call them, is the same.

While I've experienced the unknown for a lifetime, one major event in my life occurred in June 1977 while I was on active duty in the United States Air Force. I never voluntarily told a soul what my friend and I witnessed that day in a remote Arkansas wilderness. No one except my wife. I waited until six years after my retirement in 2012 before telling my story. I published *Devils Den* in 2018. I knew I'd face criticism from my peers in the legal community. Damn the consequences.

I was even more honored when Matthew asked me to read his manuscript and write a foreword for this book. In addition to the candid facts disclosed, Matthew also shares with you his personal attempts to process these encounters and events. It is truly a journey.

While many folks would have sought comfort and understanding from their religious beliefs, Matthew's life's anchor was not in organized, dogmatic religion. He chose the writings of Greek mythology and other sources of wisdom. The ideas in these writings have withstood the test of time. It's a shame they're no longer taught in secondary school in the United States. I admit, I am not well-versed in the subject of mythology. It is not necessary to have a familiarity with the topic because Matthew does such an excellent job of comparing and contrasting his reality with the characters in these mythologies.

I recall reading Plato's story about the cave dwellers and a world defined by shadows. If you have never read the story, I encourage you to read it. It's relatively short, but it is as relevant today as it was when written. I am also a lifelong fan of Dr. Carl Jung's work in symbolism and other belief systems that Matthew encountered along his journey.

I have an undergraduate degree in psychology, but I'm not a psychologist or certified therapist. However, after a lifelong career in the law, practicing as an attorney representing both plaintiff and defendants, I'm a fairly good judge of someone's veracity. Especially after several hours of phone conversation and the exchange of many emails. I use this "vetting process" to separate the "wheat from the chaff" when I interact with people claiming experiences with the paranormal.

It became obvious to me that we were "cut from the same cloth." We were both prior military and we both found ourselves trying to process our incredible esoteric experiences.

I've received over 1,400 emails from readers of my book wishing to candidly share their encounters with the unknown. Matthew was on active duty at the time we spoke. He was under certain constraints preventing his complete candor. I understood. Divulging secrets, even by a benign misspoken word, carried consequences for him personally, career wise and most importantly potential danger to the safety and security of the United States, whom he had sworn to defend.

Matthew Roberts is a 16 year veteran who served in the United States Naval Intelligence Service. When he began his enlistment, like everyone else newly enlisted, he was tested to determine his aptitude in varying areas. This is how initiates to active duty military are placed job wise. The tests used have been utilized in this selection process for over 75 years. It's how the US Navy determine who's best suited to be a cook, a radar operator, or engine mechanic.

Very few candidates possess the deductive reasoning skills Matthew's test results proved. But high test scores alone are only half of the selection process. Initiates must demonstrate high character traits and rock solid stability to be selected. They are subject to a background test that involves Naval Intelligence officers knocking on the doors of friends, neighbors, teachers and the like. They conduct personal interviews to determine what type of character traits define Matthew Roberts. Those with transgressions in their past involving truthfulness and honesty are eliminated at this step. Many are considered but few are chosen. The result is that our intelligence services are composed of the "best of the best." Honest and highly intelligent men and women

In case you're unfamiliar, "cryptology" is defined in the New Oxford Dictionary as "the art of creating and deciphering codes." In today's modern military that skill set is much broader than the simple description implies, solving word problems with paper and pencil. It's a technological world of complex digital information entrusted to the cryptographer to draft accurately and transmit securely.

So important is Matthew's message that in March of 2020 he left the United States Navy for civilian life. He decided his ability to write and speak freely about face-to-face encounters with extraterrestrial beings and their crafts, outweighed his opportunity for personal gain and financial security. His message, and its high cost, proves the urgency in this matter is justified. As we say in the legal community, "time is of the essence." Perhaps in the entire history of humanity has that never been truer.

In many ways, Matthew's book was the catalyst to share the experiences of others, people who shared their personal experiences with me and allowed me to share them with you. His accounts are so detailed as to defy credulity. Matthew is not a man subject to confabulation or exaggeration. In our 2018 telephone conversations, Matthew weighted his words carefully, correcting me if I made an unintentional embellishment.

By writing this book, Matthew assumed the risks involved. It's something that could carry consequences and expose him to ridicule. I salute Matthew's sacrifice. He was just four years away from retirement, likewise, as a veteran myself, I understand the courage it takes to write candidly about experiences with the paranormal that many cannot accept as truth.

In 2015, Matthew was aboard the Theodore Roosevelt as part of a "strike group" or collection of naval warships. He was onboard during the events that brought us the now declassified Gimbal and Go Fast footage. Unfortunately, he cannot go into the details of the events that brought us that footage. He refused even after my encouragement to do so. I respect that and consider him a patriot in that regard.

During his career as a cryptologist, he participated in numerous deployments all over the world. He was chosen to train others in the subtleties of the craft as they prepared for deployments.

After the workups and subsequent deployment of the Theodore Roosevelt strike group he transferred to his new duty station where he worked as an analyst at the Office of Naval Intelligence in Washington DC. It was during his time at the Office of Naval Intelligence that he began to experience subsequent personal experiences with the phenomenon. Speaking from experience, it's not uncommon for these esoteric events to "ramp up" after an encounter.

In March of 2020 Matthew left the Office of Naval Intelligence forever. I suspect his encounters with a blue lady will continue episodically for many years. Matthew is not the only human to encounter the blue lady. She's become well documented in the UFO world for years.

Within his experiences he found an ultimate truth that he describes simply as "consciousness." The breadth and scope of consciousness exceeds any written text. Science today does not understand the nature of consciousness. It's location within the brain has never been found. It's defined simply as "a state of awareness." Evidence now shows consciousness may reside outside and separate from the human body. The mystery crosses lines between medicine and physics.

Matthew's goal is to raise awareness of the phenomenon. Also, to help us to question and attempt to understand consciousness and its deep implications for the human race. He wants the world to know that there are dire results waiting for the human race in denying the existence of the phenomenon.

By world governments keeping knowledge of this phenomenon a closely guarded secret, humanity is denied the opportunity to embrace Whitley's "New World" and foster a global mindset of higher consciousness. I was told by an entity in 2017 that mankind "must learn to act globally and not regionally." This book may leave you questioning the world around you that we take for granted daily.

Terry Lovelace
Bestselling author of *Incident at Devils Den*
Former Asst. Attorney General
USAF Veteran
Lifelong Experiencer

NOTE TO THE READER

I wrote you this book out of my unconditional love for mankind; to be etched in the timeline of the human experience as a testament to a brutally painful truth; to the difficult journey we all must take; to the beauty of what we must become; and to the strength and resiliency of the human race. We all have value. We will all have a role to play in our journey homeward toward the stars.

Matthew Roberts 2020

Initiated:

UAP, Dreams, Depression, Delusions, Shadow People, Psychosis, Sleep Paralysis, and Pandemics

Chapter One

THE CALL TO ADVENTURE AND REFUSAL OF THE CALL

As I sit down and begin to write this book about my experiences involving what people currently describe as aliens and the paranormal, I wonder where or how I can begin to describe the indescribable. I know that no matter what words I put on paper, I can never do it the justice it deserves. I have beginnings and endings rolling through my mind. Life is full of them; endless cycles of beginnings and endings that, at times, unexpectedly come crashing through your life like a wrecking ball through a brick wall. We prefer the kinder and gentler beginnings, such as the birth of a child, or a wedding; while shielding ourselves from life's harsher moments; but if we don't view them both equally as the gifts that they are, then we have lost something very precious that we may never regain. It is through the chaos of the wrecking ball that we discover who we really are, and it is in both the gentler and the harsher moments that we should apply that knowledge of self. We tell these stories of beginnings and endings as cycles of the hero in human mythology. If we could see through to all of the veiled truths hidden in this mythology spanning the ages of human existence, we would begin to understand how to live our lives; who and what we are. Who among us hasn't envisioned themselves as the hero? It is the hero myth playing constantly in the background of the human subconscious that keeps us reaching ever onward and upward for that which lies just beyond our grasp. The myths teach us that the hero endures great hardship on their journey to becoming the savior.

We speak of freedom a lot here in the United States, yet so few of us have actually experienced freedom or can even wrap our minds around what this concept actually means. One can never know freedom unless they have known the shackles of bondage; one can never know pleasure without the knowledge of pain. I know there can be no beginnings without endings; no life without death; it is an inescapable and very painful truth. Even as mild-mannered, level-headed, and emotionally stable as I thought I was; I think about the person I once was, and will never be again; full of hate and anger; consumed by fear. I now see that for what it was; a lifelong journey to the knowledge of self—to my center. "Know thyself," is a rather famous saying and was inscribed on the wall at the ancient Greek Temple of Delphi. Just like the word freedom, it is an enigma that almost nobody truly understands. The mythologic hero understands these seemingly simple words on a level that transcends the human condition and mortal existence. Through knowledge of self he transcends it all; becoming a living god; experiencing a liberation and a freedom that few of us have actually known.

In the beginning of 2017, I knew what I was doing, and where I was going; I was sure that I had life figured out. My hubris was about to be exposed in the most humiliating, painful, and terrifying ways, as I learned the truth of what it means to be human. In understanding this truth and the immense responsibility that truth carries with it, I know that I can never again partake of any feast of hate, anger, or fear. I can never again allow these toxins entrance to my soul. It is the heaviest of burdens and the greatest of blessings.

These days, I approach burdens and blessings as I approach pleasure or pain; I embrace them as one and the same. I do so without reservation or judgment; head-on, from the refuge of my tower of inner strength and wisdom while doing my best to lead a life of grace and virtue. So many of us are lost at sea, drifting aimlessly, tossed about by the storms of life—our vision clouded by the fog of emotion. There are always beacons of light showing us the way home; if we would only bother to lift our heads and search the horizon of our inner being for them.

My goal in writing this book is that it may act as such a beacon; guiding you home; calling you home through the darkness of the storm. For me, the words of the most famous of beacons takes on a much deeper meaning; a meaning in word and physical form that too few of us have known. She stands as testament to the powerful myth playing in the collective human subconscious. Standing as a rock in the storm with her crown of golden light and immortal torch of fire held high she says:

> *Give me your tired, your poor, your huddled masses yearning to breathe free, the wretched refuse of your teeming shore. Send these, the homeless, tempest-tost to me, I lift my lamp beside the golden door!*

I currently live and work in Washington DC. It is the capitol city of a nation that possesses this beacon of wisdom that we don't understand, and I worry that we will never live up to what it truly represents. Many of us learn this poem in school and we see her form in images without ever understanding that there is a much deeper meaning that has to do with the true nature of the universe in this great statue of ours; a terrifying, dangerous, and beautiful truth. I see tour busses constantly touring the city and I wonder what future tour groups will see hundreds or thousands of years from now, and what will their guides tell them about this place as they gaze on whatever remains of our capitol.

Two possibilities come to mind. I've been all over the world on these types of tours and the story is the same no matter what the ancient city. "This is where it ended. There once was a great, wealthy and powerful civilization that existed here; and these are the ruins of their once thriving capitol city. They succumbed to their own greed and fear, destroying their civilization from the inside out." I wonder if this is what will be said of this city one day? Some may say it's inevitable. I can envision a second possibility. A tour guide leading a group through the city saying, "This is where it began. The events that transpired here are why humanity now exists as a tower of strength and a beacon of light in the universe. The spark that lit the fire of the soul of humanity was struck here; and these are the ruins of that city."

No doubt there will be those who dismiss my work as the ramblings of a madman led through delusion by the noxious fumes of swamp gas, light phenomenon through temperature inversion, ball lightning, and weather balloons that came together in a perfect storm within my bedroom to bring you this work. Nonetheless, I am going to share with you my experiences. Along the way, I will point out others that have had the same experiences throughout the history of humanity, giving us our rich history of religion and mythology that, at times, has been misguided at best, and weaponized at its worst. In doing so, I hope to instill in you the gravity and seriousness of the matter at hand. In giving you examples, my desire is that you will take a closer look and begin to scratch the surface of this for yourself. In doing so, you will become a quester of truth and will see that everything I experienced, as disturbing as it may seem to some, is supported by fact—a truth that resides in our stories of fiction and myth.

I began playing some music to set the mood as I began to write. "Heaven" by Angels and Airwaves was the first song that popped up. "Heaven" has become one of my new favorite songs, and I listen to it often. Some of the imagery in the unofficial music video is what I picture when I think about my favorite mythology from ancient Greece. For me, what comes to mind is the natural beauty of the poplar tree and its uses in mythology. Specifically what comes to mind is the quaking aspen or (Populus tremula). It is a poplar that is prevalent in North America and can be found growing in some of nature's most beautiful and striking landscapes. Places like Crested Butte, Colorado. If you look up images of the quaking aspen you will see what I mean—the autumn landscape of rocky outcroppings high in the mountains covered in these white-barked trees and yellow leaves. It arouses in the mind the air of an inspired fairy tale. It seems as though these trees must have been placed in this landscape to remind us of what heaven must look like.

The quaking aspen gets its name from the way its leaves seem to tremble noisily with fear in the slightest of shifting breezes. To the ancient Greeks however, the poplar tree was viewed quite differently. In ancient Greece, the wind was said to carry the messages of the gods. When the wind would blow, the poplar's leaves would become excited as the tree tuned in to receive its divine correspondence. Hercules was given a crown made of the poplar at the end of his hero's journey, symbolic of his successful struggle to transcend the human condition and become divine. The goddess Persephone, who was queen of the underworld, kept a poplar grove outside the gates to the underworld. Symbolic of the divinity that awaits those who successfully return from their treacherous decent into the underworld.

The true beauty of this tree is not just visual. As a living organism, it's equally stunning. This tree has the ability to prune itself, giving it its very clean, manicured appearance. Its bark is capable of photosynthesis; enabling it to produce food for itself, even in the dead of winter. It's incredibly resilient and recovers quickly from forest fires. The key to this resiliency is hidden underground in its root system. It may seem that these trees are individual living organisms at a glance above ground. Underground, however, it is revealed that a forest of these trees is in fact a single living organism that is connected through a large knot of interconnected roots. The ancient Greeks knew this and it's why they used it in their mythology. To them, the poplar represented natural perfection, independence, fearlessness, and beauty all encapsulated in this divine plant. To the ancient Greeks it represented everything humanity was capable of becoming.

There is a Greek myth concerning the Greek goddess Persephone who kept poplars outside the gates of the underworld. It is the story of how she became the queen of the underworld. I recently came across this ancient Greek myth in the form of a famous hymn. It was written in the same poetic style and form as the *Iliad* and the *Odyssey* by Homer. It is called the *Homeric Hymn to Demeter*, and I feel it fits perfectly in the beginning of this book. To understand the journey one must be familiar with this myth. The myth's importance in the hero's journey is the reason this story was central to the ancient Greek Mysteries. They were known as the Eleusinian Mysteries as they were practiced at the temple to Demeter in Eleusis, Greece at the foot of the Acropolis.

As there were in many cultures throughout the world, the Mysteries were schools that individuals were initiated into. They were central to the Greek religious experience. The *Homeric Hymn to Demeter* concerns the goddess Demeter and her daughter Persephone. To the ancient Greeks, Demeter was goddess of vegetation, harvest, sacred law, and the cycle of life and death. Demeter and Persephone were immortal goddesses that were always depicted as very beautiful young women with soft feminine features. Despite these depictions, Persephone's name in ancient Greek means *the destroyer and bringer of death.* Some of the inhabitants of ancient Greece dared not speak her name out of the fear that they might summon death to their doorstep.

In the *Homeric Hymn to Demeter,* Persephone is out picking and admiring flowers with the daughters of Okeanos on the plane of Nysa. She picks roses, crocus, violets, irises, and the hyacinth. She comes across the narcissus flower which was purposely designed by Gaia, the goddess of the earth, to be so beautiful that Persephone would be distracted by its beauty. It was Hades, the god of the underworld that directed Gaia to construct such a flower. All of this was done with the blessing of Zeus, the king of the gods and Persephone's father, who had agreed to the plan of Hades' abduction of Persephone.

As she is distracted while gazing on the beauty of the narcissus flower, Hades grabs Persephone from his chariot drawn by undead horses. Persephone screams in her immortal voice as she is abducted, but none of the other immortals or mortals hear her scream, except Hecate and Helios. The goddess Hecate was the goddess of magic, witchcraft, night, moon, ghosts, and necromancy. Helios was the god of the sun, guardian of oaths, and keeper of human and immortal sight.

Hades brings Persephone to the underworld to be his wife. Persephone had hope that she would one day see her mother again, as she continued to call out in her immortal voice that resounded throughout the world. Persephone's mother, Demeter, heard her daughter's cries and was stricken with grief.

Distraught by the disappearance of her daughter, she puts on a dark cloak and sets out to find her beloved Persephone. For nine days she wanders and nobody can tell her what has happened to her daughter. In her grief, she does not partake of ambrosia, the immortal nectar of the gods, and refuses to bathe her body in water. On the tenth day of grieving, Hecate comes to Demeter with torch in hand and asks Demeter which one of the gods or mortals has taken Persephone. Hecate explains that she heard Persephone cry out but did not see who abducted her.

Together, Demeter and Hecate set out to visit the god Helios, the seeing eye of gods and men. When they arrive, Demeter asks Helios who has taken her daughter. Helios tells Demeter that Persephone was abducted by Hades with the blessing of Zeus. Demeter is devastated by the news, even though Helios tells her it's not that bad. In her grief, Demeter shuns the company of the other gods on Olympus. Instead, she wanders the earth visiting various mortal cities disguised as an old woman.

The disguised Demeter ends up in Eleusis, where she rests near a well along the road that leads to the house of the Lord of Eleusis. As the disguised Demeter sits under the shade of an olive tree, the Lord's four daughters come to the well. The daughters ask this old woman who she is and why she's wandered so far from the city. The disguised Demeter tells the girls her name is Doso. She tells the four daughters she is from Crete but that she was kidnapped from there by pirates. The ship she was on with these pirates was beached on the shores of Thorikos. There the ship was boarded by many women from the mainland. The disguised Demeter tells the Lord's daughters that she escaped as the pirates began preparing dinner next to the beached ship. She then wandered and was unsure where she was exactly. She told the girls she was looking for a house with children in which she could do a woman's work. The daughters invite the disguised Demeter to the palace to care for their baby brother Demophon.

Demophon was not well, as he was born to their older mother. Demeter assists the girls in filling jars of water from the well and they proceed to the palace. When they reach the palace, the daughters rush into the chamber where their mother is seated with Demophon in her lap. Demeter waits in the entryway wearing her dark cloak and a veil over her face. Her head nearly touches the ceiling and the dark entryway is bathed in her divine light. When the Lady of Eleusis sees the disguised Demeter, she is struck with a sense of awe and holy wonder. The Lady offers the disguised Demeter her splendid seat. Demeter refuses the splendid chair and instead sits on a stool.

Demeter sat on this stool for a long time and made no attempt to speak. She sat depressed thinking about her daughter Persephone with her eyes cast down at the floor. An old woman, Iambe, came along and started making many jokes with Demeter. This made Demeter laugh and turned her mood in another direction. From that point on, Iambe became a part of Demeter's sacred rites performed at her temple in Eleusis.

The Lady of Eleusis offered Demeter a cup with honey-sweet wine but the disguised Demeter refused the wine claiming that it was divinely ordained that she not drink red wine. Instead, Demeter asked for some water and barley with pennyroyal to drink. The Lady of Eleusis prepares this drink for the disguised Demeter. The Lady of Eleusis then tells Demeter that she has the appearance of having been born to nobility. The Lady asked the disguised Demeter to care for her son who was not well. The disguised Demeter tells the Lady she will care for him and she has the perfect antidote for Demophon.

The goddess Demeter begins to care for the boy with her immortal hands and his family is amazed at how well the boy is progressing under the care of this old woman. The boy was growing like a daimon. His parents looked on him as they would look on the gods. The secret to his amazing recovery was that Demeter, still disguised as an old woman, decided to turn Demophon into an immortal god. She did this to repay the family for their kindness towards her. Secretly she had been delivering the boy rites by bathing him in ambrosia and placing Demophon into a fire to burn like a log every night; burning away his mortal soul.

Demeter is discovered by the Lady of Eleusis as she burns Demophon in the fire one night. The Lady of Eleusis reacts badly to this sight and screams. Demeter becomes angry at the response of the boy's mother and decides to reveal herself as the goddess Demeter. She chides the boy's mother for behaving like a silly mortal and for being unable to tell the difference from good fortune and bad. She tells the Lady she would have made the boy an immortal god. But the boy will now only be immortal for a short time just by virtue of having sat in her lap and slept in her immortal arms. Because the boy's mother had interrupted the process, Demeter was forced to halt the ritual and the action could not be undone.

Demeter proclaims that from now until the end of time the sons of Eleusis will have a great battle among themselves at the right time every year. Demeter then demands that a temple be erected to her, the goddess Demeter, at the foot of the Acropolis. She then shed her dark robes and old age. She was enveloped in beauty as her divine light shone like a bolt of lightning; illuminating the entire palace. The Lady of Eleusis fell to her knees at the sight of Demeter in all her glory; forgetting all about her son. The four daughters ran downstairs from their chambers and grabbed Demophon. They began washing him as he gasped and sputtered. They hugged him but he could not be comforted because he was now being held by nursemaids who were far inferior. The family prayed all night to the goddess Demeter as they trembled with fear. The next morning the Lord of Eleusis gathered his people and explained what had happened. He informed them they had to build a temple to the goddess Demeter as she has demanded. The people obeyed and built her temple.

Demeter remained at this temple for a year. During this year of her absence from Olympus, the human race suffered dearly as did

Demeter in the grief over her daughter, Persephone. Demeter, the nurturer of the earth, was absent from her divine duties. No seeds grew. There was no harvest. The people of the earth were starving.

Zeus noticed what was happening and sent different gods from Olympus to offer gifts to Demeter if she would just return to Olympus; but she refused. She stated that she would only return if she could see her daughter Persephone. Zeus then dispatches Hermes, the messenger and scribe of the gods, to the underworld to retrieve Persephone who was in great pain at the hands of Hades. Hermes tells Hades that Zeus requests Persephone be set free. Hades gives up Persephone and tells her to go to her mother, but before he lets her leave, Hades gives Persephone a pomegranate seed to eat. Hades did this because when one eats in the underworld, they must return, and he did not want Persephone to leave forever. He wanted her to return.

Persephone then climbs into a chariot with Hermes and they head for Demeter, who is at her temple in Eleusis. When Hermes and Persephone arrive in Eleusis, Persephone rushes to her mother telling her everything that had transpired. She tells her mother that she was about to leave the underworld when Hades gave her a pomegranate seed and compelled her to eat it, but that she did not want to. When Demeter asked her how she came to be abducted by Hades, Persephone states that she was out in the meadows picking flowers with the daughters of Okeanos. She picked many flowers including narcissus. As she did this, the ground opened up underneath her and Hades grabbed her. She explained to her mother that he then took her down into the underworld against her will. Persephone and Demeter spent the rest of the day happily enjoying each other's company.

Hecate, the goddess of magic, witchcraft, night, moon, ghosts, and necromancy welcomed Persephone back with many embraces. From that day forward Hecate became Persephone's attendant and substitute queen of the underworld.

Zeus then dispatched his mother, Rhea, to bring Demeter back to the company of the gods at Olympus. Zeus tells Rhea that she is to inform Demeter that her daughter Persephone must spend one-third of the year in the underworld and the other two-thirds of the year would be spent in the company of Demeter and the other gods in Olympus.

Before Rhea arrived at the fields of Eleusis near Demeter's temple, they were barren and dead but began to flourish as soon as Rhea arrived, like springtime. Soon the fields were overflowing with grain. Demeter and Rhea rejoiced in each other's company. Rhea asked Demeter to come back to Olympus and to make the harvest for the humans. And so Demeter obeyed. Immediately she set up the harvest and all was well.

Demeter then showed the human people how to perform the rites and rituals at her temple so they could deliver them correctly for themselves. The holy ritual could not be ignored and was not to be spoken of. Fear of the gods would hold back any speaking out. Blessed is he who among the earthbound has seen these things. But he who is uninitiated into these rites and takes no part in them; will not in death receive the things that initiates do. When Demeter finished her instructions, she and Persephone returned to Olympus where they abided at the side of Zeus.

Blessed is he, whom they (Demeter and Persephone), being kind, decide to love among earthbound mortals. To him they send riches to reside in his hearth.

Today's scholars read this mythology as a way that the ancients poetically spoke of the changing of the seasons, but it's so much more than that. As with all Greek mythology, it is in fact meant to teach. This hymn was one of 33 *Homeric Hymns*.

The Eleusinian Mysteries were known as one of the greater mysteries. The would-be initiates had to graduate from the lesser mysteries before continuing on to the greater mysteries. The truth of these mysteries were known only to its initiates and was never written down. All initiates had to be sponsored by a previous initiate who would remain at their side throughout the nine-month experience. In the temple to Demeter at Eleusis, there was an area where sacred artifacts were kept. They were only to be viewed and handled by initiates. There are accounts of children hopping the fence to the compound and viewing these objects. If discovered, they were immediately sentenced to death. As I write this, I believe the reason for this is that these artifacts were in fact artifacts of the "gods." The Knights Templar knew of this and it's what drove them to seek true religious artifacts all over the world. The same was true for the Nazis, as they understood that these artifacts could be technological and powerful in nature.

Some would argue the Mysteries were practiced in Greece for some 2000 years. Greek art found around Eleusis concerning the Eleusinian Mysteries depicts an initiate standing between Demeter and Persephone as they hold torches to him. It depicts the pain of initiation and the burning away of the mortal soul.

Plutarch was a priest at the Temple of Delphi in ancient Greece. The Temple of Delphi was the seat of the oracle, a female priestess the Greek people would consult on matters of life. Despite the threat of death, Plutarch did leave a limited description of the Mysteries.

> *The candidates were made to roam through winding subterranean passages. It was a peregrination through the dark, a journey to an invisible end, which put to the test all one's presence of mind. And then at the moment of decision, the initiates were subjected to terrors. They experienced shudders and trembling, they sweated with fear and were paralyzed with terror, until light was gradually admitted, and the day restored. With sacred chants and dancing choruses a magnificent place opened before them... The initiated was crowned with garlands, and by the side of pure and holy men he enjoyed the festival of rebirth.*

The Romans had their own version of the Mysteries that they borrowed from the Greeks, which were celebrated during the Saturnalia Festival. Later, these mysteries became the Gnostic Mysteries and made it into the Bible in the form of the Book of Revelation. Its counterpart in India is a book called the Bhagavad Gita in the Hindu religious texts known as the Mahabharata. In Egypt it was known as the Book of the Dead. I will break all of this down later in the book.

The Mysteries were always practiced around the world at the same time of year beginning around the autumnal equinox with the harvest moon through the winter solstice and ending in the spring. The Mysteries were practiced in Mesopotamia, Göbekli Tepe, Ancient Egypt, Asia, Australia, and even North and South America. I make this assertion based on some of the mythology of these cultures as well as iconography and artifacts that have been unearthed. I see evidence that they were practiced worldwide and always around the same time of year. One could argue that these mysteries have been practiced by humanity for at least the past 13,000 years. I would argue, however, that some of the cave paintings of early man also depicted some of this same iconography, dating back at least 30,000 to 40,000 years. As we will see, these traditions go back even farther than 30,000 to 40,000 years, and I would speculate many hundreds of thousands of years.

I don't seek to rewrite the many books that are out there that I know to be true treasures of humanity. Instead, I seek to share with you my own journey in the hopes it will act as a catalyst for yours. In this book I have embellished nothing, if anything I have left some things out, as hard as it may be to believe, all of this actually happened to me. I was never regressed or put under hypnosis to remember any of this. As you read this book leading up to September and then the winter solstice, I encourage you to put it down and read the books I read along my journey. The most important advice I can give is that you isolate yourself to the extent that you can with these books. Don't concern yourself with others. Turn your gaze inward. Turn off your TV. As we have already learned in the *Homeric Hymn to Demeter*, if one eats, or is distracted, while in the underworld, they must return.

While writing this little bit of the introduction, I found myself unable to sleep late one night. I turned on the TV and started flipping through channels. I came across a movie that was just starting called *2010: The Year We Make Contact*. It's the sequel to *2001: A Space Odyssey*. The main character finds himself once again heading back to the mysterious monolith that was discovered orbiting Jupiter. Throughout *2001* and *2010,* there is the air of tension mixed with a creepy uneasiness. In *2010,* the main character has a run-in with a character named Bowman who disappeared into the monolith during the first movie and was presumed dead. Bowman appears to various characters in seemingly paranormal ways. He appears as an old man, a baby, and as himself at the time he disappeared. He warns the characters repeatedly that the characters on the ships around Jupiter must leave the orbit of Jupiter in two days. When pressed on what is going to happen in two days, Bowman simply replies, "Something wonderful."

***

It was the end of September 2017. After a brush with death in the form of a massive saddle pulmonary embolism, I was being discharged from the hospital. I hadn't shaven in a week. As I looked at my reflection in the hospital bathroom mirror, I noticed that I had two bald spots on my neck and chin where I was no longer growing facial hair. It looked ridiculous. While I stood there in my hospital gown shaving with the awful disposable razor they gave me, I examined the spots with a deep sigh and thought, *What is this…? These are the scars I'm left with after all of this I suppose.* I felt a little silly to worry about the spots. It seemed so vain considering I easily could have died.

The odd part about everything I had just been through was that at no point was I ever worried. At no point did I ever feel like I was in danger. I somehow knew this wasn't going to kill me. Being the ever introspective person that I am, I also had a strong feeling that my life would never be the same. Not because of the seriousness of my situation, but because of something else I couldn't quite put my finger on as I stood shaving in the mirror at that moment, but I did have this sense that something had caught up to me, and everything was about to change. Little did I know how correct this moment of intuition would turn out to be.

In writing these words, and thinking of what I have endured, I am becoming incredibly emotional. Thinking about the worst days that were so packed with incredible pain that my teeth were chattering and filled with so much terror that all I could manage to do was lie on the floor in the corner of my bedroom shivering and crying like a baby; while everything I perceived to be reality was systematically shattered and crashing down around me. This is all so deeply personal and so incredibly painful that, when I speak about these events, I often fall into a mess of incoherent emotion. This incident; this brush with death in the form of these blood clots, only marked the beginning of my descent into hell, where Persephone, the destroyer and bringer of death, was patiently anticipating my arrival. Standing with her mother Demeter, torches in hand, ready to burn away my mortal soul and initiate me into the truth and beauty of what it means to be human.

> *Whenever two previously unrelated things are joined together a scar, or a seam if you will, is always the result; and when individuals are joined to previously unknown and unconscious aspects of themselves, scarring is the painful and inescapable result. It can only be ever thus: only when one is faced with something overwhelming can the archetype of wholeness be constellated. So do not be ashamed of scars. Valorize them; caress them; trace their course in your skin and in your mind's eye. Scars are roadways drawn onto maps of flesh, leading always to the beautiful truths buried deep within oneself.*
>
> –Bradley Olson Ph.D.
> Cultural Mythology–MythBlast | Scares and Scars,
> The Joseph Campbell Foundation

As I got ready for my discharge, the doctor that had been taking care of me walked in.

"Are you ready to go home?" she asked with a smile on her face.

"I am," I said in a raspy, weak voice. She was thin and young. She was wearing blue scrubs with a white lab coat and long blonde hair pulled back in a ponytail.

"Well, I have your discharge paperwork here and I just need to go over it with you before you go. The saddle pulmonary embolism you suffered was very serious and it could happen again," she explained. "Because of this you will have to take blood thinners for the rest of your life, which makes you non-deployable as you will need to be stationed near a medical treatment facility at all times. Unfortunately, because of the blood thinners and the inability to deploy, your medical record is going to be submitted to a medical review board and you may not be able to continue military service, depending on the findings of the board." She paused waiting for some reaction, but I had none. "How long have you been in the navy?" she asked.

"Fifteen years with ten years at sea," I said.

"It would seem a shame to kick you out so close to your twenty-year retirement mark, but I don't know what the board will decide, I've seen these things go either way," she said. I told her I understood and signed my discharge paperwork. As I sat waiting for my ride, I reflected on everything that led me to go to the hospital.

I woke up in the middle of the night, a week prior, gasping for breath. I couldn't get air into me. I felt as though I had just been sprinting a marathon. In a panic, I threw the comforter off of me and scrambled for my phone to call for help. Before I could make it out of bed I saw my bedroom closing in and becoming dark. I was losing consciousness and I knew it. I started slumping over in my bed. Despite the violent surprise that woke me up: not being able to breathe; I felt a calm wash over me as my body went limp, and the room closed in. The last sensation I felt, as I slumped over, was a feeling of incredible peace as the left side of my face came to rest on the mattress.

The next morning, I decided I should go to the emergency room on base. I was still feeling incredibly short of breath. I drove myself there thinking that this was possibly some allergy or maybe pneumonia. When I checked in at the front desk they handed me a sheet to fill out. The sheet I was given stated that if you are short of breath to check in with the nurse at the front desk immediately. I didn't really feel like it was necessary to make a big deal of this, so I didn't, and chose to simply list shortness of breath among the symptoms I was having. I decided it would be best to wait my turn as there were people ahead of me who were already waiting when I arrived.

I was called back by a nurse and put on a bed behind a curtain. This was an emergency room on Andrews Air Force Base but had no hospital attached to it. After several minutes, a doctor came in and asked me about my symptoms. The doctor told me he thought I should get a CT scan of my chest and would also order some blood work.

After the scan and blood tests, I lay there behind this curtain awaiting some news as to what was going on. I wasn't waiting long before the doctor came in carrying a syringe.

"I have some bad news and it's pretty serious, but I have to give you this injection immediately, just lay back and relax," he said as he lifted my shirt and gave me an injection in my stomach.

"You have some massive blood clots in both your lungs. This injection I am giving you is a blood thinner. There is an ambulance on the way that will transport you to the hospital. You're going to spend some time in the intensive care unit there. I want you to understand that this is serious and incredibly life-threatening but we are going to do everything we can for you," he said.

Nurses walked in with various types of equipment to hook me up to. By the time they were done, I was covered in wires and tubes of all sorts. One nurse started to give me oxygen through a tube across my nose. She explained that the oxygen levels in my blood were low and this would help me breathe. I had been very short of breath, so this was something that I welcomed. I found it easier to breathe with the oxygen flowing and drifted off to sleep while I lay there waiting for the ambulance.

I was woken when the ambulance arrived as they unhooked all of the tubes and wires and then hooked me up to the tubes and wires of the machines and IVs that were going to accompany me in the ambulance. I felt so stupid. *Why was this happening? What had I done to myself that caused this?* These were the thoughts that were running through my head as I was loaded into the ambulance. I felt embarrassed and humiliated.

The hospital they were transporting me to had lost power and we were diverted to a different hospital. The woman who was caring for me told me to just relax because the trip would be a bit longer than they expected. She kept asking me if I was comfortable. I was, but I couldn't really talk as I was wearing a mask over my face for oxygen as opposed to the small tube across my nose.

I spent my birthday that year hospitalized in the intensive care unit recovering from the saddle pulmonary embolism that had nearly ended my life. I woke to a group of doctors examining me one morning. They explained a procedure they were going to do in which they would insert tubes into the arteries of my neck. They would then push those tubes into the arteries of my lungs and drip blood thinners directly on the clots extending into the primary, secondary, and tertiary arteries in both of my lungs. There was an opening just big enough to allow blood flow all the way through. I was told I was lucky to be alive and that my recovery would be long and difficult. One doctor even told me that he'd never seen anything like this in anyone that had lived. He recounted the story of a man he was treating that died on the table right in front of him gasping for breath. The hematologist that saw me said that there was a young lady he was caring for that had a stroke and was now in a coma and her lungs didn't look as bad as mine.

I don't remember much of my hospital stay. I mostly slept and didn't even really eat anything. I woke occasionally to see various medical professionals standing over me pushing buttons and adjusting equipment around me.

One night, a wire that was connected to a node on my chest came loose. I was awoken when a nurse came in and started pulling at the blanket I was wrapped in, to get to the loose wire. I opened my eyes to the sight of a dark shadow standing at my bedside with only the light of the open door behind her partially illuminating the room. I was suddenly very uncomfortable with this. I didn't understand the reaction I was having. I was absolutely terrified as she tugged at the blankets. My heart was pounding and I had a rush of adrenaline that shot through me. I could see my heartbeat in my eyes and was beginning to see stars as I panicked and thought about how I could escape.

"Are you ok?" she asked. "You're white as a sheet. Are you feeling alright?" she said as she walked around the foot of my bed looking into my face. I lifted my hand to my face to rub the sleep out of my eyes and I noticed it was shaking with weakness and fear. I could feel my heart pounding in my chest. "Can you breathe all right? Your heart rate is up there," she said.

"Yeah, I'm fine thank you, I think you just scared me coming in here in the middle of the night, I'm sorry," I said.

"I'm going to give you a bit more oxygen… you'll be more comfortable." She said as she walked around the room checking the machines and pushing buttons.

After my discharge, I spent the next several days at home recovering and taking it easy, I began to notice an intense ringing in my ears. One of my ears was irritated and felt like there was water in it. I wondered if, on top of everything else, I might have an ear infection too—but I wasn't in a rush to go back to the doctor any time soon.

I found that I was hyper-paranoid at night. The slightest creek in the house and I found I was jumping out of bed full of adrenaline and ready to fight. I recalled having a spell like this when I was a teenager. In one instance, I jumped out of bed so terrified that I grabbed a baseball bat and went down to the kitchen where I heard some rustling. I came around the corner ready to swing, but it was just my dad rummaging in the kitchen for a midnight snack.

"Oh!!" I said as I exhaled with relief.

"What, were you having a nightmare or something?" he asked; laughing as he made a sandwich.

The hyper-paranoia was worse this time. I was having nightmares as well. My dreams were terrifying to me. So much so that I was having difficulty sleeping. I would wake up covered in so much sweat that it looked like I had just been standing in the shower and I would have to change my t-shirt and shorts.

In one dream, I was inside a cave hiding behind a boulder. There was a man in a white lab coat who was laughing madly as he tortured a naked woman that was chained to a table. All I could do was hide terrified behind a rock inside the cave. In another dream, my parents were being hacked to death with an axe. This dream was really puzzling to me as my mother had passed away in 2015. I didn't understand where these dreams were coming from, they weren't me at all.

Thoughts like this never occurred to me, so why was I dreaming this? I had another crazy nightmare in which I was running around my house looking for a weapon I could use to defend myself, but stopped for a moment to look at a news report on TV as it was the latest breaking news. The footage showed bodies hanging from nooses in the trees around the White House lawn. The camera panned around the scene. There were crowds running through the street with weapons, covering their faces with rags as the air was heavy with smoke from tear gas and burning cars.

When I was younger, I would have recurring dreams every night. When I was very young—perhaps in kindergarten—I would have dreams of standing barefoot in a white robe talking to throngs of people about God on top of a mountain. I saw the Pope one night on the news and told my mom that I wanted to be the Pope, she laughed at me, so I kept my dreams to myself. Later, the Pope came to our town. I was watching footage of him on the local news as he walked with reporters across a grassy lawn. I could see his white shoes popping out of the bottom of his robe as he walked. I remembered feeling upset that he wore shoes. I felt like he was a fraud. I remembered asking my mother why he was wearing shoes. I again told her that I needed to be the Pope.

One recurring dream that returned from my childhood was less pleasant. The dream begins with me sliding down this slope towards a cliff that looks like it is part of the Grand Canyon. I can't stop myself from sliding toward the cliff, down this slope, because it is too sharp of an incline and littered with small rocks, pebbles, and sand that enable my slide. When my feet reach the edge of the cliff, my body jerks and I wake up.

I began to consider that this pulmonary embolism had really messed me up pretty bad. It was changing my personality, my ears were ringing, I had these bald spots on my face, and I was having terrible nightmares of unspeakable violence. People being chopped up with chainsaws and axes. I didn't know where all of this was coming from. My thought was that maybe I had some oxygen deprivation due to the blood clots, and it had caused all of this somehow. At the time, it was my only explanation and it was very depressing. I was devastated at the prospect that this current state could be the reality of the rest of my life. I couldn't keep doing this. I was becoming depressed... severely depressed.

The first time the disciple is consciously aware of it the suffering is terrible, because it seems to be a final state. It is known as the Ceremony of Terror, and two stanzas of the birth litany belong to it. LITANY:

I. I am nothing, save as a fragment to be burned and consumed.

II. I, alone, am as nothing.

–Mabel Collins
When the Sun Moves Northward:
The Way of Initiation c. 1923

One night, in December 2017, as my ears rang, I was sitting around as I took stock of my life, which I had pretty much done every day since my discharge from the hospital. As I pondered my life, my phone beeped; it was a text message from my older brother. He works as a middle school teacher, and we often text back and forth on a daily basis. I come from a very close family, and we were all still reeling from the loss of my younger brother, in 2010, and my mother in 2015.

My younger brother passed away after a two-year-long battle with colon cancer at the age of 29. My mother passed away five years later. She had taken his death very hard, as we all did, and I believe it contributed to her own early demise. She died of heart failure due to complications with Addison's disease. Our family of five was now down to three in just five years, and had nearly gone down to two with my own death.

I had just transferred to a new duty station at the Office of Naval Intelligence (ONI) in Washington DC. I had only been there six months before I got sick and was thinking things weren't off to a great start here.

When I arrived in DC, I didn't have much with me. I piled just a few belongings into my beat-up 13-year-old truck and I drove to DC. I found a furnished room in someone's house for $525 a month on Craigslist. It was my plan that this was just temporary for me. I would move into a house of my own and bring my dogs up here. I left them with a friend when I left for training several months before transferring. I was coming off yet another three-year sea duty tour and a lengthy deployment during which my mother had passed away, but at least I wouldn't be going anywhere for the next three years. My thought was that maybe I would have the opportunity to work on me during this shore duty tour.

We weren't a spiritual family growing up, in fact, we were proud and devout atheists. My father, having been an astronomer teaching at a university for the past thirty years, and my mother a nurse; in our household, if it wasn't provable by science then it didn't exist. My father was very interested in mythology, particularly as it pertains to the night sky, so Joseph Campbell was a household name growing up.

I hadn't taken any real interest in mythology or spirituality, so I wasn't really sure what "working on me" meant. All I knew at this point was something had to happen. I was falling apart, no doubt a physical symptom of the issues I hadn't dealt with. I thought often about my brother, his illness and early death, my mother and her death. I missed them terribly and not a day went by that I didn't think of them. I also often thought about how, following my brother's cancer diagnosis, the route that took me to and from work passed a large cemetery. I started taking a different route after his diagnosis. I couldn't face the fact that my younger brother might not survive and passing the cemetery was a daily reminder of that.

Before I had left my last command, I was sitting around talking to the junior guys I was in charge of when something unexpected slipped out. We were talking about how difficult military life is and how to deal with its complete lack of frills and comfort. I was giving them advice. Just little tidbits that had helped me cope along the way.

I said, "If you don't enjoy anything, then the Navy can't take anything from you, in fact nobody can." When I said this, I immediately felt the awkwardness of it. It's not what they wanted to hear. So, I added, "You need to find something in this experience that you learn from, something that, mentally, will allow you to chalk this up as a win for you." After my conversation with them, I thought a lot about what I had said. I thought about how awful it sounded to say that if you don't enjoy anything nobody could ever take anything from you.

My thought was, *What is wrong with me? Why don't I enjoy anything?* I thought about how this was something I had always struggled with. Growing up, I always dreaded the first day of a class or the first day of school. Inevitably, there was always the routine of having to stand up in front of everyone and talk about who you are and what kinds of things you like to do. I would always struggle deeply with this. The truth is that there was nothing I enjoyed.

My outlook on life also kept me from hating things as well. I began to think that I was really becoming a terrible person. I was starting to think that maybe I needed therapy. I did know there was one thing I hated. I hated my life. I hated everything about it. But how could I improve that feeling if there was nothing that I liked or enjoyed? I would wake up in the morning and my first thought was always, *I hate my fucking life.* I thought about going out and getting a Mercedes or a Jaguar. I have money, a net worth like others do not, a good job… But I pictured myself crawling into that fancy expensive car, pausing before I started it, and thinking once again, *I hate my fucking life.* At that point, I knew the fancy nice things weren't going to save me and they didn't matter anyway. *Something isn't right*, I thought as I sat there.

I looked down at my phone and read my brother's text message. As I was reading, the messages were coming in fast. He was clearly excited. He was texting me about a news article in the *New York Times* concerning a Pentagon UFO program. His next message stated that there was footage that had been released. The message after that stated that the former Senate Majority Leader, Harry Reid, was quoted in the article. I texted back and let him know that I would check it out. I secretly didn't want to have this conversation with him. My family always asked me about things they read, or would see in the news, concerning the military. I loved to impart my wisdom when they would ask me things, provided they didn't get into anything that I wasn't at liberty to discuss. This was something I thought I definitely wouldn't be able to discuss.

I read the article and watched the footage. My heart sank into my stomach as I watched what is now referred to as the "Gimbal footage." I had seen it before and was starting to become a bit emotional as it took me back to the memory of this experience. I knew my brother would be calling any minute to ask me about it. I was in a panic and my heart was pounding. I didn't know what I was going to tell him. I was thinking maybe I would just play it off. I went back to the article to try to make sense of why this had been released… Was it declassified? Could I talk about it?

I had been present in the battlegroup when the footage was collected and remember the incident as though it were yesterday. Until this point in my career, work had always been work. It was a place where I was a cool, calm, and collected professional above all else. I was happy to discuss generalities about the military, but when it came to anything I had actually seen or done, I would again speak in generalities or dodge the question completely. The nature of my job or its specific details were something I had never discussed with my family. For me this incident was different. It was inexplicably very emotional.

I was reliving the first time I had seen this footage as this encounter was unfolding. I had found that the footage spoke to me on some level. As I studied it one day, I found tears were welling up in my eyes as though I knew something about this, but I didn't. I was unable to eat for several days, as my appetite had disappeared completely. At one point, the thought entered my head that I had brought them here. I was unable to shake this feeling because it was so powerful. This feeling grew stronger and more intense as the events unfolded. I remember feeling afraid to sleep. The feeling they were there for me was unsettling. I felt guilty about it and worried that I would be found out. These thoughts entered my head for some unknown reason.

One day, I walked past a couple of the pilots who were talking about it. As I listened to them discussing it in passing, I looked down at the floor and tried to sneak past them without being noticed. I was shaking with fear that someone might find out that I had something to do with this. I couldn't understand this reaction I was having; it was nonsense, yet the emotion was very real. How could I feel this way?

Out of everything I had done in the military, this was an instance where I was having a lot of difficulty. For many years it was always in the back of my mind. At the time, I studied this footage extensively looking for signs of propulsion. Watching it over and over again trying to make some sense of it. I remember driving home from work one day listening to an NPR story about black holes, concerning the discovery that gravity existed in waves. It was proven by measuring the waves as two distant black holes collided. I then understood that's what the propulsion was. It was anti-gravitic.

I was very aware of how communications worked. Communications also travel in waves. If you can broadcast on the same frequency as an unwanted signal with more power, you can block the unwanted signal. This discovery meant that you could essentially do the same thing with gravity. It was something that I thought about often. I never bothered to dig into the whole UFO thing, not because I didn't want to know, but rather because I didn't know where to start. There was so much garbage out there… fake CGI videos… bogus abduction stories… it was a circus of tinfoil hats that I didn't want to follow down the rabbit hole.

My phone started to ring. It was my brother. I had no idea what I was going to say. I let it ring a few times before I answered, because the prospect of discussing something that had to do with work on this level made me feel sick to my stomach. I answered the phone with the thought that maybe he wouldn't even mention it. Maybe he'll talk about something else first.

"Hello," I said.

He asked, "Hey, did you read the UFO article?"

"Yeah I read it, it's pretty interesting," I replied.

"Have you ever encountered anything like that?" he asked. My esophagus was suddenly in a knot and I started to choke.

"I..." There was a long pause because I didn't know what to say. I was becoming emotional. I started to cough. My brother knows me very well and I knew that he knew something was off about my reaction. I was so pissed in that moment that I had paused. I wondered in that instant why I couldn't have just played it off and not let on that I knew anything. I was so disappointed in myself.

He asked, "Matthew? Are you there?"

"Yeah, I'm here," I replied.

"Have you ever encountered anything like this?" he asked, again. I thought about the article... thought about how Harry Reid had been quoted... this was all out there now... declassified... people were talking about it... I cleared my throat and choked a bit more. I was breathing very heavily and my heart was pounding out of my chest.

"Yes," I replied. "I was there in the battlegroup when this particular footage was collected." Now the pause was on his end. I don't really remember much about the rest of the conversation. He had a few questions. I had no answers, because I didn't know anything more than he did.

Several days passed before our next conversation. It was unlike him to not communicate for several days like this. I decided to call him. He answered the phone and sounded very down in the dumps.

"What's wrong?" I asked.

He stated, "Oh, just trying to take all this in." At this point, the major news networks were all running the story of the Pentagon's UFO program. CNN, MSNBC, and Fox were all running it… it was everywhere. We talked for a bit about an organization that was mentioned in the article called To the Stars Academy of Arts and Science that my brother and I were going to look into.

I was actually excited, and I visited their website in the hopes of finding some answers. I hadn't bothered looking into this before, because I wasn't sure what was fact and what was fiction, but now I finally had a place to start. A place that had some association with the Pentagon, and for me, was sure to have more credibility than the grainy CGI videos, and aluminum foil hats that were all over the internet. The first thing I came across was the launch video for To the Stars Academy of Arts and Science. As the video opened there was a quote by Mark Twain up on the screen that read: "The two most important days in your life are the day you are born… and the day you find out why." It was something that stood out in my mind. In front of the screen there was a stage with a seated panel. I saw that this panel was made up of heavy hitters at the Pentagon. I was sure this was all legitimate.

In exploring the website for TTSA, I found that there were two books for sale. One was called *Sekret Machines Chasing Shadows* by Tom DeLonge and A.J. Heartly about the reverse engineering of alien tech by the government. And the other was called *Gods: Gods, Men, and War* by Tom DeLonge with Peter Levenda. I ordered them both and I read them both. They made a lot of sense. *Gods* spoke a lot about consciousness, religion, shamanism, and mythology. It was interesting but I didn't really understand where it was going. It also contained a phrase that I didn't really understand, "That which is below is like that which is above, and that which is above is like that which is below." I didn't fully understand what that meant at the time but it was something that stood out to me as it is mentioned several times.

Years ago, I watched a show on TV about otherworldly encounters. In the show there was an interview with an airline pilot who was flying around what we now call Area 51. He claimed he was diverted around the base by air traffic control. He made his course corrections, glanced out the window and saw what he described as fireflies lighting up in the sky around the base. He saw a giant landing strip illuminate on the ground as these fireflies zipped in at incredible speeds toward the runway one by one. At the time, I didn't think much of his experience, but now, in light of the books I read, I was starting to think about it differently. In an interview with Joe Rogan, Tom DeLonge mentioned he was detained and questioned by the government about the book. In reading and hearing these things I was very excited. In the interview, Tom DeLonge mentions how Greek mythology plays some role in this but he was very vague about it. He talked about how the wreckage at Roswell had the word "Freedom" on it in ancient Greek. My reaction to hearing this was mixed. Freedom from what? What, was there some kind of war going on? Were there slave races out there that were fighting for freedom? Or was Tom DeLonge just a crazy nut? What was going on?!

I tried to look a bit into Greek mythology at this point but quickly discovered that it's so complex that you could honestly get a Ph.D. in Greek mythology and still not completely understand it. In looking this stuff up, however, I found the writings of Plato and Democritus interesting. In looking at mythology, I was taken off on this internet tangent and I began watching some documentary about Angkor Wat in Cambodia. There is a bas-relief that runs along an entire wall of the complex called The Churning of the Sea of Milk. It depicts an important part of Hindu mythology and explains the process of the origination of Amrita, which is the nectar of immortality. It depicts the Hindu gods churning the Sea of Milk, or Milky Way, in the making of this nectar of immortality. At one point, the gods begin to fight over the nectar. A bit of this nectar spills and hits various places. Some of it hits earth. I thought it was a neat story in terms of human mythology but I felt like I was getting sidetracked. Although, I thought it was incredibly interesting to be looking into all of this mythology that was impossible to grasp because of its infinite complexity.

On the website for TTSA there is a quote from one of its members, Steve Justice, about the changes this stuff will bring about for humanity, stating, "Revolutionary is too mild a word." This is what appealed to me. It was hopeful and I loved it. I was so happy that this was finally coming out into the public sphere. It means so many things—new energy technology, new propulsion—it could truly revolutionize the way we live our lives. All of those things are wonderful, and truly revolutionary, but what made it appealing to me was what it would mean for humanity going forward.

I began to comb through the staff that was listed on the TTSA website to see if any of these individuals wrote any books in the past. I came across Dr. Colm Kelleher, which led me to a book he wrote called *Hunt for the Skinwalker*. As I read, it all seemed pretty unbelievable and creepy at the same time, but I couldn't deny the credibility of the people involved. The book seemed to imply that what we call paranormal was somehow linked to all of this. It seemed the more I read; the more I realized that all of this stuff was already out there in the public sphere. Still, there was a part of me that was skeptical. *Okay, so some of this stuff it turns out is true, but there's no way all of it's true,* I thought.

Another source for me was Jacques Vallée as he had written the foreword for *Volume 1 of Gods, Man & War*. I read *The Invisible College* and *Confrontations* both authored by Vallée. All of these books were a wealth of knowledge. I was reading things that I had thought existed only in the realm of tinfoil hats. Stories of abduction. The loss of control of one's body. The feelings of an urge to get in your car and drive. Feeling paralyzed as aliens conduct experiments on you. There were so many interesting abduction stories in *Confrontations,* but there were two that stood out to me as being particularly interesting for some reason. One of the accounts was that of Sergeant Herbert Schirmer who was on patrol near Ashland, Nebraska at 2:30 am on December 3rd 1967. The part of the story that sent a chill through me was the following:

> *Schirmer recalled being taken out of the patrol car, unable to use his radio or his gun. He was given a tour of the saucer. The operator asked him, "Are you the watchman over this place?" And when they reached the top of the craft the man told Schirmer, "Watchman, some day you will see the universe!"*

This stood out to me because it seemed so profoundly poetic. But it didn't make sense. Poetic, yet it was nonsense as it was 1967, and no human would be exploring the universe with the technology we possessed at that time. It's not like Sergeant Schrimer was some kind of astronaut, he was a police officer. He wasn't even in the right field to be exploring the universe, even if it were possible. The other account that stood out is in the next chapter of *Confrontations* called "Happy Camp." The account is as follows:

> *The main event took place five days later, on November 2, 1975, when the same principals (Steve, Stan, and Helen) and two other people drove down a dirt trail into the canyon at the base of Cade Mountain. They were still trying to find an explanation for what they*

had seen earlier, and they explored the area in more or less systematic fashion.

In the canyon, however, they found an area of heavy fog that forced them to turn back, and they became very confused about subsequent events. They remember heavy boulders falling off the cliffs and bouncing around the truck. They remember the door locks being opened and a strange being telling Steve "you won't need that" when he reached for his gun. They believe they saw a hovering object. Helen recalls being lifted inside a room, but she is confused about the time sequence. One occupant had a dialogue with her, in the course of which he described a transparent object as being made of gold. Helen answered that she knew what gold was like, and it surely was not transparent. The being answered simply, "There is such a thing as gold that you can look through. It's in your Bible." Steve thinks he was in a craft with a transparent window on top and bottom, through which he was able to see China Mountain.

Their next conscious memory is of driving down the mountain, singing a chorus of an old church song. I find it interesting that the hymn they were singing was "There is Power in the Blood of the Lamb."

It struck me as an odd encounter because of the whole gold description. And why would this being tell her it's in her Bible? What's that all about? As a devout atheist, I found it intriguing yet incredibly disturbing at the same time. Intriguing because it was coming from an otherworldly being, but disturbing that he would bring up the Bible. In doing so, it occurred to me that he could be misinterpreted to be endorsing one religion over another. To me, all religions are nonsense so I found it disgusting that such a being would even mention this. I decided to look into this because that prospect seemed so awful to me. It also struck me as odd that some being from some other place in the universe would have such an immediate and intimate knowledge of something like the human Bible or even the English language. I looked for the part of the Bible that was referenced by this being and found it in Revelation 21 in the King James Version of the Bible:

The New Jerusalem

***9** And there came unto me one of the seven angels which had the seven vials full of the seven last plagues, and talked with me, saying, Come hither, I will shew thee the bride, the Lamb's wife.*

***10** And he carried me away in the spirit to a great and high mountain, and shewed me that great city, the holy Jerusalem, descending out of heaven from God,*

***11** Having the glory of God: and her light was like unto a stone most precious, even like a jasper stone, clear as crystal;*

12 And had a wall great and high, and had twelve gates, and at the gates twelve angels, and names written thereon, which are the names of the twelve tribes of the children of Israel:

13 On the east three gates; on the north three gates; on the south three gates; and on the west three gates.

14 And the wall of the city had twelve foundations, and in them the names of the twelve apostles of the Lamb.

15 And he that talked with me had a golden reed to measure the city, and the gates thereof, and the wall thereof.

16 And the city lieth foursquare, and the length is as large as the breadth: and he measured the city with the reed, twelve thousand furlongs. The length and the breadth and the height of it are equal.

17 And he measured the wall thereof, an hundred and forty and four cubits, according to the measure of a man, that is, of the angel.

18 And the building of the wall of it was of jasper: and the city was **pure gold, like unto clear glass.**

19 And the foundations of the wall of the city were garnished with all manner of precious stones. The first foundation was jasper; the second, sapphire; the third, a chalcedony; the fourth, an emerald;

20 The fifth, sardonyx; the sixth, sardius; the seventh, chrysolyte; the eighth, beryl; the ninth, a topaz; the tenth, a chrysoprasus; the eleventh, a jacinth; the twelfth, an amethyst.

*21 And the twelve gates were twelve pearls: every several gate was of one pearl: and the street of the city was **pure gold, as it were transparent glass.***

22 And I saw no temple therein: for the Lord God Almighty and the Lamb are the temple of it.

23 And the city had no need of the sun, neither of the moon, to shine in it: for the glory of God did lighten it, and the Lamb is the light thereof.

24 And the nations of them which are saved shall walk in the light of it: and the kings of the earth do bring their glory and honour into it.

25 And the gates of it shall not be shut at all by day: for there shall be no night there.

26 And they shall bring the glory and honour of the nations into it.

27 And there shall in no wise enter into it any thing that defileth, neither whatsoever worketh abomination, or maketh a lie: but they which are written in the Lamb's book of life.

It was clear to me in reading this that it was referring to a cube-shaped craft of some kind. Perhaps this is why the being had mentioned it during the abduction experience. Perhaps this part of the Bible describes an otherworldly encounter and the author didn't understand what he was looking at thousands of years ago. It seemed a little less creepy to me now. This was just an example of someone encountering a cube-shaped craft in antiquity and not having the vocabulary to describe what he was seeing. I still wasn't sure about why they would be singing "Power in the Blood of the Lamb." Perhaps mentioning the Bible made them think this was a religious experience of some kind?

In *Confrontations,* Vallée includes a list where he classifies anomalies related to UFOs or UAPs, as they are now called. It includes lasting side effects. Physical effects, reality transformations and injury. He lays this out in a chapter called "The Price of Contact." Vallée states:

> *My own private conjecture, which deviates considerably from the accepted dogma among UFO believers, is that **we are dealing with a yet unrecognized level of consciousness, independent of man but closely linked to the earth.***

I went online looking for other sources and came across a YouTube video of an experiencer named Suzy Hansen. In it she claimed all kinds of crazy things. Abductions, tests, being allowed to pilot ET craft. It seemed like the type of madness that the internet was full of when it comes to this subject. At the end of her presentation she began crying and talking about the spiritual aspect of this. I didn't want to pursue anything like that. I needed credible sources. The things she was claiming were way too out there for me.

I was online one night combing through some stuff and came across an experiencer checklist. I knew it probably carried little credibility but decided to open it just out of curiosity. I sat there reading this and, to my surprise, I started to feel very uneasy. Some of the questions seemed very familiar to me. It mentioned blood type, blood clots, nightmares, hyper-paranoia at night, and Addison's disease. It said that Addison's disease was a side effect of the constant tapping of the adrenal gland; this caused the gland to begin to not function properly over time. I had opened this with the expectation that it would have nothing to do with me. Or at the very least, I thought I would get a good laugh out of it. I choked as I realized it had everything to do with me and my stomach sank. "No," I said softly as I looked up at nothing in particular off in the distance. I was trying to wrap my mind around this. "No, it can't be…" I said aloud to myself. I looked down at my hands as they started to shake. My heart started pounding. I didn't want to believe it but deep down I knew it was true. I was worried.

At one point I came across Dr. Steven Greer in a YouTube video. He was taking people out to the desert and meditating. In this meditation he would have people project themselves astrally and ask for assistance. I saw one video where he was able to make craft appear in doing this. In another video I saw Tom DeLonge talking about his experience in doing this with Dr. Greer. It seems to work, so I decided to give it a try. I lied down in the bed of my truck one night and followed Dr. Greer's instructions. I asked for help in understanding what this was all about. I wanted to do something that would benefit the human race. I was very careful. I did just as he suggests. I did this with love in my heart. As I did the meditation, I was tearing up a bit. It seemed a bit corny. It was in fact the first time I had ever meditated and it was surprisingly relaxing. I was, however, not surprised when nothing happened, but was a bit disappointed as I thought I had really tried. I figured if they had been abducting me I deserved answers. I began to think they were responsible for the death of my mother, possibly the death of my brother, and they had almost killed me with blood clots. I demanded answers and I was determined to get to the bottom of this. At the time, I even told my brother that I knew I would never be able to let this go until I knew the truth.

On the night of February 14, 2018, I was sitting in my truck, having a smoke before I went to bed, running out of options for credible sources, I remembered reading at the end of *Sekret Machines* about some tablets. Ancient tablets that were held in a glowing sapphire metal frame. It was a bit of a cliffhanger as that is where the book ended; without telling the readers what these tablets were and why they are significant. When I looked up ancient sapphire tablets, the first thing that popped up was the Ten Commandments. I was pretty disappointed. My immediate thought was, *It can't be the Ten Commandments, that's just the corniest thing I've ever heard.* I began looking up ancient tablets of all kinds. I came across the Tabula Smaragdina or Emerald Tablet. I began reading about it.

This tablet is what gave birth to alchemy in the middle ages. When I read that, my thought was, *Well alchemy is just what became modern day chemistry.* Or at least that was my idea of what alchemy was. It seemed interesting. Although they were the wrong color; green as opposed to blue, as described in *Sekret Machines*. I found translations of the tablet on a Wikipedia page. One was Isaac Newton's translation into English. My immediate sense was that this was just internet conspiracy theory nonsense. But I was forced to rethink that theory when I found a digital image of the translation in Isaac Newton's own handwriting at a major university, the text is as follows:

Tis true without lying, certain and most true.

That which is below is like that which is above & that which is above is like that which is below to do the miracles of one only thing.

And as all things have been and arose from one by the meditation of one: so all things have their birth from this one thing by adaptation.

The Sun is its father, the moon its mother, the wind hath carried it in its belly, the Earth is its nurse. The father of all perfection in the whole world is here. Its force or power is entire if it be converted into earth.

Separate thou the earth from the fire, the subtle from the gross sweetly with great industry. It ascends to the Earth from the heaven & again it descends to the Earth & receives the force of things superior and inferior.

By this means you shall have the glory of the whole world & thereby all obscurity shall fly from you.

Its force is above all force, for it vanquishes every subtle thing & penetrates every solid thing.

So was the world created.

From this are and do come admirable adaptations whereof the means (or process) is here in this.

Hence I am called Hermes Trismegistus, having the three parts of the philosophy of the whole world.

That which I have said of the operation of the Sun is accomplished & ended.

In reading this I didn't understand how this gave birth to what I thought alchemy was. It seemed to speak to something other than turning base metals into gold. I was shocked at the realization that of Isaac Newton's personal papers, the majority of them were writings about the study of theology and alchemy. The Emerald Tablet also contained the "as above so below" text that I remembered reading in Tom DeLonge's book. I didn't at the time understand it as I do now, but I did know at the time it was significant. Isaac Newton was the father of so much in the way of science. He was a genius, so why would he be investigating something like this? I had a kind of emotional response to reading his translation. It smacked of some kind of truth; but what? It was clearly cloaked in some esoteric meaning. I looked for books concerning Hermes and ran into Hermetic teachings. The first book I came across was a book called *The Kybalion* by Three Initiates.

As I was sitting there in my truck smoking, looking all of this stuff up on my phone; I looked up in contemplation of all of this. I let my eyes wander across the backyard. I was parked in front of the 3-foot chain-link fence that enclosed the backyard. The previous owners of this house kept horses and there is an old stable off in the distance toward the back of the property. In the doorway of the stable I saw a shadow. It looked like a very tall, thin, all-white person that was bending down to look out through the doorway. I found myself fixated on this figure I was seeing, trying to make sense of it. I suppose I could have turned on my headlights to see what was going on, but I didn't. In the end, I figured it was just light playing with my eyes.

I looked back down and read the synopsis of *The Kybalion* on my phone. I wasn't impressed. It seemed a bit out there. In the synopsis I read about the seven universal principles it covered. It spoke to the fact that there is no such thing as chance, and that everything happens for a reason. There is only cause and effect. I read about how people have a hard time with this because it implies we have no free will. I definitely wasn't going to read it. It just didn't speak to me, so this was a dead end.

I wondered if there was a chapter of MUFON here in Maryland, as I was eager to dig into this stuff. I was finding posts and activities listed under MUFON Maryland that were a decade old. It didn't seem to me that there was an active chapter in the area, so this was again another dead end. I felt at this time that I was out of options for credible sources. I was still sitting in my truck and it was getting late. I decided to go to bed as I had to get up early in the morning for an appointment I had in Patuxent River. It was an hour and some change south one-way so that meant over two hours driving the next day. I resigned myself to the fact that I would just have to wait for more releases of information from TTSA. I decided, with that, I would call it a night and went to bed. Ignorantly unaware that the next day my life was going to change forever. In my hubris I decided that *The Kybalion* was something I could dismiss and brush aside; just as I had done with so many things up to this point. The experiences of people like Suzy Hansen and *The Kybalion* were nonsense to me. The next day, the universe would begin to bare down on me with all its weight, in an absolutely terrifying demonstration of *The Kybalion*'s principles; just for me.

Chapter Two

SUPERNATURAL AID

It was the morning of February 15, 2018, and I got up knowing I would spend a good chunk of my day driving. I went in to work in the morning just to remind everyone that I would be at my appointment in Patuxent River and that I likely wouldn't be back till after lunch. When I got these blood clots in my lungs a few months earlier, I was told my medical file would be presented to a medical board for review. The board would determine if I would be allowed to remain in the military.

Because of the severity of my clots, I was told I would need to take blood thinners for the rest of my life. This would make me non-deployable. At this point, I had about 15 years of active duty service under my belt. I could retire in just five years, so I decided to let the board know it was my wish to remain in service. I had spent about a decade of that on ships out to sea and I could go overseas for shore duty without breaking my duty assignment rotation. The board had come back with their findings and found me fit to continue active duty. I had decided I was going to stay in and retire. My appointment in Pax River was to sign the paperwork from the board finding me fit for duty.

In looking back at that decade at sea, I realized that there's nothing like military service. I really learned very quickly what I do and do not need. Out to sea there are no luxuries. Out to sea, every day is Monday. I would regularly work 12-20 hours a day depending on what was going on. At times I would only sleep every other day. There are no days off. Sometimes, on a deployment, we would leave homeport and not get a day off until we pulled into our first port call four months later. The big joke is that it's like the movie *Groundhog Day*, waking up every day to exactly the same routine as the day before.

Looking back on it, as I write this book now, I know all of this to be a significant life lesson; in doing this, I learned to cultivate many important personality traits that were key in enabling my journey. Despite the hardships, I found a way to enjoy what I was doing. I learned to disregard hardships; in fact, I had such disregard for them that I didn't even notice or mind them. The ordinary person is plagued by the monsters they allow to run wild inside themselves. Monsters that paralyze them with fear, anger, or worry at the slightest experience. In reflecting upon my life, I can appreciate its difficulties. At the time, it didn't seem difficult to me but I think about how few would have chosen the path I did. Or how few would have survived. How many people could work a 12-hour shift where you must be continuously alert followed by a five-hour watch outside the skin of the ship in 110 degree weather wearing 50 lbs. of gear behind a 50 caliber machine gun; the air thick with the smell of burning oil from the burnout stacks of drilling platforms littering the horizon off in the distance? And this followed by three hours in the ship's medical facilities standing suicide watch over someone who wasn't quite strong enough. And to do this every day, for months?

I'm going to quote a silent movie star here named Douglas Fairbanks because the quotes go a long way in explaining the type of person I've always been. I have already used a quote from a woman named Mabel Collins in the first chapter. Later in the book I will explain this. It may seem like this is coming out of nowhere but it's not. In *Laugh and Live* Douglas Fairbanks writes:

> *People are divided into two classes -* ***those who profit by experience and those who do not.*** *The unfortunate part of it all is that the latter class is by far the larger of the two.*
>
> *The man of vigorous purpose, fine constitution, and the full knowledge of self, sees through an experience as clearly as through a window. The glass may be foggy, but he knows what lies beyond. Self-reliant and strong he seeks knowledge through experience, while the weak man, the unhealthy minded, the inefficient, stands aside and gives him the right of way. In later years, however, they bitterly complain that they were not given the same chance to succeed.*
>
> *The man of experience having long since passed through the stages of indecision has, through careful self-analysis learned to bridge difficulties that would make others tremble with fear. He knows that every lane has a turning. He may not see it at*

the moment. He may not know where it is. **But that doesn't worry him.** *He picks up his bundle and trudges ahead, confident that victory awaits him somewhere along the line.*

The fact that he believes in himself, sets him apart from ordinary mankind. Many great men have been at a loss to understand why they attained success. It is well nigh impossible for them to outline the causes that led them to the top rungs of the ladder. The reason is **their lack of fear** *of experiences was an unconscious one, rather than a conscious one. However, they are willing to admit that acting on the principle of profiting by experience* **loaned them initiative** *with which to proceed. They soon came to know opportunity at sight and had only to look around to find it.*

In *Making Life Worth While* Douglas Fairbanks writes:

In **Laugh and Live***, my sole purpose was to emphasize our first duty toward ourselves, which consists of doing our level best at everything we undertake, and making the best of every situation that arises to confront us.*

All through my early life I read inspirational books and liked them best of all. They seemed to beckon me on. I could feel myself being pulled along by an unseen hand.

My drive to Patuxent River was long and uneventful. I arrived there and signed the forms with the medical board's findings. I could remain on active duty. I felt good about it. I didn't want to have to look for another job right away and I was still in need of the paycheck the military offers, as I had been investing in real estate since 2007. It was my retirement plan. I still had one house in Portsmouth, Virginia that was gutted and I needed to put it back together so I could get tenants in there. After leaving the military, I would work some other job and live off the supplemental income the rental properties offered. This was my plan. These were the thoughts that were rolling around in my head as I drove back to Washington DC.

While contemplating the rest of my life on this long drive back to DC, I was cut off by this small hatchback that had zoomed up on my left side and pulled closely in front of me. On the back window was a giant graphic. It read "MUFON Maryland, find us on Facebook." *Oh!* I thought. *That's why I didn't find them when I looked them up last night, I don't have Facebook so that's the one place I didn't look.* Just then I looked off the road and saw I was passing a Hobby Lobby. I had never actually seen one before but I was aware of the controversial Supreme Court decision concerning that chain of arts and crafts stores. Just as a side note, I'm watching the protests on TV as I write this. The protests concerning another controversy involving the Supreme Court, the swearing in of Justice Kavenaugh. It's funny that this type of coincidence should happen in this part of the book. As though to remind me that there is no such thing as chance or coincidence, as you also will begin to see as you read this book.

I followed behind this hatchback for several miles. My thought was that if he turned off into a gas station, I would get out and talk to the guy, but it didn't seem as though he would turn off, and he was going too fast. I was in uniform at the time so it might be weird if I got out and started asking him about the MUFON chapter. He would likely be suspicious of the uniform. It started to seem like not such a good idea after all. He'd probably think I was working for the government on some kind of fact-finding mission. I watched the hatchback disappear down the road speeding ahead faster than I was willing to go. At least I knew now that there was a Maryland chapter. I could create a Facebook account just to check them out.

I returned to work and things were pretty uneventful there. When I got home I spent the rest of the day doing laundry and cleaning. It was getting late and I was almost out of cigarettes so I went and picked up a pack at the gas station down the street from the house. I smoked a few cigarettes before heading in to go to bed. It was about 10:30 on a Thursday night and I had to be up early for work. I did what I always do. I walked in from the kitchen door and set the alarm, as I wouldn't be going out again.

I walked into the living room where my roommate was watching television. He was watching some talking heads on CNN. He's a liberal just like I am, so this was in no way surprising, but he normally wasn't up this late. I had to walk in front of the television to go upstairs. As I headed up the stairs my roommate suddenly asked, "Do you know what this is all about? All this stuff with the Republicans?"

I stopped on the first few steps of the stairs, looked at him and said, "No, what?"

"Hobby Lobby!" he exclaimed. He then went on to explain how that Supreme Court decision had allowed all this dirty corporate money to pour into political campaigns. I agreed. We spoke about it for a few minutes before I went up to bed. I shut my bedroom door behind me and was going to get changed and crawl into bed, but I paused. I started to think about how the night before I had looked up MUFON Maryland but didn't find anything on them, and how that car had cut me off with the MUFON Maryland, Facebook graphic. I had seen the Hobby Lobby and my roommate had just brought that up. It suddenly seemed like a day of coincidences.

As I pondered this for a moment, my heart began pounding. It was jumping out of my chest. I looked down and I could see it thumping under my t-shirt. It was alarming and uncomfortable. It was like the kind of pounding that would happen after a rush of adrenaline, but I didn't feel any rush, just the pounding in my chest. I wondered if it was because of the blood clots. Maybe they were back. I was getting worried. My hands started to tremble. I sat on the edge of my bed trying to remain calm. I then felt a powerful urge to get in my car and drive. *Now that is weird,* I thought. I lay carefully on my bed for a bit to see if this would just subside. I believed that I might die if it was the clots returning. The urge to get in the car and start driving was becoming more intense. I had never "FELT" the urge to go drive before. It was something that I had read in some of Jacques Vallée's books concerning alien abduction. I was scared. Terrified would be more like it. The urge to go drive and the pounding in my chest were not subsiding, so I decided to relent. I thought that if I just did this I would see there's nothing to it and it's just a silly thing.

As I exited my room and slowly walked down the stairs, pausing on each creaky step, pondering what I was about to do, I noticed my roommate had gone to bed. I wondered what would happen to me if I did this. What did this mean for me? More importantly, what did it mean for my sanity? This was a wild goose chase in the middle of the night. The house was completely dark and I used the light of my cellphone to navigate the darkness. I walked through the living room into the kitchen and disarmed the alarm. I set it again and walked out the side door and across the gravel driveway.

I could hear the gravel crunching under my feet with every step as I made my way slowly to my truck. I got in and started the engine. I noticed that my heart was no longer pounding, but I still felt the powerful urge to go driving. That feeling was now mixed with a sense of urgency. It was incredibly powerful. I started crying.

This is madness... I thought, as I put the truck in reverse and backed out of the driveway into the first point of a three point turn to get out of the driveway. I hit the brakes and put the truck in drive. I paused. I began to think this was going to be unhealthy for me. Leaving the house late at night on wild goose chases that existed only in my own head. I thought about how I had been reading these books with all these strange stories of abduction and it was getting to me. I began to really break down. I was sure this would drive me to madness. I'd be in a straitjacket before long if I kept this up. I couldn't give in to this for the sake of my own sanity. The nightmares I was having, the nighttime paranoia, the ringing in my ears, the severe depression; all led me to believe I was starting to go crazy just like everyone I knew that has PTSD. If I did this then it would never end and I was already disappointed in myself for going this far. I had absolutely lost my shit. I wiped the tears from my face. It was then that I decided I would just pull back into my spot in the driveway, go upstairs and go to bed, forgetting this whole crazy thing.

In that instant, I felt one of the most uncomfortable sensations. The only way I can describe it is electrocution. I've touched live electrical wires before and felt that buzzing feeling. It was unlike touching an electrical wire in that it wasn't painful, but there was that uncomfortable buzzing feeling. It shot through my body as though I was attached to a light switch and someone had just flipped it. I could feel my toenail beds buzzing, they felt raw and exposed, as my foot involuntarily stepped on the gas pedal, and my hands turned the steering wheel toward the road. The buzzing stopped as the truck drifted toward the road and I slammed on the breaks. It seems as though someone had turned off the switch.

My ears were ringing pretty badly. I began taking these heaving deep breaths with tears rolling down my face. "What… is… happening… to… me?" I said, now in all-out panic, pausing between each word with a deep heaving breath. My entire body began shaking with fear. I knew then that none of this was in my head. In my life I have felt many things, but never have I been able to induce the feeling of electrical shock in myself. I was feeling a very strong sense of urgency now. It was rather intense. "Ok… ok I'm going," I said and stepped on the accelerator.

I didn't know where I was going. As I drove down the road trembling and wiping the tears from my face, I felt a sense of euphoria, it felt as though I was being rewarded for doing the right thing. I figured I would drive back down to Patuxent River, as I had been there earlier, and it seemed right. I wasn't sure how long this would take, so I decided I would stop at the gas station just before the Maryland 5 South to pick up a drink for the road.

I pulled into the gas station and parked at one of the pumps in front. My heart began to pound again. I froze. A feeling came over me that whatever reason I was made to leave the house was going to take place right here at this gas station. I was frightened by this. What was going to happen at a gas station, near the freeway, in a not-so-great part of town, nearing midnight on a Thursday? I was shaking with fear. My mind became full of possibilities. Was someone going to rob the gas station and I had to stop them? Maybe someone would start shooting and I was meant to die here? My eyes were welling up with tears as I was once again becoming emotional. I turned around and looked behind me, scanning the intersection to see what was coming. I looked out the side windows. I then scanned the front of the gas station. Looking inside to see if there was something going on in there. Then I saw it… I had parked right in front of it. It was clearly out of place.

The gas station also sold fried chicken and had some tables on the sidewalk in front where people could eat. There was trash all over—chicken bones, empty fried chicken boxes, napkins blowing across the parking lot in the breeze. It was clear that given the time of night and location there was no way I should be seeing what I was seeing. Actually, even during the daytime this would have been odd.

Seated at the table by the door outside were three people; a man and two women eating together. The man was clearly homeless. I could see that from across the parking lot. The two women were immaculately dressed. They looked like many of the civilian women I worked with. Women like this would not be at a gas station near the freeway at midnight eating with a homeless man. They were dressed to the nines in a smart and professional manner as though they were about to go brief Congress or something. I also knew that I was supposed to hear what they were talking about. I was afraid to leave the truck. I looked down at the door handle. I heard a voice say very forcefully "GET OUT." I collected myself for a moment then reached for the door handle with my trembling hand and pulled it as I once again felt this powerful urgency. I stepped out of the truck and shut the door.

As I slowly and cautiously walked across the parking lot, my knees were trembling with fear. I was choking back tears as I tried to compose myself. I was a mess. My senses were heightened, and I was in a state of absolute terror. As I walked toward the table I noticed more detail. The homeless man was filthy. There was dirt and grime literally caked on his clothing. His stained jeans were shredded around his ankles and he had grass in his hair. I could see clearly now one of the women was a thin, light-skinned African-American woman with short straight hair and not a single one of those hairs was out of place. She was wearing a tweed skirt with purple, black, and cream-colored threads woven into it. A matching short jacket hung on the back of her seat. She was wearing a long sleeved satin cream-colored blouse that tied in a loose bow at the neck. Her makeup was perfect. She was clearly a very classy lady. As she spoke, she was very animated with her hands. The other woman was dressed similarly. She was Hispanic and had long hair that was pulled into a bun at the back of her head. She was wearing simple pearl earrings and her makeup was also perfect.

As I passed them with my ears wide-open, the African-American woman lifted her hand and pointed at the homeless man as she began to speak. She was clearly responding to something he had just mumbled. I could see a thin diamond tennis bracelet hanging around her wrist. There was a small hanging gold chain at the bottom that made up part of the clasp. It was stunning to me that these two women were seated there with this homeless man, but they seemed so comfortable and fearless.

With her arm stretched out pointing at the homeless man, the African-American woman said, "You see! There's no such thing as chance! Everything happens for a reason. I never sit at places like this but something told me to sit here tonight."

With that I entered the store to purchase my soda. Taking a deep breath, I headed for the coolers in the back as I choked back tears. I thought about what the woman had said, and the coincidences throughout the day. It became clear to me that I needed to read *The Kybalion. The Kybalion* stated exactly what this woman had just said. The coincidences and electrical shock that had brought me to this gas station in the middle of the night were no accident. I wanted to completely break down. How could all of this have happened and come full circle back to this book I was looking at the night before. It was purposeful. I knew then that I would begin reading this book the next day.

Standing in line at the gas station, I had hoped that the night was over. I thought about how I couldn't take any more; mentally, I just couldn't handle any more tonight. I wondered if I should join this conversation at the table outside but a feeling washed over me that I had heard what I needed to hear, and had figured it out; there would be nothing else tonight. As I left the store still shaking and weak-kneed, I could hear they were discussing God. Being a proud atheist, I didn't think I would want anything to do with that conversation. I felt relieved and calm as I drove home. I went to bed and fell asleep almost immediately.

The next morning, I awoke and went to work just as I would any other morning. I thought about what had happened to me the night before. It made me feel incredibly uneasy. I knew I couldn't tell anyone about it. People would think I was crazy. I knew the events of the previous evening were significant and I needed to think about them. It was sobering to say the least, but I was very curious, and I looked forward to leaving work and cracking open *The Kybalion*. All-day at work my mind was elsewhere. *What happened last night? What was that? How was all of that even possible?*

I came home for the weekend and found a copy of *The Kybalion* online. I listened to a LibriVox recording by Andrea Fiore. I was struck immediately by some of the eerie parts of the first few pages of the book. Given the very purposeful means by which this book was placed in my lap; these parts caused the hair on the back of my neck to stand up.

> *The lips of wisdom are closed, except to the ears of understanding – The Kybalion.*

The book starts with this quote. Given the manner in which I came across this book, I wondered if I had ears of understanding, and what did that even mean anyway?

> *The Hermetists have never sought to be martyrs, and have, instead, sat silently aside with a pitying smile on their closed lips, while the "heathen raged noisily about them" in their customary amusement of putting to death and torture the honest but misguided enthusiasts who imagined that they could force upon a race of*

barbarians the truth capable of being understood only by the elect who had advanced along The Path.

I found this to be particularly confusing. It seemed cold to me. If there were people who didn't understand something then why not teach them? All of the hostility that the above statement implied was something I couldn't really wrap my mind around.

And the spirit of persecution has not as yet died out in the land. There are certain Hermetic Teachings, which, if publicly promulgated, would bring down upon the teachers a great cry of scorn and revilement from the multitude, who would again raise the cry of "Crucify! Crucify!"

Crucify? What, like Jesus? I was becoming increasingly uncomfortable with the idea that there were some kind of religious implications here. It wasn't something I had ever believed in. The idea that this could have to do with Christianity made me very uncomfortable. But the book did mention occult teachings. I wasn't sure which one of those made me more uncomfortable.

The passage of this book to those ready for the instruction will attract the attention of such as are prepared to receive the Teaching. And, likewise, when the pupil is ready to receive the truth, then will this little book come to him, or her. Such is The Law. The Hermetic Principle of Cause and Effect, in its aspect of The Law

> *of Attraction, will bring lips and ear together-pupil and book in company. So mote it be!*

When I read this, the hair on the back of my neck and arms stood up. I understood the method by which I had come to be reading this book, and I knew it was no accident. I didn't understand how someone could have written a book over 100 years ago, and know that it would be purposefully distributed in such a seemingly paranormal way. What is going on here? "When the pupil is ready to receive the truth…" I thought about this for a moment. Everything in this book must be truth… And for some reason, I must be ready to learn these things.

> *If you are a true student, you will be able to work out and apply these Principles—if not, then you must develop yourself into one, for otherwise the Hermetic Teachings will be as "words, words, words" to you.*

For me, the book was a hard pill to swallow.

The first principle of the book is mentalism which states that the universe can be thought of as a mental creation that stems from a single consciousness. While reading this I thought to myself, *How could one even know that? How could you even prove this?* I found it hard to believe while also pondering the fact that I couldn't dismiss the means by which I came across this information, which I found incredibly unsettling. I found the following words incredible and of little comfort. I felt terrified at the prospect that this was true.

And death is not real, even in the relative sense-it is but Birth to a new life-and You shall go on, and on, and on, to higher and still higher planes of life, for aeons upon aeons of time. The Universe is your home, and you shall explore its farthest recesses before the end of Time. You are dwelling in the Infinite Mind of THE ALL, and your possibilities and opportunities are infinite, both in time and space. And at the end of the Grand Cycle of Aeons, when THE ALL shall draw back into itself all of its creations-you will go gladly, for you will then be able to know the Whole Truth of being At One with THE ALL. Such is the report of the Illumined-those who have advanced well along The Path.

And, in the meantime, rest calm and, serene-you are safe and protected by the Infinite Power of the FATHER-MOTHER MIND.

I did not feel rested, calm, or serene. I was uncomfortable. Incredibly uncomfortable. It was late and I was lying in bed listening to this. I wanted to climb the walls. I didn't understand how anyone could ever know this. What did that mean for me? Was I a good person? What about all that talk of eternal punishment that exists in so many religions, what is that? Granted, my experience didn't involve abduction or anything, but if it were otherworldly beings that were pointing me in the direction of this book… I mean from everything I understand about these craft is that they ride around in a space-time bubble that the craft generates. Any being that had the smarts to be able to figure this out probably knows what they're talking about. More so than I ever would. It was shocking. I felt sick.

The principle also speaks to the fact that everything is alive and has consciousness. Everything from humans to the smallest possible particle of matter. In thinking about this it does in fact make sense. There are some things in physics that we don't understand, such as particle entanglement and the double slit experiment. I won't go into any detail of those two examples here but you can readily look them up yourself. They do imply a consciousness to the universe.

The second principle is correspondence, which states that there are other planes of existence and that there is always correspondence between these planes. Most humans are currently only aware of the physical plane. As above, so below; as below, so above.

The third is the principle of vibration. This states simply that everything is in a constant state of vibratory motion. This makes sense scientifically as well, in terms of atomic structure. Atoms are in a state of constant motion within themselves.

The fourth principle is polarity. This principle states that everything has poles and therefore has its opposite. Opposites are not completely different things, they are the same thing that just varies in its degree. The principle applies to everything, but I found it most useful in terms of human emotion. The example given in the book that people can apply in their everyday lives, just as I have, is that of love and hate. If you think of love and hate as the same emotion and that love and hate vary in degree, you can begin to conceptualize that; as someone who controls one's own emotions, you can, in fact, choose where on that pole you will rest.

The fifth is the principle of rhythm. It states that there is a rise and fall in everything. A swing backwards and forwards. A pendulum movement, as it were.

> *Everything flows, out and in; everything has its tides; all things rise and fall; the pendulum-swing manifests in everything; the measure of the swing to the right is the measure of the swing to the left; rhythm compensates.*

The sixth, the principle of cause and effect, states that for every cause there is an effect and every effect has its cause, even though causes and effects may not be readily apparent to us. When reading this it occurred to me that this is true. Nothing is random. Even the lottery isn't random, it's just complex causes and effects. The balls are released into a tumbler moving at a certain speed, they slam against each other, against the tumblers, and the sides of the container at certain angles based on the speed and mass of the balls. The outcome is actually a certainty based on the physics and math given differing variables of the positions of the balls upon their release, the speed of the tumbler, and the time at which the balls are sucked into the selector. It would actually be possible to predict the results every time.

It was getting really late as I listened to the seventh principle, the principle of gender. I was laying in my bed by this point. The principle of gender refers to generation. Generation on the physical plane manifests as sex but it in fact refers to creation. It also applies to everything. The mind can create and generate thoughts and ideas on the mental plane. In terms of the mind, it speaks of the female and male aspects of the mind or the desire and will. People have sex and generate life. This principle is evident in even the smallest particles. Atoms and particles becoming entangled in the conscious effort of creation with their likes and dislikes, known in science as chemical affinity.

As I lay in bed listening to this I was looking at the wooden frame around one of the windows to my left. I had the thought that the atoms within that wood came together to create its structure. A human came along and had the desire to create the trim, his will allowed him to follow through with the desire to make it happen, and trimmed it down to create the frame from the conception that was created in his mind. It was all the principle of generation through and through in everything. The significance of this thought that I had was not immediately known to me and will become apparent in the next chapter. Although, when I was living the next chapter, I didn't immediately understand this until I started to put things together much later, as you will see. When I was living through it, however, I was always one step behind what was happening. I would experience something, then come across the explanation as to what it meant.

Although there was a lot in the book that seemed a bit out there, I could see its truths. There was quite a bit in *The Kybalion* that I knew through personal experience were true such as the following:

> *The normal method is for the Masculine and Feminine* (will and desire) *Principles in a person's mind to coordinate and act harmoniously in conjunction with each other. But, unfortunately, the Masculine Principle in the average person is too lazy to act-the display of Will-Power is too slight-and the consequence is that such persons are ruled almost entirely by the minds and wills of other persons, whom they allow to do their thinking and willing for them. How few original thoughts or original actions are performed by the average person? Are not the majority of persons mere shadows and echoes of others having stronger wills or minds than themselves? The trouble is that the average person dwells almost altogether in his "Me" consciousness, and does not realize that he has such a thing as an "I." He is polarized in his Feminine Principle of Mind, and the Masculine Principle, in which is lodged the Will, is allowed to remain inactive and not employed.*

My jaw dropped at this statement. I have always found the above statement to be true. Particularly when it comes to money. When the bottom fell out of the housing market many years ago, I had steady income and saw opportunity. I began buying real estate. It hadn't been this inexpensive in a long time and likely wouldn't be again. In doing so, I was able to acquire several rental properties that I gutted, put back together, and subsequently rented out. It was a lot of hard work, blood, sweat, and tears but I persevered. I had a thought of buying these properties and turning them into rentals. It was something I knew could sustain me and my family into old age. I had a thought and followed through with action. It was something that had always been true of me. I can see how difficult it is for others to do this. I always supposed that the reason for this was because of failure.

If anything fails in any process then you would be forced to take responsibility for that failure. But if you are following someone else; well, you can blame them for that failure and wash your hands of any wrongdoing. The big thing the public doesn't understand is that there is no failure. It doesn't exist. I know this idea also to be key in my journey. You may make mistakes and slip up here and there, but you get up, dust yourself off and learn from your mistakes. If, in your error, you learned anything, then it is not failure, it becomes a learning experience and you can therefore chalk it up as a win.

What people fail to see in these situations is that even if you blindly put your faith in someone or something else, was it not you who decided to do this? And therefore you also share the blame. This has been one of my dearest philosophies in life and here it was in this book. The desire to do something and having the will to follow through with that desire. I was also constantly checking myself against these types of philosophies I had read about in *The Kybalion* and also in the writing of Douglas Fairbanks. (At this point I had not yet read any of the books by Douglas Fairbanks but I have decided to interject these quotes because they belong here at this point in the book.) Douglas Fairbanks addresses this in his book *Live and Laugh*:

> *In taking stock of ourselves we should not forget that fear plays a large part in the drama of failure. That is the first thing to be dropped. Fear is a mental deficiency susceptible of correction, if taken in hand before it gains an ascendency over us. Fear comes with the thought of failure. Everything we think about should have the possibility of success in it if we are going to build up courage. We should get into the habit of reading **inspirational books**, looking at **inspirational pictures**, hearing **inspirational music**, associating with **inspirational friends** and above all, we should cultivate the habit of mind of thinking clean, and of doing, wholesome things.*
>
> *"Guard thyself!" That is the slogan. Let us "take stock" often and see where we stand. We will not be afraid of the weak points. We will **get after them** and get hold of ourselves at the same time. Some book might give us help - a fine play, or some form of athletics will start us to thinking. Self-analysis teaches us to see ourselves in a true light without embellishments or undue*

optimism. We can gauge our chances in no better way. If we grope in the darkness we haven't much of a chance. "Taking Stock" throws a searchlight on the dark spots and points the way out of the danger zone.

I had always felt the same way about spirituality that I did about money. I could never bring myself to sit and listen to someone tell me the way things are. I need to see the proof. I can't just blindly follow. I've never been able to do that. I need to know or have some idea based on my own experience. Even as I sit and write this book I have a problem with religion. The churches' stance that the only way to God is through them has never sat well with me. I've seen too many occasions in history where this is twisted to manipulate the public for the financial gain of a few. That being said, I have always had an open mind.

If someone could show me proof, then I was willing to entertain the thought. This is exactly what had just happened. I had come by this book that smacked of some truth. I couldn't deny that I had come by this knowledge by some extraordinary means. So, I am willing to entertain the thought even though it was unsettling and uncomfortable. When I finished the audiobook, I put my phone on the nightstand, and tried to go to sleep. I must have stared at the ceiling for several hours. It was dark in my room and my eyes were wide-open. There was nothing I could do to make myself comfortable in any way. I was screaming inside.

After listening to *The Kybalion* audio book several times, I thought I had a pretty good grasp on it. At the time I thought, *Okay, I've got it, now I'm ready for more conscious experiences from which I can learn.* With that thought began my entrance into the belly of the beast. I was not prepared in any way for what was about to happen next or the events of the next several months. I had no idea what was about to happen. As unsettled as I felt, it was mild, things were going to get much worse. I had no idea at the time but the events of the next several months were going to completely destroy me.

Chapter Three
PASSING THE THRESHOLD INTO THE BELLY OF THE BEAST

I don't exactly remember the date when it comes to this next experience, because it threw me into a state of absolute shock and an emotional crisis of epic proportions, but it was only a few days after the gas station incident. I didn't even talk to my brother about this experience for several weeks as I didn't want to scare him and I felt ashamed. I eventually had to tell him because it was so devastating and disturbing to me at the time. I felt this inner emotional turmoil that was boiling over after this. The incident that led me to *The Kybalion* was scary in itself, but the events that followed caused fear to begin to consume me completely. For the next several months, I was a thirty-nine-year-old male that slept with the lights on because the dark terrified me.

The dark became a place where the comfortable reality to which I was accustomed no longer existed. Adding to the terror was the fact that there was nobody that could help me. My nighttime hyper-paranoia increased 100 fold after the events that followed and I began to have nightmares every time I went to sleep. At times, I found I was struggling to wake from a nightmare but I couldn't. At times, I would even open my eyes and fight to try and push myself up out of bed, but there was some unseen hand pushing me right back into the nightmare. I felt as though my body weighed a thousand pounds as I would collapse right back into my night terrors. I was not in a good place, mentally. There were nights I would sit up all-night long, on the edge of my bed and cry because I couldn't bring myself to lie down. Just the possibility of having a nightmare or another terrifying experience was more than I could handle some nights.

***

To take my mind off things I decided to go to an after-work get-together with some coworkers. In the haze of not getting enough sleep, I forgot to bring civilian clothes to work with me, so I had to go home and change. I came home from work in a rush and changed quickly. I got dressed but didn't like the shirt I had put on, so I changed it. Feeling rushed, I threw it over the closet door. It's not something I ever do because I like to keep the closet door closed and you can't do this if there's something hanging on it. It's sloppy. I'm one of those people that doesn't care to see the messy disorder of a closet, so I keep it shut.

I got home late that night and remember being exhausted, so I took a shower and went to bed. I was tired and I didn't bother to hang up that shirt hanging on the closet door. *I'll take care of it tomorrow,* I thought as I looked up from my bed at the open closet door. This wasn't the type of thing I would normally do. I had adopted this philosophy about life that if I ever had the thought of procrastination, I would take that as my cue to take immediate action. Nonetheless, I threw my head into the pillow and fell asleep rather quickly.

At some point that night I woke up. I could feel a hand touching my arm. I opened my eyes. The first thing I saw was my window off to the left. I was in my room, in my bed, on my back. I was looking at the trim around my window as I thought about how I must have snored myself awake. I inevitably do this when I sleep on my back. I am a stomach sleeper because of that. I then noticed that my eyes were going slightly blurry. I couldn't see the detail in the trim around the window anymore. I tried to raise my hand to my face to rub the sleep out of my eyes and realized that it just flopped there at my side. I couldn't move. I glanced down toward my hand and noticed that I was no longer under my comforter. My body felt very heavy.

I then remembered that I woke up because I could feel this hand on my right arm just below the shoulder. It was still there. I felt like I should be scared and alarmed that there was someone in my room and they had their hand on my arm, but I wasn't. It seemed as though my emotions were also paralyzed. I fought to turn my head to the right. As I did, the room became blurrier and the grip on my arm became tighter. I turned my head slowly; I was scanning the room. I could see my shirt hanging on the open closet door. By the time I finally was able to get my head turned to the right, everything was out of focus. I was squinting. I could see the dark shadowy outline of someone standing over me bent slightly. They began to move closer looking into my face. I could make out two arms, a torso, and a head. As soon as I was able to make this out, the room behind this very tall shadowy figure began to slowly light up with this golden light.

I saw the being begin to lean back and away from my face. I saw the golden light on the walls behind this figure. It was as though this figure had a light source on its back that was turned on and became more luminous as it slowly began to warm up. I could see it begin to turn its head towards the window. The light became blinding and then became organized into rays of golden light that were extending out of the blurry dark head of this being standing over me. All the while its hand was on my arm. I saw the being turn its head back in my direction. Suddenly, an image appeared over the face of this being. It was the image of a face. It appeared as though there was an extremely high definition screen in front of the face of this being and it was displaying various pictures of faces of people that I knew.

The image was so sharp and defined that it occurred to me at the time that I had never seen a device with this type of clarity before. It stopped on a picture of an ex of mine from 20 years ago. It wasn't as though I could have thought this image was this person in any way. I mean, it seemed so fake. You can't just hold a tablet in front of your face with the image of someone else's face on it and pretend to be this person. In looking at this scene and taking this all in, I thought to myself, *What is going on?!!* I then lost consciousness and drifted back to sleep as I felt the extreme weight of this very large being crawling onto my bed.

I began to have a sexual dream with me and my ex from 20 years ago. In the dream it was me and my ex surrounded by nothing but complete darkness. There was no floor, no bed; there was nothing.

I was barely asleep. The dream seemed so real, as though I was actually feeling the things that were happening in the dream. I opened my eyes as I started to regain consciousness. I could see that there was a female on top of me. I was back in my room out of the dream. This female had blue skin. I could see her legs were straddling me. My hands were on her legs and I could feel her skin. It was not like human skin. It was clearly thicker and felt tighter than ours. I could see a belly button. I remembered seeing that there was even a slight layer of fat under her skin because I could see the cellulite dimples even though she was thin and had an amazing body. She was wearing a top. The top had red and silver stripes in a vertical zigzag pattern and appeared to be made of the most impossibly tiny beads. It appeared as though it might have been handmade, and of the finest craftsmanship. The way her top glistened in the light of my TV made me think that the beads may have been tiny rubies and actual silver beads or perhaps some other precious metal.

As I scanned up toward her face it was a blur, although much clearer than before. It was obvious that she did not want me to see her face. I could only see the outline of her face and a very large black mass around her head. I couldn't make out what this black mass was. Maybe she had a lot of black hair on her head? Maybe she was wearing something on her head and perhaps that mass on her head is some kind of technology? Maybe it was the technology she didn't want me to see? Perhaps her face is very alien and would be shocking if I saw it? Maybe she had giant black wings? Or it's a combination of all of that. I wasn't really sure, but as I write this now, I know what it was.

Whatever was going on up there she wasn't going to let me see it. I was in and out of this dream state several times as the experience wore on.

At one point, I felt her breath on my face. I remember thinking that I couldn't believe this was happening. I knew even in this state what she was. I knew she was not human. I knew there must have been some craft parked in the back yard. In my dream I did climax, obviously. She wasn't going to leave without that I'm sure.

The next thing I remember was waking up the next morning. I was once again looking at the window when I woke up and daylight was coming in through it. I went downstairs in a daze, went out to my truck and stood there dry heaving. I wanted to vomit; but there was nothing in my stomach. I climbed in my truck and lit a cigarette. I was confused. I was angry. Most of all I was terrified. I was basically raped and there was absolutely nothing I could do about it. I had zero recourse. It was sinking in that there was absolutely nothing that anybody could do about this. I couldn't even tell anyone. I found all of this very, very, deeply disturbing. I was devastated. I wanted to understand all of this and I was just raped rather than given any understanding.

I began to unwrap the experience in my mind. How would this being have known about an ex that I had 20 years ago? Why was there a complete disregard for me? What does this mean for humanity? The thought occurred to me that this has been going on a long time. Religious art and even cave paintings have always depicted deities and divine beings with golden halos around their heads. Golden rays of light extending from the head. It was exactly the same light show I had seen as this being stood over me. The whole story of fallen angels having sex with the daughters of men went rolling through my head. This is a fucking nightmare!! Were we just fuel for some kind of slave race and didn't know it yet? What - the - fuck - is - going - on?!!

I began to comb through the entire experience. My mind was racing. Lying there paralyzed…that feeling of heaviness…feeling like my body weighed a thousand pounds. This was what medicine would describe as "sleep paralysis." The dream state surrounded by nothing… I've experienced that before… This isn't the first time this has happened to me. Tears began rolling down my face as I recalled another time I felt this heaviness. I started shaking. I was terrified as I recalled these experiences I thought were just weird dreams in my past.

I must have been about 26 at the time. I had just moved into a condo with two coworkers. The condo had just been built and we were its first residents. Just inside the front door was a small foyer with a set of stairs that went up. We were on the second floor and there was another condo underneath us that had an entrance in the side of the building that was occupied by an older single man. Next door was the reverse floor plan with whom we shared a wall. The unit upstairs was occupied by an older lesbian couple from South Africa. I knew this because I would hear them coming and going speaking to each other in Afrikaans. It sounds like it should be Dutch or German but it's different and particular to the South African white population. The condo had an open floor plan. At the top of the stairs was the kitchen to the right and the living room to the left. Beyond the living room was a sunroom that was wrapped with windows, but all of this was essentially one large area that was airy and bathed in natural light during the day.

It was summertime heading into fall. I had just come home from my usual daily five-mile run. My roommates were both out of town and I was home alone for several days. As the sun was getting low on the horizon, I sat in a big oversized chair in the sunroom with my feet up on the ottoman. I could feel the warm light on my skin as the sky was beginning to turn shades of orange and red with the setting sun. I felt myself drifting off to sleep.

Suddenly, I was having a nightmare where I was running through complete darkness. There was no ground…just me and nothing. There was something chasing me. It was grabbing at me from the darkness as I ran. I couldn't see its body but its arms were swooping in from the darkness trying to grab me. The only light that existed in this dream was directly around me, although I couldn't see a source for this light. The arms were covered in green skin. The hands were long and thin with fewer than five fingers on each hand. The fingers had large bulbous knuckles with conical fingernails on the end of them. At the time, in what I had assumed was the same nightmare, I woke up on my back on the floor of the sunroom.

As soon as I opened my eyes, I took in a giant gasp of breath and felt as though the wind had been knocked out of me. I couldn't see very well. I looked to my right and saw a face that was definitely not human. It looked somewhat human but had very pale skin. It had a large wide nose with ridges on it. Its eyes looked human in size and shape but not in their content. It opened its small mouth and hissed at me. It had what looked like small pointed and well-manicured sharks teeth in its mouth. It appeared to be wearing something on its head that was ridged and metallic. Later, I saw drawings of the beings at Holloman Air Force Base and realized this is what that face looked like. The condo was completely dark so it didn't make much sense that there was so much light on this creature's face. I hadn't turned on any lights before I drifted off to sleep in the chair earlier, and it was now nighttime.

I was feeling the heaviness of sleep paralysis as I struggled to get up. I rolled over onto my stomach and was able to get to my hands and knees but it was incredibly difficult and slow. I was panicked. I could still feel the presence of the monster that was pursuing me. It was behind me and I had to get away. I could feel its intense frustration with me. I looked back and could see a pair of legs standing in my peripheral vision behind me with dark pants on. I was terrified as I crawled across the floor in a desperate attempt to escape. I felt so heavy that I couldn't move quickly. I couldn't even lift my knees as I crawled. All I could do was scrape them across the carpet. My knees were raw with rug burn as I slowly made my way to the back of the couch in the living room to pull myself up off the floor. As I crawled,

I could feel the floor was wet because I was slobbering and couldn't swallow. I struggled to look up at the back of the sofa in a series of jerking movements with my head. As I did this I felt the stream of slobber hit my chin. I slowly struggled to lift my hand toward the back of the sofa. I grabbed it.

I woke up in my bed the next morning fully clothed. I felt disgusting. I wondered if I was getting sick. I had fallen asleep in that chair and had a vivid nightmare that seemed so real. It stood out in my mind because it was in fact a nightmare in which I woke up in another nightmare. Strange… a nightmare within a nightmare. I didn't even remember going into my room and getting into bed. I was sure by the end of the day I would have some kind of fever, sore throat, or something. I felt groggy and dehydrated. I took a shower and felt my knees burning as the soap and water washed over them. I wondered if I had been sleep walking and crawled into my bed. I got dressed and headed out.

It was the weekend and I was going to grab a bite to eat. When I got out to my jeep, the downstairs neighbor came out of his house. He started yelling at me. He was livid.

"Your kids were running around upstairs all night, and at one point it sounded like they threw a goddamn bowling ball down the stairs!!" he yelled.

"Wait a minute, calm down," I said. "I don't know what you were hearing but I don't have any kids. I was the only one home last night, and I fell asleep before the sun even set."

I was thoroughly confused. I must have given him a look like he was crazy because he immediately shut down and had a look like he was doubting his own sanity as he turned around and walked back to his condo. When my roommates returned, I told them to watch out for him because he was a little off his rocker. I told them how he had come out yelling at me about "my kids." We had a good laugh. Forever after that he was known to us as the crazy guy downstairs.

Looking back, I now have no doubt that the guy downstairs wasn't crazy. There was a struggle inside the condo that night, although I can't remember all of what happened.

In remembering this experience, I recalled one of the accounts Jacques Vallée documented. It took place in South America. A young boy came across a craft with a being standing outside it. The being was covered head to toe in some kind of uniform and wearing a helmet and gloves that did not allow the boy to see its face or any of its skin. The boy approached the being standing next to the open door of the craft. The being told the boy he could go inside. The boy entered the craft and saw a small robot that was busy cutting up bones. A few days earlier the boy's family had livestock that had disappeared. The boy became frightened by all of this and quickly exited the craft. The being stood outside the craft with the boy. The being bent down and took off his glove. The being's hand had green skin with conical fingernails. The being poked the boys arm with the tip of one of its fingernails. Over the course of the next several days the spot where the being poked the boy's arm swelled up and scabbed over. When I read this story it sounded like an inoculation of some kind. Like a smallpox vaccination.

After the above realization and the nighttime visit from the blue being, I was overcome with fear. I began to sleep with my bedroom light on. Any creek in the house and I was jumping out of bed fully awake, heart pounding and full of adrenaline. A few days prior to the experience with the blue being in my room, I had awoken to some loud noises downstairs and my roommate's dog was barking very aggressively. I heard him open the door in his room that went out to the back deck. I heard his dog barking as she ran toward the back of the yard. He texted me to say he woke to her barking and saw the shadow of someone standing on the back deck by the door but couldn't find his glasses on the nightstand. In the scramble to find his glasses he had knocked over the lamp and it shattered on the floor.

Some nights, after this visit by the blue being, I would sleep very little or not at all. I began to sleep in my comforter wrapped up like a burrito. I kept all of the ends of the comforter underneath me. My thought was that if anything was going to come for me they would have to jerk the comforter out from under me. This would surely wake me. It was very exhausting to be in a constant state of fear.

I had yet another disturbing realization as I ritually prepared myself for bed. I had wrapped all the comforter ends under me. I wanted more coverage over my head so I pulled the top of the comforter up over my ears as I had done when I was a young child. In doing this I remembered why I had done it before. I remembered being in bed very young, not even in school yet, pulling the comforter up over my ears with the thought, *I don't like it when they whisper in my ear; if they can't whisper in my ear then they can't take me.*

I remembered one occasion as a very young boy when I awoke and heard whispers down the hallway through my open door. They were calling my name. I had the impression that they wanted me to come to them. I ran across the hall to my parents' room. I woke my mom up and brought her into the hallway. I pointed down the hallway toward the family room and told her there was a monster in there. I asked her if she could hear it. She kneeled down and listened, but at this point all I could hear was my father snoring from their bedroom.

My mom said in her usual nurturing and tender way, "No, that's your father snoring... Listen... that's not a monster." She walked down to the end of the hallway and looked around then back at me. "See, no monsters here, Matthew." She picked me up, carried me into my room, and tucked me back into bed. I remembered being very young in that house and being afraid of the window in my room at night. I have vague recollections of lights in it.

I felt overwhelmed with this realization. What did this mean for me? Was I now destined to live the rest of my life in fear? I was becoming angry. It was intense anger mixed with frustration. Frustrated because I knew there was nobody out there that could help me with this. These beings can come and go as they please. What am I going to do, call the police? I'm sure the police will get right in their spaceship and take care of it. Not to mention the fact they would just think me to be crazy anyway.

As I lay in bed wrapped like a burrito, my mind started racing with various thoughts of things that happened to me as a small child. Even more shocking than the realization that this has been going on since I was a young boy was the realization that I had been indoctrinated into this by my own mother.

My mother was a wonderful woman and there's no way she consciously did this, but she would make this *pssst pssst pssst* noise from across the room when I was a baby in my crib. She thought my reaction to it was cute. It was something her mother's family did to her as a small child, and my mother would have the exact same reaction. When my mother would make this sound from across the room it would resemble the sound of someone whispering in my ear. This would cause a memory reflex that would tickle my ear and neck and cause me to smile and laugh while pushing my head into my right shoulder. She would then say, "Tight, tight, tight," as I would wrap my arms around myself in an attempt to get the tickling to stop. I remember my mother doing this as she would tuck me in at night. She talked about how she would do this to us as babies. She told us that her mother's family also did this with her. There are pictures of me in my crib doing this.

I threw the comforter off of me in a rage at the thought of all this. I had volunteered for the Special Olympics recently. The high school where the event was held was out in the middle of nowhere. Lackey High School in Maryland. I got dressed and decided I was going to go out there. I wanted answers, I was furious, and in fact, I demanded these answers. If they had been doing this my whole life and knew everything about me then surely they would know I was driving out there. They would know I wanted answers. I got dressed and headed out.

The entrance to the high school campus was completely dark. It was late. I pulled over and sat there. I was so exhausted. I hadn't slept well in weeks. I was so tired of being afraid. I could feel myself falling apart more and more every day, but they clearly didn't care. I sat there on the side of the road in the darkness terrified, angry, completely exhausted, and crying like a baby. I wasn't going to get any answers. As I drove back home I felt dead inside. I was lost as to what to do. I turned on the radio and decided to listen to some music to take my mind off things.

I never listen to music. I prefer listening to NPR. Listening to music was something that I never did just because it didn't fit in with my philosophy about life. My whole thing had always been that if I wasn't learning something from what I was doing then it wasn't worth doing. Right then, I wasn't in the mood to learn. I wasn't in the mood for anything heavy anymore. I turned on the radio and began listening to music. It seemed that every song on every station that happened to be playing at that moment had some kind of "Awwwww, poor you" type of theme to it. I heard a song beginning with what sounded like these chiming bells with birds singing and turned the station only to hear these bells on the next station as well; I shut the radio off. "What, is that supposed to be funny?" I said. I opted to drive home in silence and anger trying to think of nothing.

As these things in my childhood were coming to light, I began to recall other strange events that, at the time, I couldn't explain, but now seem so obvious. One such event involved only my mother.

We had been spending the summer on the East Coast. My mother had to return a week before the rest of us, so she flew back home alone. I woke up one night during that week of my mother being home alone to the sound of some conversation down the hall in the kitchen. I left my room to see what was going on. When I entered the kitchen, I could see my dad was on the phone and seated at the kitchen table with my older brother standing next to him looking very concerned.

"What's going on?" I whispered to my brother.

"Oh," he said. I could feel the hesitation in his voice. He didn't want to tell me. My heart sank as I realized it must be serious. "Mom woke up and saw someone in the room with her. She called the police," he said.

"What?! What happened?!" I asked insistently.

"She woke up and saw the figure of a man standing in the doorway. She started screaming at him to get out. She grabbed her glasses from the nightstand and saw the figure take off down the hall before she could get them on," he said. He explained that she had already spoken to the police and they had combed through the house and didn't find any signs of an intruder, and that she had then called my dad to tell him what had happened. I was concerned.

"Who was it?! What did they want?!" I asked.

"Dad and I think it was probably someone that had the wrong house, they were probably looking for the house down the street where they're always having parties." He said. At the time this seemed a somewhat reasonable explanation. It was a college town. And there were constant parties at the house down the street. Looking back, however, I don't think that's what happened there. Nobody looking for a party would have entered a house that was dark, with no music playing, no people around, and then proceed into the farther reaches of the house. It doesn't make sense. And what about that had woken her up anyway? By the time the rest of us flew home later that week, my mother even seemed to believe this story as the most likely explanation.

In another disturbing occurrence; we were at home one evening playing board games in the dining room. I was in elementary school, perhaps second grade. It was a cool evening so we had all the windows and doors open for the breeze and fresh air. We had various chips and snacks in bowls on the table, enjoying the evening as we often did as a family. We were having a good time playing board games and talking when suddenly, this man stumbles through the front door.

He was covered in blood and yelling for help. His face was swollen and bloody, his eyes were black and blue. He had gashes all over that were dripping blood on the carpet. He was yelling about the demons in our front yard that had beaten the shit out of him. My mother was on the phone in an instant calling the police. My dad was trying to calm him down and keep him distracted by giving him a glass of water. The police showed up and took him away. In thinking about this I wonder if there wasn't something more to this than just some crazy guy.

I recalled another documented Jacques Vallée case from *Confrontations* in which he described a nurse that was in the home of one of her elderly patients. The nurse was thrown to the floor and badly beaten by an invisible entity. The nurse suffered a broken leg as a result of the encounter. In light of that I had wondered if that, "crazy guy" that ran into our house had been up to no good. Perhaps he was seeking to harm us. Why was he *in* our front yard when he got beaten up anyway? A few days later a mangled and beaten body matching the description of this guy was discovered in a back alleyway or near some drainage ditch. My parents had read about it in the papers and wondered if it wasn't the same guy.

Thinking about the incident with my mother brought out memories of a dark family secret. The details are vague, not because I can't remember, but because nobody wanted to talk about it. I've had to piece things together.

The event occurred sometime in the early 1920s as it concerned the birth of my grandfather. His father worked in the family business and at some point became ill and died young. Somewhere during all of that my grandfather was born, my great-grandmother went crazy, and was committed to an insane asylum where she was never heard from again. My grandfather was raised by his grandmother. I tried to ask my grandfather once what had happened there, but he wouldn't talk about it at all. From what I remember, I asked him and he just looked at me and walked away. My mother's family was considerably wealthy with a good household name, so I didn't understand why an insane asylum would be the best they could do. At the time of my grandfather's birth, they were probably one of the wealthiest families in the major metropolitan area. It didn't make sense, and now the story was very unsettling to me because of what I was going through.

From all accounts, my grandfather had nothing good to say about his family. He left for the war and had very little to nothing to do with any of them after that. He was shot down during the war and spent some time as a POW and eventually retired from NASA in the 90s.

Given everything that was happening to me; I wondered why my great-grandmother was committed to an insane asylum. How could a family of considerable wealth feel their only option was to commit her? What was that really all about? Would this be my fate as well?

I was beyond paranoid at the prospect of all of this. Not only had this been going on since I was a baby but this has been happening to my family for who knows how long. I woke up one morning during this phase of heightened fear and paranoia to a disturbing feeling. This feeling that something bad was coming for me. It was intense. I came down the stairs that morning and my roommate's dog was laying on her pillow in the living room. She saw me coming down the stairs and she wasn't happy to see me. She looked away from me as soon as she saw me looking at her. I went over to her and attempted to pet her, but she got up and walked away from me as though she were afraid. She hid from me behind the dining room table, which is something she had never done before. I could see her behind the table as I made my way to the kitchen. She was looking straight ahead at the wall with her tail between her legs. I could tell she was watching me through her peripheral vision so she didn't have to look directly at me as I left the house through the kitchen door.

I went out to my truck to think. I wondered once again what all this was about and my mind was racing with all kinds of awful possibilities. I imagined that there was maybe some giant pile of half-human bones discarded on some distant planet somewhere after medical experimentation. Were these beings actually evil? All of this stuff in *The Kybalion* suggested at least that the universe was in fact created. Was it created with evil beings as well?

    I tried to call a friend of mine to take my mind off things. I wanted to talk about anything. I certainly wasn't going to talk about any of this. I was standing outside by my truck with the phone to my ear as it rang several times. It appeared he wasn't picking up. I had my back to the house when I felt someone push on my phone with such force that I had to tighten my grip on it so it didn't fall out of my hands. I turned around with a smile on my face expecting to see my roommate standing there; but there was nobody there. A rush of adrenalin shot through me; I was terrified. I looked around but there was nobody anywhere. I quickly walked inside. My roommate's dog quickly ran away from me as I came in. I went up to my room and curled up in a ball in the corner. I sat there crying and shaking with fear for hours. How bad was this going to get? Why was I being tortured? I couldn't shake this horrible feeling of impending doom.

    I went down to my truck for a cigarette that night and I called my brother. I was a mess. I was broken. As the phone began to ring sitting in the truck with the phone to my ear, I felt someone once again push on the phone from behind me. It was becoming too much. There was no room for there to have been someone behind me, so I didn't bother to turn around. I knew what it was. I unloaded all of the dots I had connected on him. I was forced to tell him everything that had happened. I was in a panic and crying uncontrollably. I was hyperventilating and felt like I might pass out. I was a bit upset by his reaction when I told him about the sexual experience with the blue being in my room. His reaction was "Holy shit, are you kidding me!! That's amazing!! Your DNA is in space right now." The implication being that there would be a child, or children, born from my DNA that is not completely human on some other planet somewhere. I was fully aware of this and it was of no comfort to me.

I was terrified and told him that I was afraid for my life. I told him that I thought they might kill me and I felt something bad was coming for me. I told him about the phone incident and the fact that the dog was suddenly afraid of me. He stopped me and said, "There's got to be something you're missing. Something you're misinterpreting. These beings don't have these crafts just so they could come here and terrorize you," he said. After discussing it for several more minutes he was able to talk me down.

After I got off the phone with him, I decided to go back through *The Kybalion*. Maybe there was something I was missing. It was worth another look. Something had to give because I couldn't take much more of this. My world was unraveling, and even at work I was finding it difficult to keep myself together. The constant fear, being unable to sleep, and my depression was becoming incredibly intense. I used to pride myself on my ability to remain calm and collected in stressful situations. I had been told by many people in the past that I was the most level-headed person they had ever known. This was obviously no longer true and to me that was devastating.

As I lied in bed that night, I put on *The Kybalion* audiobook in my headphones. I was starting to get tired, as it was getting late. When I was listening to the principle of gender, I found my eyes scanning the room. I was once again looking at my window just as I had the first time I listened to it. I remembered looking at the woodwork frame around the window thinking about creation. Suddenly, it occurred to me that when I was awoken by this blue being I was also looking at the woodwork around my window. This was how I was aware that my vision was going blurry, because I couldn't see the detail in the woodwork. It made me think back on what had occurred to me the first time I listened to this looking at that window. In *The Kybalion,* the principle of gender refers simply to generation or creation which manifests as sex on the physical plane. It occurred to me that maybe these beings don't view sex the same way we do. Maybe to them it's something that is viewed as simply creation just like the frame around my window. This brought me a bit of comfort, but I was still upset. We don't, as humans, view sex this way and I still felt violated. I had the thought that this couldn't continue. It was an outrage that they were doing this to people.

I listened to the portion of *The Kybalion* that speaks to the hierarchy of life that exists in the universe and where humans fall into that hierarchy. It explains that there are some beings so high in the hierarchy that they appear to be bathed in white light. I thought back on the experience I had with the blue female in my room. The rays of golden light that were radiating from her head reminded me of the halos in religious art. The first book of the *Gods, Man, and War* trilogy theorized that this whole phenomena was responsible for all the world's religions. The fact that this being had displayed these rays of light coming out of her head was, for me, confirmation of this.

At this point, I thought about the Book of Revelation in the Bible. The light that lit up my room… In Revelation, it talks about no need for sunlight or moonlight in the New Jerusalem because the light is God and the lamp is the Lamb. I recalled the light around me as the green skinned being was chasing me. Its hands swooping into the light that seemed to only exist around me. I knew at this point I had to understand Revelation. I began to realize that these beings were the angels of the Bible. The blue-skinned Hindu gods of India. The gods of ancient Egypt. *But why?* I thought. *What did all this mean?*

Were all the religions concerning this stuff true? Or were people in antiquity unable to express what was actually happening because the vocabulary for this kind of thing didn't exist yet? There had to be more that I was missing. Clearly, I didn't have a very good grasp of what was happening here but I knew I needed to. I decided to dig into who had written *The Kybalion* and came across William Walker Atkinson as one of its authors. He had a publishing company based out of Chicago in the early 1900s called the Yogi Publication Society. He authored some 105 books under various pen names like Yogi Ramacharaka, Magus Incognito, and Theron Q. Dumont just to name a few. I decided I was going to start reading these books; perhaps I would find more answers. I would think it would be difficult to write 105 books about nonsense. Most people would be unable to write a single book about nonsense much less 105 of them.

As I sit and write this book, I believe this point in the story to be as far as most experiencers get in the journey.

Before I went to sleep one night, I decided to have one last cigarette as I was combing through thoughts in my mind. I went out to my truck and I turned on the radio. I wanted to listen to something positive. For some reason, "Where Is The Love" by the Black Eyed Peas came on. It was a song I had heard before and I always liked it. After it was over I played it again on my phone via YouTube. As the song came to an end, I decided I would let YouTube run and play whatever song happened to be lined up next. I thought, *Well, if there's no such thing as coincidence or chance, then whatever song pops up next will be significant.* The next song began to play. It started off with the sounds of some birds then moved into the sound of chiming bells. I immediately recognized it. It was the song that had started that night I drove out to the middle of nowhere angry and looking for answers.

The song was Coldplay's "Hymn For The Weekend." I grabbed my phone and watched the video. I was shocked as I listened to the words because they seemed to speak to the experience I was having. In fact every drop of this song spoke to this. I became very dizzy. There was so much going on here and I didn't understand why.

How could all of this be happening? The music video takes place in India. It wasn't lost on me that this being had blue skin as the gods of India do. After hearing this song I understood. These experiences I was having were learning experiences. I had to learn from them as I was beginning to do. I understood that I was going to be taught some things and I needed to pay attention.

Chapter Four

CHALLENGES AND TEMPTATIONS; ABYSS DEATH AND REBIRTH

Thumbing through the titles of the books by the Yogi Publication Society, I came across several titles that stood out to me. I turned off my television and decided to get to work. No distractions... I was going to get to the bottom of this.

The first book I decided to read was *Mind Power: The Secrets of Mental Magic* by William Walker Atkinson. The book seemed to speak to Eastern philosophy. Not only did it speak to Eastern philosophy but it seemed to speak to the way I viewed the world.

The book was about the power of the mind and the amazing things it can do. I read the chapter titled "Desire and Will in Fable." It was about a husband and wife; but really what he was demonstrating in this was an important lesson in human psychology. It speaks of will and desire as being the two parts of the human mind; the male and female mind that exist in everyone. The fable Atkinson made up was the same story of Adam and Eve in the Garden of Eden. It all spoke to the fact that when desires rule the mind completely, bad things can happen. The story conveys the principle of polarity with the two parts of the mind; desire and will. These stories were just examples of what happens when one lives their life ruled by their every desire. Your life is, at that point, out of control. Constantly being jerked around by your emotions; living life from one emotion to the next. I began to think about people who I knew that clearly lived in this manner. It was sad to me. I could look at their lives and see how chaotic an existence this was. How it prevented them from accomplishing the simplest of tasks.

In a later chapter, Atkinson described the abilities of mystics in India. One such mystic had cultivated the ability to induce illusion into the minds of his audience. It was a skill this mystic had refined over the course of many years; some fifty years in fact. The mystic began the illusion by planting some mango seeds. The seeds would then sprout into a mango tree from which the mystic would pick the mangos and throw them out to the audience. The mystic was able to accomplish this by means of imagination. Creatively this mystic had imagined this. Memorizing every inch of this mango tree as it began to spring up. Every leaf and every piece of fruit was recalled in vivid detail in the imagination of this mystic. Atkinson explains that if you were to take a photograph of this event mid-illusion, you would see the mystic sitting in a chair on the stage staring intently at the audience. The illusion exists only in the mind of the mystic and he is projecting the illusion into the minds of his audience.

At first I thought, *Well, that's impossible.* As I thought about it for a moment, I began to understand that it is not. I had in fact experienced this. The blue female in my room that night had done exactly this to me. The image over her face… the blurriness over her face. It was an illusion that she had induced in my mind. The reason it appeared as though there were some incredibly high definition screen in front of her face when she presented the image is because she had in fact memorized this picture. She memorized the image to such a degree that I could see the glass surface of the screen on which she memorized it. Not only did that strike me as amazing but I also knew I was reading this book so I could discover this. My experience that night was a theatrical performance that was also being used to teach me.

While reading this book on mental abilities, I recalled seeing an episode of the History Channel's *Ancient Aliens* where they discussed an incident that had happened with some divers in the Soviet Union. We now know about this because the documentation of this event was uncovered when the Soviet Union collapsed. There were some military deep-sea divers practicing in the deepest freshwater lake in the Soviet Union at the time. There were several of them going down at the same time. While down there, the divers came across a group of beings that also seemed to be wearing scuba gear of some kind, although it didn't appear that their scuba gear included air tanks. Two of the divers decided they were going to try to grab one of the beings and bring it to the surface. As they went to go grab it, one of the beings held out its hand. This action had the result of sending out a shockwave through the water that ejected the Soviet divers to the surface. Some of the divers died as a result of the bends. My thought was that if they could do this, why can't we.

I was out smoking a cigarette in my truck one night, as all of this was running through my head. There was an empty soda bottle in the cup holder. I put it on the edge of the seat so it was teetering on the edge. I wanted to see if I could WILL the bottle to fall. I didn't know how to do this, or what I was doing; but I was going to try. In Atkinson's book he describes mental abilities as being closely linked to will and desire. He describes how to use these qualities and encourages readers to "read between the lines." I understood what he meant by this. I tried it. I tried using different breathing techniques as I did it. I was concentrating on this bottle to the point that I was getting a headache, but I knew there was something to this. The bottle fell. I did this several times. It was giving me such a bad headache I had to stop for the night.

I came back to it later the next day. I was again trying to force it to fall with all my might. I heard a voice in my head say, "You're trying too hard, relax." I then decided I would relax and calm myself. I would relax completely as I stare at the bottle and let my will act upon it. In doing this repeatedly I recognized that I could do it. I could will the bottle to fall. It wasn't always immediate and the bottle had to be teetering on the edge ready to fall anyway. Sometimes it would fall on its own. When I made it move or fall I could feel it in the center of my chest just below the ribcage. It felt a bit like what would be described as butterflies in the stomach. I found I would have to concentrate on nothing else but this bottle and my will for 30-45 minutes before I would see action in the bottle and even then I couldn't do it every day. I had to be in exactly the right state. I found that the bottle began to fall as I willed it to do so, far more than would be associated with pure chance.

I did little experiments where I would go out to my truck and get the initial concentration and relaxation out of the way until I could get the bottle to fall. I would then set the bottle on the end of the seat and let it sit there while I read for 20 minutes or so. I would then look at the bottle and will it to fall. And it would. It became obvious to me that the ability to do this really well depended on the cultivation of attention, desire, and will to an extreme degree. The correct state of mind for doing this is what I have heard described as being in the right side of the brain. It's a state that is associated with concentration. Concentration to such a degree that it would seem an absurdity to do so in our culture as we would see no reason for it. This is evident when you put an audience in front of the most boring speaker on some boring topic. You'll find that within the first 20 minutes or so, most people have begun to daydream about something else. I can see that in the future of humanity, the cultivation of the will, attention, and concentration will become exceedingly important. I could easily see a day where lessons and exercises in the cultivation of these qualities will be taught beginning in pre-kindergarten. In the future, we will understand that the survival of the human race depends on the cultivation of such things from a very early age.

Atkinson describes a teacher in the cultivation of these qualities. The teacher places a dead fish in front of his student. He asks the student to describe the fish on some sheets of paper and leaves the student for several hours. When the teacher returns he looks at the report his student has made. He is incredibly disappointed and tells him to start over. This process continues between teacher and student. Several times he is told to start again until, after several weeks, the student has drawn every scale and shadow of the fish so that the drawing resembled a photograph.

It was after reading this book that I decided I would begin to cultivate these qualities in myself. I would also begin to take control of my emotions by calling into action the principle of polarity. I had always been mindful as it was something my mother instilled in me from a very young age; and was always incredibly important to me. I would begin controlling my emotions to an extreme extent. I decided I would completely cast out emotions like hate and anger. Instead, I would choose to rest on love as I selected the next book to read from the various titles put out by the Yogi Publication Society. I went online and ordered several books that I knew I needed to read. Among the titles I ordered were *Life Beyond Death*, *The Hindu Yogi Science Of Breath*, *Light On The Path*, *Our Glorious Future*, *Fourteen Lessons In Yogi Philosophy*, *Divine Pymander Hermes Mercurius Trismegistus*, *Advanced Course In Yogi Philosophy and Oriental Occultism*, *The Science Of Psychic Healing*, *Bhagavad Gita*, *Jesus: The Last Great Initiate*, *The Illumined Way*, and a hard copy of *The Kybalion*. I noticed that three of the titles were written by a woman named Mabel Collins.

I ordered these books before I discovered that you could buy the complete works of William Walker Atkinson in digital form for just a few dollars.

As I awaited the delivery of all of these books, I was going about my life in a controlled way. I was no longer acting out the emotions I was feeling and found I was falling deeper into depression. I was in a constant state of intense emotional pain. I figured it was the result of everything that had been happening to me.

I was in bed one night, I was still wrapping myself up like a burrito, just waiting and anticipating the next terrifying experience. I was on edge. I woke up because I felt the comforter jerked out from underneath me. I opened my eyes as I felt the comforter being taken out from under my feet. I was lying on my right side as I looked down and saw the comforter being tossed over in front of me by someone standing behind me. I couldn't move. Once again I felt heavy. I heard a soft calm female voice say, "Shhhhhh, don't be afraid." I was fighting to stay awake. As I drifted off back to sleep, I could feel my body sliding across the bed towards the wall. In a flash I saw the whole halo light show again and the next thing I knew I was waking up in my bed the next morning. I examined my bed and saw that the mattress was slightly pushed off the box spring in the direction of the wall. Whatever they had taken me from my bed to do to me, I could not remember. This happened often throughout the course of the next several months.

As my books began to arrive, I decided I would read *The Life Beyond Death* first. It goes into great detail as to what happens to people beyond death. It's not something that I would have taken seriously prior to my encounters. In this book, Atkinson explains that death is an illusion. He uses the example of a caterpillar surrounded by his caterpillar friends as he seals himself in his cocoon saying all kinds of depressing things as he will never see any of them again.

Atkinson states that all of us are immortal souls that are constantly being recycled. He explains that you consist of the soul, your astral body, and your physical body. When one dies they are freed of the physical body, they then shed the astral body in the astral plane. The astral body being an exact replica of the physical body just as is true in form on the astral plane. "As above so below..." The astral plane mimics the physical plane. Once the astral body is discarded the soul enters a phase of sleep. It awakens again on the astral plane to work out the things that happened in life. The soul then sleeps again and prepares for rebirth.

Atkinson also describes beings that assist in this process and may become apparent to those who are dying. They may see these beings as apparitions that are not perceptible to the living. He also explains that, in mourning people who have passed, you can in fact keep them from their slumber. This mourning can be so powerful an emotion that the soul will feel this and be pulled back from slumber in the astral plane.

As I read this book, one of my coworkers went on leave because his grandmother had just passed away, so it was interesting to read in light of all of that. It was after reading this book that I began having more nightmares. They were bad. Apocalyptic-type nightmares. At the same time I continued to be in excruciating emotional pain. Most days I would come home from work, curl up in a ball on my bedroom floor and cry like a baby, as I was unable to do anything else.

One night, I was having such horrible nightmares that I was fighting to wake up. I was beginning to open my eyes and pushing myself up. I said, "Why are you showing me such horrible shit?" I felt once again like I weighed a thousand pounds. I fought hard; I was overwhelmed and forced right back into the same nightmare.

I read through many of these books in quick succession. Reading about psychic healing was a big moment of realization for me. It took me back to all of the baggage I had from the death of my brother. He was diagnosed with stage-four colon cancer at the age of 27. I was remembering the last weeks of his life. He was in so much pain. He was at my parents' house receiving palliative care. My mother was a registered nurse so she was assisting in his care, administering pain medication and so on. I was sleeping in the bed with him should he wake at any point and need anything. One morning, he was staring at the doorway to the bedroom when my older brother walked in and stood in the doorway. As he stared from the bed, he motioned with his hand for my older brother to get out of the way of the doorway as though he was staring at someone who was standing there behind my brother.

I was watching my brother as he lay there sleeping. I could see his pulse in his neck and I could feel him slipping away from us. He was just a shell of who he was. His eyes were sunken. His skin was starting to turn yellow as the cancer began to consume his liver. I loved him so much and, as I watched him, I felt instinctively as though I should be able to put my hands on him and heal him. I didn't, because it occurred to me that this was ridiculous. In retrospect I should have tried. Maybe things would have turned out differently. As I thought about all of this after reading it, I was just overcome. I was openly sobbing in a way I don't think I ever had. My thought was that maybe I was supposed to have done that. I was repeatedly crying out, "Oh my God, I'm so sorry!!!" as I sat hunched over sobbing. I was already a basket case of fear and emotion, and to add this too…

I began to look at the other books I had purchased to decide what I should read next. I also noticed something odd. There was another book that I didn't remember ordering called *Idyll Of The White Lotus* also by Mabel Collins. I looked at the inventory sheets and it was on there but I don't remember selecting it to purchase. I had to look it up and figure out what it was about. It was also an original print from the early 1900s. It was the story of an ancient Egyptian Priest that Mabel Collins had channeled. At the time it seemed a bit out there but as I write this I see it for the beautiful story that it is. It's packed with wisdom, symbolism, and important life lessons.

The story opens with a young boy, Sensa, who is taken by his mother to the temple to receive religious training. The priests see little promise in the boy and assign him to work in the temple gardens. He was out working in the gardens one day when he sees a beautiful young woman sitting on the lotus flower tank. The boy approaches the young woman and starts a conversation but begins to feel heavy and tired; he falls asleep by the lotus tank mid conversation. The next thing he remembered was one of the other older adult workers in the garden shaking him awake. He sits up and looks around for the beautiful woman he had seen on the tank and asks the man where she went. Sensa describes this woman he saw seated on the lotus tank, and the conversation he had with her. The man is amazed. He tells Sensa the woman he saw was the Goddess of the White Lotus, and that nobody has seen her in many years, much less spoken to her. With that begins the boy's training as a temple priest. The story then unfolds into a mystic drama about hubris, greed, lust, and destiny; leading up to the collapse of the Egyptian empire, when the goddess abandons the temple and the people completely. In reading it, the thought occurred to me that it would make an excellent movie, and I would really love to see that happen someday.

Next, I read *Light On The Path*, *The Illumined Way,* and *Our Glorious Future*. In reading them they brought tears to my eyes. Many of the things written in these books were things I had done naturally. I had always viewed my philosophy on life as a simplification of my life rather than anything spiritual. I felt like these books were written for me, about me. The books clearly outlined the steps to accomplish something but, what that something was, I had no idea.

Clearly these books comprised a step-by-step guide of some kind. *Light On The Path* talks about killing out the desire for comfort and ambition. Killing out the sense of separateness. Some of it made sense, but some of it was still a bit mysterious to me. The books spoke of reaching into the soul and uprooting the source of evil. It stated, when you do this the heart will bleed, and it is only when the feet have been washed in the blood of the heart that you are worthy to stand in the presence of the masters. I had absolutely no idea what that meant. I couldn't tell where I was in this process or if I was even in this process at all.

The books explained that "The Path" is different for everyone. Perhaps this is why I couldn't tell where I was in the process. Of this process Mabel Collins writes the following in *Light On The Path*:

> *Seek in the heart the source of evil and expunge it. It lives fruitfully in the heart of the devoted disciple as well as in the heart of the man of desire. Only the strong can kill it out. The weak must wait for its growth, its fruition, its death. And it is a plant that lives and increases throughout the ages. It flowers when the man has accumulated unto himself innumerable existences. He who will enter on the path of power must tear this thing out of his heart. And then the heart will bleed, and the whole life of the man seem to be utterly dissolved. This ordeal*

must be endured: it may come at the first step of the perilous ladder which leads to the path of life: it may not come until the last. But, O disciple, remember that it has to be endured, and fasten the energies of your soul upon the task. Live neither in the present nor the future, but in the eternal. This giant weed cannot flower there: this blot upon existence is wiped out by the very atmosphere of eternal thought.

An important point in *Our Glorious Future* speaks about how when any civilization is at its height, it stands between two fires. The civilization can choose to live, or the civilization can choose to destroy itself. The only way to survive is to find the light on the path. It's the road to the salvation of humanity. Mabel Collins describes people going through this as being the threads through which humanity clings to the divine. I also had no idea what that meant. Having been an atheist my whole life, I couldn't even wrap my mind around that. I even said out loud, "What the fuck does that even mean!?"

It goes on to describe that, thus far in human history, we have always chosen to destroy ourselves. It was a humbling thought that smacked of truth. I began thinking often about humanity and its survival after reading this. How could we survive? I wasn't sure. The books spoke about these qualities that one must kill out. Leftovers from evolution that hinder us. To think of them as the lower emotions that form a handle on your back. This handle, it will be grabbed by others who will use it to move you as they wish; and you will be ruled always by other men. Chained to the earth as a slave to your own emotions. These things will cloud your judgment making you unable to see truth.

I was thinking a lot at this time about how we could survive as a race. My thought was that I knew people were losing jobs because of mechanization. When people lose their jobs it leads to anger. If that anger gets bad enough in a large enough swath of society; it's over. What was the solution to this? I decided to look into mechanization. I was watching YouTube videos of robots that could do amazing things. I saw a video of a robot standing on a conveyor line. It was catching boxes and putting them on a conveyor belt. In another video that same robot was catching boxes and putting them on shelves. In other videos, robots were laying bricks to build homes or pouring small lines of concrete, layering one on top of the other, building up a concrete wall that resembled something like a cinderblock wall. I watched other videos of plants being grown in hydroponics in an automated process using machines and robots.

It occurred to me in watching these videos that the answer to mechanization is in fact: mechanization. We could have robots that build housing, make clothing, manufacture what we need. We could mechanize the world. Food and housing could be free. Robots and machinery can take care of all the mundane and routine things we do throughout the day. We, as humans, could then concentrate on matters of a higher order. This prospect was amazing to me. I was excited and wondered why people weren't talking about these things in the same way I was envisioning them. I was becoming obsessed with this prospect. I was watching discussions of silicon valley billionaires that were discussing artificial intelligence and its uses. I was absorbed in this for a while but that soon came to an abrupt end.

I drove out of DC one Friday to tend to my rental properties out of town. When I arrived for the weekend, I was greeted by a friend of mine. As I unloaded my truck, I happened to look up in the sky. Off in the distance just above the horizon, I saw a craft moving slowly across the sky. It was brown and shaped a bit like a football. I didn't have my phone on me unfortunately, I had already put it inside. It was moving slowly, but fast enough that if I had gone in to grab my phone it would be gone. My thought was that they had followed me down here. They were watching me and they wanted me to know they were watching. Given everything that had happened, I knew they were watching me constantly for the past 39 years, but today they wanted me to know that.

On Saturday morning, I woke up and took a look at my phone. It wasn't working. Throughout the day I messed with it. Returned it to factory settings. Nothing worked. I picked up my tablet to start reading. It wasn't working either. I messed with the tablet for a bit before I realized my phone and tablet were linked. It was a virus. A virus had destroyed my phone and my tablet. As the day went on I got angrier and angrier.

I wasn't angry because I'd have to pay to replace them; it wasn't about that. It was the fact that someone sat down and created a virus that would destroy these things just for the sake of destruction. Or, the manufacturer of these items had released a virus to destroy older models; forcing one to buy the newer phone or tablet and increasing their sales. In realizing this I started crying. Everything I had been looking at in terms of mechanizing society was impossible. I was incensed at this realization as I yelled, "We can't do this, we will always destroy ourselves." There will always be someone who will want to destroy things just for destruction's sake. I grabbed my phone and tablet that were worthless at this point and, in a fit of rage, I smashed them against the brick front steps of my house in Portsmouth, Virginia; yelling various obscenities. A few friends of mine witnessed this spectacle. I told them to write to me if they wanted to get in touch with me. I grabbed my bags and hit the road back to DC leaving my shattered electronics on the front steps.

On the way back I decided I was done. I was in a state of constant emotional pain. Humanity couldn't resist destroying itself and there was certainly nothing I could do about it. I was going to throw away all these books and just forget all about it. I was so tired of it all. The constant fear and emotional pain made me feel like I was balancing on a razor's edge and I couldn't take it anymore. I was devastated now, on top of it all, because I had lived and breathed all of this stuff for the past several months.

I tried to put on some music to help me calm down. I kept hearing "Something Just Like This" by the Chainsmokers and

Coldplay, "Titanium" by Sia, and "Whatever It Takes" by the Imagine Dragons. I swear they were the only three songs on every station. I knew it was for me, but I wasn't interested anymore. I turned off the radio and just sat in silence with my anger as I drove back to DC. I pounded on the steering wheel in a fit of rage and yelled, "Leave me alone!!"

I got home late, so I decided I'd throw the books in the garbage in the morning. I went to bed angrier than I think I ever had and I don't know how I even went to sleep in that state, but I did. I mentally told the powers that be that I was done and not to bother me anymore. Humanity was way past the point of salvation and I couldn't change that. As I fell asleep, I felt so angry that I had been roped into this like some kind of dope… Whatever THIS was… I didn't even know; and that was disturbing to me as well.

I woke up that night with that heavy feeling. I was immediately fucking enraged by this. I thought, *What now! Can't you just leave me alone?!!* As I opened my eyes, my room was very blurry. *Here we go!!!* I thought angrily. I wanted to punch something. I couldn't move. My room began to slowly come into focus. I was laying on my right side. My nightstand began to come into focus. Then the room beyond my nightstand began to come into focus. I was struggling to see what was about to happen. I wasn't scared. I was angry. I could then see something on the other side of my nightstand coming into focus. It wasn't what I was expecting and I was a bit puzzled by it. Was I really seeing this?

Just on the other side of my nightstand was a face that was sticking up just above it. It was a small man. He resembled a yard gnome. He had a white locked beard. His hair was also locked and white. I stared at him for a moment in puzzled amazement; and he at me. There were large black circles where his eyes would be but I don't believe those were his eyes. He appeared to be wearing large, thick, black glasses. In the black glasses I could see a dim orange/red glow the size of the eraser on the end of a pencil. It resembled the glowing cherry on the end of a lit cigarette. He appeared to be completely white. He was monochromatic… all white. It occurred to me later that he looked a bit like the king from a deck of playing cards in that respect and he was completely expressionless. Although, the beard he had was longer than the kings on playing cards. It did seem to have curls on the ends of the locks and he looked quite clean. After I had studied him for a moment, he spoke, but his lips didn't move. He spoke to me telepathically.

"Don't give up, keep going," he said, as he began to induce me back to sleep.

"Go fuck yourself," I thought quickly before my eyes shut.

I woke up the next morning and looked at the books on my bookshelf. *He's right*, I thought. I began thinking about polarity and how I didn't have to get that angry about the virus on my phone. If his civilization was able to succeed, then perhaps there's a chance for us. Maybe he knows something I don't know. I thought about how this whole operation they were pursuing has been an enormous investment in humanity that has been going on for tens of thousands of years if not millions of years. I understood it wasn't up to me to stand in the way of that. I couldn't let my anger stand in the way of whatever needed to happen. All of this was clearly much bigger than me. I had to do whatever I could to help. In *Light On The Path*, Mabel Collins writes, "Work as those work who are ambitious; desire only that which is beyond you and unattainable." I was starting to get it. I didn't want to keep going because it was so exhausting. I was starting to understand that there is no one of us that can change the world, but all of us together can. All of us have to do all that we can on an individual basis pushing ever onward.

  A few days after this incident, my brother came to visit me in DC with his girlfriend. On my drive to pick them up at the airport. I kept hearing Imagine Dragons' "Whatever It Takes," on the radio. I knew it was for me because I could feel it in the same way I felt the other music. My brother's girlfriend is a Lutheran pastor. I enjoyed talking with her about my experiences. She believed me. Further, she stated that the angels of the Bible are not from here. They were not born on earth and they aren't human. So, obviously, that would mean they could in fact be considered aliens. She went on to explain that a lot of people don't see it that way but it was something that made sense to her.

  During their visit with me, we did a lot of sightseeing and spent a lot of time together. One of the days they were visiting, I had to go into work for a couple of hours and told them I would meet them later. They told me to meet them at the National Cathedral. From work I hopped on the metro. I was on the last 15 minutes of my bus ride out to the National Cathedral when a young African-American family got on the bus. They had a younger baby boy and a toddler. They got on the bus in a not-so-nice part of town. I could see this young mother interacting with her children. I could feel the love she had for them. They were all singing "The Wheels On The Bus." As I sat and watched this I had the thought that, *If we all loved each other as a mother loves her child, what a world this would be...* We could, if we chose to; but tears rolled down my cheeks because I knew that we don't.

Chapter Five
TRANSFORMATION AND ATONEMENT

My emotional pain after my brother and his girlfriend left was so much more intense. I was tired. I would come home from work every day and collapse on the floor of my room, curl up in a ball, and cry. It became so intense that I could often feel it creeping in the second I left the building and I would be in tears by the time I reached my car in the parking lot. The pain was so acute that not only would I be lying there crying on the floor in my bedroom but I would also be shivering and shaking as well. My teeth would chatter as I would shiver on the floor.

    I sat on the edge of the bathtub one day with my head in my hands wondering what would be the least painful way to die and end this. I started to think about how I could just open a vein and bleed out, but I knew, having read *The Life Beyond Death*, that this was not something I could ever escape, even in death, because there is in fact no death. I also knew I could never go back the way I came. I knew too much now, so there's no way I could go back to the life I had before. Instinctually, I did the only thing I could do as I dangled there on the edge of a cliff made of my own pain and fears—I let go… I let go of everything I once believed, everything I once was, everything I perceived to be reality, but most importantly, I let go of fear; it was fear that bound these things to me, and I fell into the abyss. My surrender was absolute.

I had reached into my soul to uproot the source of evil within me. I handed it to Charon as my fair across the River Styx for the last time. As I fell into the abyss, I experienced an acute and immediate moment of clarity and absolute truth. My emotions were mine and mine alone. They had nothing to do with anything external to myself. My life, up to that point, had been a physical manifestation of my own emotional self. I could see clearly what my emotions were and how I would project those emotions onto others. My fear, my anger, my insecurities, my jealousy, they were all manifesting in my life in outwardly destructive ways, and they were all mine. The result of a lazy unclean mind.

These emotions are powerful and I would project them onto others as the imagined source of those emotions because it was impossible to contain them once they existed. The only one that can make one feel emotions is oneself. When one experiences hate, fear, anger, or jealousy in themselves, refusing to kill out these emotions before they come to fruition, they become little better than a child throwing a temper tantrum. With this thought, I surrendered these lower emotions completely. I began to simply BE, as I worked through my life's truths. I had done as Mabel Collins suggests in *Our Glorious Future*. I stood aside to let the warrior within me fight by surrendering all emotion.

In letting go I was beginning to see things differently. I came to the realization that it is much easier to destroy yourself with alcoholism, drug addiction, and suicide than it is to come to the hard realization that it's all your own fault for not controlling your own thoughts and emotions. This is an incredibly painful truth. Being forced to examine one's own life through this prism will change you in powerful and unexpected ways. I realized that I had never been a victim of any circumstances; I had only ever been a victim of myself. Circumstances became clear tests. How I reacted to those circumstances was up to me. I could accept and study them, or I could react emotionally; but reacting emotionally clouds the vision and enables one to make all the wrong decisions.

Many self-help authors espouse the idea that it's healthy to view the world through positive rose-colored glasses rather than through negative, dark-tinted ones. I now knew that both of these perspectives were incorrect. To see the truth one must take the glasses off altogether and view the world for what it is. To see the world as a physical manifestation of our uncontrolled emotion and the only emotion anyone is ever justified in feeling or projecting is love. Love is all encompassing and unconditional. When you truly accept this in your life it becomes impossible not to forgive anyone anything. As I sit and write this, I know all of this analysis of emotions or perceptions to be a very old concept. I adopted this philosophy and lived my life this way to some degree without understanding that it was in fact an old philosophy. The Greeks and Romans called it Stoicism. It is in fact a more advanced form of psychology than we practice today.

I isolated myself and doubled down on the books that implied this was the path to something much greater. I reread *Light On the Path*, *Our Glorious Future*, and *The Illumined Way*, carefully; while taking notes, and underlining things that I felt were important to me. I wasn't sure what I was doing or where I was in this process, so I aimed to find out. I listened to the music that had come to me in the usual purposeful way. One day, I was listening to "Where Is the Love" and "Hymn for the Weekend." Once again I decided to let YouTube decide what I would hear next. "Diary" by Angels and Airwaves came on. I had never heard it before, but once again, I knew it fit. I was alone with these books, some music, my own thoughts, and my journal. William Walker Atkinson writes about the importance of keeping a journal for posterity and future generations. I journaled dreams, nightmares, and things that happened throughout the day. Mabel Collins and William Walker Atkinson both write about turning your gaze ever inward and journaling helped me to focus in that direction.

In driving to work I found myself having a different experience than I had in the past. I would see cars darting in and out of lanes around me; cutting people off; cutting me off. It no longer troubled me because I had stopped concerning myself with the actions of others. Instead, I tried to see the pure truth in every situation. I would see these people and feel sorry for them. To live such a chaotic life. Constantly being jerked around by their every emotion, too weak to control themselves and their own mind. Their minds were so uncontrolled that their mental demons were manifest for the whole world to see as they made their way to work in the morning. I began to feel a calm coming over me.

One day, I was driving home from work and I was beginning to feel a bit better. I started to wonder where all of this was going. I was so confused. What was the point of all of this? What was I supposed to do with all of this? I heard a voice. It was just like the voice I had heard at the gas station when all this began that told me to "GET OUT" of my truck.

The voice told me, "You are to act as a shepherd of men. But there is not much time."

"What?" I said. I was very uncomfortable with the Biblical tone of this statement. "What do you mean by 'not much time'? Does that mean I'm going to die?" I asked.

"Yes," the voice said.

As I drove down the freeway I was instantly transported to another place and time. I was shown my death. It felt real. I was suddenly driving very fast through an intersection at night. I was being pursued by cars behind me and I was attempting to escape. There was a car approaching the right side of my truck at a very high rate of speed that I knew was part of the pursuit. I was hovering above myself watching through the back window. I could see the car heading quickly for the right side of my truck. I watched as the car hit me in slow motion and began to tear through the cab. I was suddenly seated inside the cab and felt the glass hitting me in the face as I watched the front of this car come towards me. The slow motion sped up and it was over in an instant. I suddenly was back in my truck driving down the freeway.

I asked how long I had and if there was anything they could do about it. The voice gave me a timeframe and said there was nothing that could be done because I was on borrowed time. I thought about this for a moment and, oddly, I had no reaction. I was at a point, after having read *Life Beyond Death,* that I knew it didn't matter. I wasn't afraid of death. It doesn't exist.

As I began to exit the freeway, I was hit with this brick wall of emotion that was not my own. It knocked the wind out of me for a moment. It was a lot to feel all at once. It was the most beautiful thing I had ever felt in my life. I suddenly realized I could FEEL the trees on the side of the road, the bugs in the grass, and the drivers around me. I could feel life as it was happening around me. This feeling gradually subsided as I drove home, but it brought me to tears. It was then that I realized everything I had been reading about the true nature of the universe was true. The only way I could have felt that was if there was a singular consciousness that connected everything. It's why I could hear the words of the small man in my room. He didn't move his lips when he spoke. He was using his mind to communicate through the Source. His immortal voice as the *Homeric Hymn to Demeter* implies.

The following week at work, I had to take a day-long class. It was a class about leadership that was taught by a couple of senior enlisted members that had been in the Navy some 25 years. Many of the concepts, I could see very clearly, had roots in Eastern philosophy, although it wasn't delivered as such. The instructors reminded me a lot of myself. They spoke about letting go of anger, and how work shouldn't be personal. Treating others like human beings and the acceptance of diversity. They became emotional in talking about their families. They talked about how they believed in the concepts of the course and how important it was to them. I really liked it. At the end of the day, as we were leaving, I approached them and told them about these books by the Yogi Publication Society I had discovered. I wrote down the names of a few books. With a deadly serious look on my face I looked them in the eyes and I told them *The Kybalion* would teach them the true nature of the universe.

I walked down the hall and out the building to head home for the day. As I got in my car a very powerful thunderstorm erupted. The sky opened up in this torrential downpour with terrible lightning and thunder as I was driving out of the parking lot. I could feel this storm in a way I had never before. It felt as if the storm was inside me even though it was external to myself. I thought it was a fitting backdrop to what I had just done. It represented the storm on their horizons. The storm that awaited them in their discovery of truth.

When I got home, my roommate was standing in the kitchen complaining about the severity of the storm. I went upstairs and got changed, I was about to make something for dinner but I started to feel overwhelmingly tired. I felt incredibly weak and sluggish. The storm outside was still raging, so I lied down and went to sleep at about 4 pm.

The next morning I woke up feeling rather rested, as I slept for quite some time. Much longer than I was accustomed to sleeping. It was a Saturday morning, so I got up and went about my day. About 10 am it started raining again. And again, I could feel the storm internally. I suddenly felt tired and my body was beginning to feel sluggish, again. I figured I would take a short nap. I had slept well the night before and I had in fact slept about 14 hours, which is more than twice as long I normally would. Somehow, I was feeling tired again, so I took a nap.

I began to have a dream. The dream seemed like it might have been the type of astral projection I had been reading about. I was flying through the clouds, and I was tethered to the small man that had been in my room. The one that told me "don't give up, keep going." We began to descend through the clouds. I could see he was taking me to work. We landed out front by the flagpole. He showed me a giant dead beetle at the base of the flagpole. It was odd because I had seen that beetle there a couple days before as I was walking into work. It was a very large beetle that was nearly the size of my fist. He stood there at the base of the flagpole looking at me and pointing at the beetle. He said nothing. We then went inside and he took me into the room where I had been in the class the day before. There was a very tall being in a white hooded robe floating in the room that radiated the most brilliant white light.

Nothing was said as we went outside to the back of the building. We stood at a table where I would take my cigarette breaks near a parking lot between the metro line and the back of the building. There was another white light being standing there. It had occurred to me that these were places where I had spoken to people about the books by the Yogi Publication Society. I remembered I had mentioned them to someone out there as I smoked one day. She was having a hard time and I told her these books that were based on Eastern philosophy had helped me.

As I stood out there with the small man, the being that radiated white light spoke to me, I had originally written here and in my journal that I couldn't recall what he said to me and what I asked him. I do remember what I asked him and what he said. I asked something that I read later in one of Mabel Collins' books should never be asked. I don't feel it necessary to repeat, because it was a disgusting question loaded with ambition, so I received a very disturbing and unnerving response. I was told I would be given the answer if I did something awful that I also won't repeat. I told him that there was no way I was going to do that so I was fine with not knowing, and looking back on it, I know that it was a test for me. I did receive the answer to this question when I asked it later for want of clarity and understanding rather than ambition. I learned that it's not the question that is the problem. The problem is why you want the answer. If you ask for your own ambition then you're wrong and you invite bad things.

We then went inside. We entered the space where I work and I assumed we were heading to my desk. The wall to the right was gone and there was just a wall of white light there; I noticed an elderly lady seated at the desk of one of my coworkers. The small man that had brought me there was gone. I knew immediately who it was. She was my coworker's grandmother that had passed away. She was seated at his desk. As I approached her, she stood up. She was wearing a pink skirt and a matching pink jacket with a white blouse. Her pink hat had red berries in it.

She looked at me and asked, "Have you seen my grandson?"

"Yes, I have," I said.

"How is he?" she asked. She was very emotional and insistent.

"He's doing well, he's going to be just fine," I said. I looked down at her and told her in a gentle voice, "It's time to sleep now." She stared up at me a moment, then nodded, and held her right hand out to me. I smiled at her, took her right hand in mine, wrapped my left arm around her, and we walked together into the wall of white light.

When I woke up, I began to examine what had just happened. I thought about how my coworker must have been mourning his grandmother very strongly because it had been a few months since his grandmother had passed, but she was still in her astral body, and looking specifically for him. This is a situation that William Walker Atkinson describes in his book, *The Life Beyond Death*.

The soul of the higher Astral planes, dwells in the idealistic condition, concerning itself not with the affairs of the world it has left behind it. It, of course, maintains a sympathetic connection with those near and dear to it by ties of love or friendship who have been left behind on the material plane, but such sympathetic connection is entirely of a psychic or spiritual nature, and has no connections with nearness in space, or physical proximity. The ties and bonds between the disembodied soul and the soul still in the flesh in earth-life may be thought of as spiritual filaments - something like a transcendent form of telepathic rapport. When the disembodied soul is thinking of the loved one on earth, the latter frequently experiences a feeling akin to the physical nearness of the disembodied soul, but this merely arises from the sensing of the mental and spiritual rapport of which we have just spoken. In the same way, the disembodied soul experiences a sense of "call" or message from the person in the flesh when the latter is thinking intently on the former.

The following Monday, I was going to talk to him about his grandmother but I wasn't sure how. Would he just think I'm crazy? Was it even worth trying to do this? I wasn't really sure. When I got to work, I discovered he was out for the next week attending some training offsite, so I had a week to think about it. I was thinking about calling him but decided I needed the week to think about how I was going to talk to him about this.

Later that day, I went out behind the building to the table that marked the smoking area. I was standing there smoking and thinking. Suddenly this hornet aggressively began flying at the center of my chest. I shooed it away. It quickly came back right at the center of my chest. Again, I tried to swipe it away but it came right back to the center of my chest. I did this many times with the same result. It was insistent and so aggressive that I put out my cigarette and quickly walked back to the building. I knew that whatever was happening with the hornet, it was FOR ME. I decided I would look up symbolism for the hornet when I got home.

As soon as I got home I began to search the web. I came across a book called *Ancient Egypt: Light of the World* by Gerald Massey. In it, he describes the symbolism of the hornet and the bee in ancient Egypt. Apparently, they had only one word for the bee and the hornet. The hornets in Egypt are not the typical hornets we are accustomed to here. The hornets there are much larger. They were considered sacred insects because it was said that they led the souls of the dead to the flowering fields of reeds, Aaru, the land of milk and honey.

In this book, I also found symbolism involving other insects. I read that the beetle was symbolic of the Egyptian god Kephri, whose symbol is the beetle, the sun, and rebirth or resurrection. I remembered how the small man had been pointing at the dead beetle at the base of the flagpole. I wondered if this symbolism meant something.

In the days that followed, I saw these giant dead beetles on the walkways outside the building. I also read the mythology of how spiders became the weavers of the web of destiny. Spiders will come in to play later in the book and knowing that they were the weavers of the web of destiny was helpful.

I began to understand in my experiences that sleep is not what I thought it was. It is a restful state, but it is so much more. I began to think of it as a state of deep meditation and decided to read a book called the *Hindu Yogi Science of Breath* to assist me with breathing techniques during meditation. A couple of the books I had read pointed out how important breathing was in meditation.

In one of the techniques there is a description of breathing rhythmically. Just as in *The Kybalion*, it states that everything is in a state of vibratory motion. When meditating, you can breathe with the vibratory motion of the body by breathing with your heartbeat. In practicing this breathing technique, I learned that it's not as easy as it sounds. A deep breath in for six beats of the heart; hold your breath for three beats; exhale for six beats; hold for three beats; repeat. Throughout the meditation, one is supposed to breathe in this way. Atkinson warns that this is a very powerful form of spiritual meditation when breathing rhythmically. He warns that if you do this you must take it seriously and complete the session as it is not to be entered into flippantly.

I was standing in my room practicing as I read just so I could get the breathing technique down. I was taking my pulse in an attempt to get the timing of my heartbeat and the breath down. I was standing there and glanced at myself in the full-body mirror in my room as I was doing this. I stopped and walked over to the mirror. I looked at the placement of my fingers on my neck as I took my pulse. I couldn't believe what I was looking at. I removed my fingers and put them back again several times. I stood there in shock. The spots on my face where I was no longer growing facial hair corresponded exactly with my fingers as I had placed them to take my pulse. I suddenly recalled the voice I heard as I drove saying that I was already on borrowed time.

I saw a flash and, suddenly, it was nighttime in my room. I was standing at the foot of my bed watching myself slumped over in my bed the night I woke with blood clots in my lungs and lost consciousness. There was a tall being that radiated white light standing over me with his hand on my throat. He looked different than the other white light beings I had seen at work. He wasn't wearing a hood and he wasn't floating. He turned his head and looked at me standing there at the foot of my bed as he had his hand on my neck... I died that night... he was healing me through his fingers on my neck so he could feel a pulse.

Suddenly, I was back in my room during the day. I started shaking and my heart was pounding. I didn't really understand... Why did they do this? Who do they think I am? I'm nobody, there was no way I could possibly be anything big, or do anything significant for humanity. In Mabel Collins' books, she states that the beings that appear to be bathed in white light are not seen by everyone and only become involved with people on matters of critical importance to the whole of the human race. It was a very sobering moment to understand that I was supposed to be dead; but I wasn't because they had something for me. Something I was supposed to do, but I didn't know what or how.

It was spring and I was starting to feel much better by this time. My depression had completely subsided and I was in a good mood. Not only was I in a good mood but my mood was amazing. I felt so incredibly relaxed. I was starting to feel that feeling that hit me as I drove down the freeway that day; but now I felt it all the time. All tension had left the muscles of my body. I was feeling better than I ever had in my entire life.

I was able to feel the emotions of others. Around this time another of my coworkers was arrested for a DUI. I found it difficult to be around him because I could feel that there was so much pain there. I asked him how he was doing one day and he gave me this enormous grin and threw two thumbs up. I knew better. His actions were not reflecting his true mood because I could feel his mood. I told him that I knew this. I told him that if he ever needed anyone to talk to, I was there for him. Further, I told him that I hoped he would be able to find the strength to turn his gaze inward so he could begin to heal himself.

In a separate incident at work, I had a coworker that told me something one day that he shouldn't have known. I asked him how he knew this. He then told me he couldn't reveal his sources. I looked up at him, slightly annoyed, with the intent of getting this information from him. When my eyes met his, I instantly I saw it. The conversation he had and who he had this conversation with. I even saw where they were in the building when it happened. I knew it had taken place earlier that day as well because he was wearing the same clothing. In fact, I knew that he had just come from that conversation.

It was during this time that I could look back on my own life and see it for what it was. In my journal I wrote that I had been drowning my whole life but, in this current state, I was finally able to breathe and I knew I was going to live. For the first time in my life, I knew what freedom felt like. I had freed myself from false ideas, the emotions and perceptions that imprisoned my mind and limited my field of vision.

After these realizations and understandings, I began to sleep with my lights off. I had killed out the fear in me. I had reached into my soul and uprooted the source of evil. My heart had been bleeding for months. My feet had been washed in the blood of my heart. Just as Mabel Collins writes. It was then that I stood in the presence of the masters and it was in the following events that I understood what that meant.

I awoke in the middle of the night with the heavy feeling typical of the presence of beings. I felt my comforter thrown off of me. I could see my room was brightly lit as I drifted back to sleep. I saw the golden halo and I could feel my body being lifted from the bed. I woke up somewhere else and still had that heavy feeling. As I opened my eyes, I could see dim lighting and felt like I was lying on what I think was a table. There were several beings surrounding me that radiated brilliant white light, looking down at me and also looking at each other. They all looked like the one that was in my room the night I died. I could tell they were communicating with each other, although I couldn't hear them as they examined me. They said nothing to me and I drifted off to sleep.

I awoke again and found that I was no longer lying down; I was standing, although I still felt heavy. I was in some kind of a massive room that extended off into the darkness. I could see the immediate area was lit by two giant fires that were burning inside these huge pedestals on either side of me. In front of me were several beings that radiated white light standing shoulder to shoulder. They were flanked by the beings I had seen with blue skin that were radiating golden rays of light from their heads. They had brought me here to this council.

Behind all of these beings, I could see there were two giant columns as though we were in a large temple of some sort. One of the white light beings stepped forward towards me. The white light was so strong, I couldn't see a face; just the outline of two arms, a torso, and a head. He must have been wearing a robe of some kind because I couldn't make out legs. The being that had stepped forward then spoke. He spoke of mission and purpose. He paused, a long uncomfortable pause, as he looked at me, then he said, "This life you have does not belong to you; it belongs to all of humanity. Your days of judgment begin tomorrow." He then put me back to sleep and I woke up in my bed the next morning.

I thought about what had been told to me. It was humbling. In all of the books I had been reading it was clear to me what I had gone through. It was an awakening into a higher consciousness. It's described by Atkinson as a natural progression in humanity. He described it as a natural part of evolution. At some point in the history of human evolution, we became self-aware. This new consciousness is simply the next step up. In the East this has been described as Nirvana or Enlightenment. In recent years it has been referred to as Cosmic Consciousness. It was also clear to me what consciousness is. One could think of it as perspective. A new and higher perspective. The purposeful nature of things becomes clear and the universe begins to make sense in new ways.

Having killed out the old self, one gains a higher perspective where you are no longer inhibited by old primitive ideas and emotions that hindered and blurred your vision. My mood continued to improve. It became so good that there was nothing that could happen that would change it. I felt this connection to everything that was so powerful I could almost see it. It was a strange sensation to be able to actually feel something internally that is physically external to myself. I could sit in my room alone and know that I was not alone… ever. I began to understand what Atkinson and Collins were trying to communicate when they spoke of the peace and calm that follows the storm. It was a peace and calm unlike anything I had ever known.

In reading the *Bhagavad Gita,* it is clear to me how I got here. The *Bhagavad Gita* is a book in a series of Hindu religious texts called the *Mahabharata*. William Walker Atkinson published his preferred translation through the Yogi Publication Society and it was this version I read. In his introduction he writes about the beauty of this book. He explains that no matter what your level of unfoldment on the path, you will get something from this book. In fact, as you unfold you can read and reread this book several times and it will have a whole new meaning to you each time. Reading it now, I can see the multilevel truths within this precious gift to humanity. In its description of the many paths, I can see clearly the one I took.

In the beginning of my experiences, I was wondering why it was I didn't enjoy anything, and why I also didn't hate anything. What was that? What did that mean? Was there something wrong with me? I know now that this is all psychology based. As one begins to do the psychological work, changing their worldview, changing their perceptions, there are things that begin to fall off. In the *Bhagavad Gita*, God is speaking to Arjuna, Prince of Pandu, about a battle he must fight against a rival faction. I, of course, recognized that this battle is the inner battle which I had just fought. The pain one must overcome. It involves the daily psychological battle that happens as one begins to rein in their mind.

For, verily I say unto you, that the man whom these things have ceased to further torment - he who stands steadfast, undisturbed by pleasure and pain - he to whom an things seem alike - such an one, say I, hath acquired the road to Immortality.

That which is unreal hath no shadow of Real Being, notwithstanding the illusion of appearance and false knowledge. And that which hath Real Being hath never ceased to be - can never cease to be, in spite of all appearances to the contrary. The wise have inquired into these things, O Arjuna, and have discovered the real Essence, and Inner Meaning of things.

Know that the Absolute, which pervades all things, is indestructible. Noone can work the destruction of the Imperishable One.

These bodies, which act as enveloping coverings for the souls occupying them, are but finite things of the moment - and not the Real Man at all. They perish as all finite things perish. Let them perish. Up, O Prince of Pandu, knowing these things, prepare to fight!

He who in his ignorance thinketh: "I slay," or "I am slain," babbleth like an infant lacking knowledge of a truth, none can slay - none can be slain.

– Bhagavad Gita

This experience is not relegated to Hinduism. The following can be found in the Bible. But really this is all about psychology and the way you view the world:

> *22 And the Lord God said, Behold, the man is become as one of us, to know good and evil: and now, lest he put forth his hand, and take also of the tree of life, and eat, and live for ever:*
>
> *23 Therefore the Lord God sent him forth from the garden of Eden, to till the ground from whence he was taken.*
>
> *24 So he drove out the man; and he placed at the east of the garden of Eden Cherubims, and a flaming sword which turned every way, to keep the way of the tree of life.*
> —Bible King James Version Genesis 3:22-24
>
> *7 He that hath an ear, let him hear what the Spirit saith unto the churches; To him that overcometh will I give to eat of the tree of life, which is in the midst of the paradise of God.*
> —Bible King James Version Revelation 2:7

In trying to explain some of the knowledge that is inherent in this profound change, I find it's a bit difficult to do; I liken it to trying to describe color to someone that has never before had the ability to see. I could witness a situation which you may have two people who might bicker back and forth. When I witness a scene such as this I could actually FEEL the universal forces at work behind the scenes. But if you were to try to warn them of this, and explain why you know this, they wouldn't understand. What I just described to you is the reason that Plato wrote the *Allegory of the Cave*. One can't possibly explain what this change is to someone who has never experienced it. They are like the people in the cave watching the shadows on the cave wall, having no ability to conceptualize what the shadows even are or what lies outside the cave.

I was now looking at the world through new eyes. Reading religious texts became something that became very interesting. In reading them, I separated fact from fiction. I was learning through these books that there is some truth to all the world's religions and there are untruths in all the world's religions. I could see clearly how these religious texts were describing what I had just gone through. I could also see that these texts are grossly misinterpreted. I could see the message of this awakening into higher consciousness everywhere. It pervades everything as the myth of the hero's journey. I could see it in art, movies, books and hear it in our music. In fact, I could also tell who in history had been awakened, based on their works.

I put the book down that I was reading at the time to pursue other things even though I only had three chapters left. It was a book called *Raja Yoga or Mental Development (A Series of Lessons In Raja Yoga.)* I had been practicing the mantras in the book. Particularly the "I AM" concept. I mention this because this concept was the one thing that carried me over the top. I think this book in particular carried a lot of people over the top based on its last chapters. For me this book is where everything snapped into place.

I AM is a concept that Mabel Collins expresses in *Light On the Path* when she writes about killing out the sense of separateness. When one thinks, I AM, they should think of themselves as a part of everything. There is nothing separating you from everything you see around you. I had always thought this to be the case to some extent. I have had many debates with people over the years that thought of things that are man-made as being somehow unnatural. I would point to a light fixture and ask if it was natural. They would respond that it was not, it's man-made. Then I would ask if an ant hill or a beaver dam is natural. The response is always yes. I would then ask what the difference is between an ant hill and Manhattan. The response is always that Manhattan isn't natural because its man-made. When you take this view, as so many people do, it fractures the psyche. The home in which you are reading this book and everything within it, to include yourself, becomes unnatural. There is nature outside this place and it is separate from myself.

The reality is that each one of us is simply a concentration of the single universal consciousness that touches everything. You can see this concept in Ancient Egyptian art in the form of the Aten. Scholars misinterpret this as a representation of a sun god because its depiction is that of a disc in the sky with rays emanating from it. If you look closer at the rays, you can see that they are in fact not rays of light; they are hands that touch everything. It is depicting the source touching everything. It is likened to the light of the sun, because when there is light, you can see; unlike the absence of daylight, where you can't see as well, which is also an analogy for what happens when one attains a higher consciousness. When you awaken into this consciousness you are given a peek behind the veil of the universe through a connection to the singular consciousness that snaps in place internally and can be felt. There is a fairly well-known piece of art that I believe depicts this. It's called the Flammarion engraving. It depicts a man on his hands and knees that has reached the point where the sky touches the horizon, he has lifted the sky as though it were a curtain to view what lies beyond; peaking behind the curtain at the inner workings of the universe with its machinery, belts, and turning wheels.

    I read something that had been written about this state of Nirvana or Enlightenment. The author described it as the architect of creation closing up all of the doors of suffering. In doing this the individual feels a sense of incredible joy and unwavering peace. It's powerful. So powerful that it was the driving force behind the building of giant megalithic structures that marked its time of year. Many scholars believe the ancients were simply worshiping the cycle of life and death, the changing of the seasons because their lives depended on the cultivation of crops. If it's crops you are worried about, then you would devote your efforts in that direction. You wouldn't stop that to move millions of tons of earth to create these huge complexes that exist all over the world. Today, we still depend on the cultivation of crops in the same way. Nothing has changed in terms of our dependance of crop cultivation. The current scholarly explanation doesn't hold water.

This connection is so powerful that there is no doubt as to whether or not you have felt it, nor is there any doubt as to what is happening to you. I knew in this state that if a bomb went off next to me I wouldn't flinch or react to it in any way because I was so at peace. When I first read *The Kybalion,* I thought it seemed a bit out there. It described the universe as a mental creation that stems from a singular consciousness and I wondered how one could ever make such a claim; or even know that. In this current state I knew. I knew it for myself. I also knew that this was the only way anyone could know; the only way to know is to know it for yourself.

As a child, I would look up at the night sky and wonder what was out there. My father would sometimes take me to his planetarium shows followed by rooftop telescope sessions with the night sky. The universe seemed so vast, cold, and mysterious. So unknowable. Now, having awoken into a higher consciousness; I knew. Suddenly the universe seemed much smaller. Having realized my own immortality and destiny, I could lie there under the stars and feel the life out in the universe raining down love from the sky.

In meditating under the stars one night, I was listening to "Diary" by Angels and Airwaves. When the song ended, I decided to let YouTube decide what I would listen to next. It was a song called

"Heaven" also by Angels and Airwaves. I lied there breathing rhythmically while meditating under the night sky. Breathing in the divine breath of love that created the universe and breathing it out; sending this love out to all of humanity. I had read in *The Hindu Yogi Science of Breath* a quote, "*Lucky is he who can breathe through his bones.*" I now knew what this meant. I could feel it through my whole body. Lying there under the stars, feeling the universe, and listening to "Heaven," I recalled with a smile the encounter with the police officer that was described by Jacques Vallée. I thought about how the being told the officer that he would one day see the universe. I now understood what the being was trying to tell him. The universe is small, warm, full of life and love; it is my home; and I knew that one day soon I would be exploring its farthest reaches just as *The Kybalion* states.

> *And Death is not real, even in the Relative sense-it is but Birth to a new life-and You shall go on, and on, and on, to higher and still higher planes of life, for aeons upon aeons of time. The Universe is your home, and you shall explore its farthest recesses before the end of Time. You are dwelling in the Infinite Mind of THE ALL, and your possibilities and opportunities are infinite, both in time and space. And at the end of the Grand Cycle of Aeons, when THE ALL shall draw back into itself all of its creations-you will go gladly, for you will then be able to know the Whole Truth of being At One with THE ALL. Such is the report of the Illumined-*

those who have advanced well along The Path. And, in the meantime, rest calm and, serene-you are safe and protected by the Infinite Power of the FATHER-MOTHER MIND. "Within the Father-Mother Mind, mortal children are at home."

The Monday following being told that my days of judgment had begun, I was heading into work when something strange happened. I had entered the building and began to walk toward my workspace down a main corridor. There were several groups of people walking about 100 or so feet ahead of me. Suddenly, a black spot shot in front of my face and I heard it smack the wall to my right. Before I could even turn to look, I realized what it was. I had spider web in my eyelashes and across my face. I knew immediately it was for me. I knew the symbolism of the spider in mythology. They were said to be the weavers of the webs of destiny. So, I interpreted this to mean that after having been told that my days of judgment had begun, I was now walking into my destiny. I had been told that I was to also act as a shepherd of men, so I understood that I could no longer remain quiet about everything that had happened to me. I decided I would begin talking about these things openly. I would talk about all of it. The visits by the beings in my room, the books by the Yogi Publication Society, everything.

In doing so, I was asked to go to medical and get checked out by psych. It was disappointing that some people had this reaction, but

I can't say it was completely unexpected. They knew I had been present for the Gimbal footage and they never denied that, because there was video I could show them on YouTube. I agreed to go get checked out if it would put them at ease. I knew I wasn't crazy. There was too much to all of this.

I first had to see my primary care doctor to get a referral. While I was in the waiting room, I saw my coworker whose grandmother had passed. He asked me what I was doing there, so I told him about the beings that had been visiting me and teaching me about the universe. He was surprised at this but not completely shocked. I didn't at this time tell him about the incident involving his grandmother. The corpsman had called me back and it was time for me to go see the doctor.

My primary care doctor gave me the referral I needed to visit a psychologist. He also wanted me to have a CAT scan on my head. He explained that with blood clots it could be possible that a clot would travel to the brain and cause delusions. I agreed to that as well to put them all at ease. I knew this was no delusion. I wasn't imagining these books by the Yogi Publication Society that would explain things that I had just seen or gone through.

I returned to work later that day. I was sitting at my desk and my coworker that I had seen at medical approached me. He asked me if I could help him.

I said, "Sure, what do you need help with?"

"You know all that stuff you were talking about earlier."

"Oh," I said. "I can try."

He then went on to tell me that his grandmother who had just passed was someone who he knew had "visions." He told me that she had these visions involving the people around her. She was told she had to share these visions with people or this ability would be taken from her. I understood what he was telling me about her. I then used that opportunity to tell him that I knew he was grieving her death too much.

With tears welling up in my eyes, I told him how I knew he was grieving too much because of my encounter with his grandmother. He became emotional and admitted to me that instead of taking a lunch break; he would go out to his car and cry because he missed her so much. He had been doing this for several months since her death. I told him that she would be just fine and he didn't need to do this anymore. I explained that these strong emotions can be felt by those that have passed and it keeps them from moving on. I told him that he needed to let her go, and let her rest.

Later that week, I had my appointment with the psychologist. He explained that he couldn't get an accurate picture of what was going on with me until he had a couple of sessions in which to evaluate me. He was a thin man with a beard. He sat me down and asked what was going on with me.

I was a bit apprehensive because there was no telling where this would go. Psychology, as a profession, is all over the place. And, just as with any profession, you have people who are good at what they do and others that are not good at what they do. With this in mind, I began to tell him what was going on. I told him everything. He sat expressionless. It occurred to me when I was talking to him that there would have been a time that I would have been afraid to say such things; but fear was something I no longer had in me.

By the time I finished speaking the appointment time was almost over. He asked me if I had ever read a book called *A Crack in the Cosmic Egg*. I told him I hadn't heard of it. He told me that it was a book he read many years ago and seemed to be in line with what I was talking about. He described to me that it speaks to the illusory nature of the universe. He told me about an account in the book in which a guy could put a lit cigarette out on his arm without suffering any ill effects. No pain or burn marks. I told him I would read *A Crack in the Cosmic Egg* ahead of our next meeting. At the end of the second meeting He asked me where he could view the footage that was taken by the aircraft onboard the Theodore Roosevelt. I showed it to him on his computer in the office. As I left him, he smiled at me, shook my hand and said, "I think you're on to something here. Who do you plan to work with on this? I think you need to work with someone on this. Maybe you should write a book."

The next day I had a sleepy feeling that came over me at work just before the day ended. As I left the building a bad thunderstorm began. I knew the storm combined with my sleepiness was a sign that I needed to take a nap because something was going to be revealed to me. When I got home, I was so tired I could barely stay awake. I ran into the house and up the stairs as I began to feel the heaviness increasing. I threw open the door to my room with the storm raging outside and jumped on the bed. Instead of hitting the bed, I went right through it and landed in my dream.

I found myself walking up a staircase inside a large house. The house had gas lighting and the walls were covered with green and red wallpaper. Everything seemed new. The dark wood floors were not worn and the wallpaper looked as though it had been hung yesterday. The gas lighting fixtures did a good job of illumination. I was surprised how much light they threw out. I looked next to me as there was someone coming up the stairs with me. It was my coworker; the one who asked me to help him. I could see at the top of the stairs, beyond the landing, was a wide hallway with several doors on either side. We began to walk down the hallway. The doors were all closed and we could see some liquid flowing out from under the door to our right. "What is that?" I said as I bent down to examine it.

"It looks like blood," my coworker said as he stood off to my left.

I stood up and opened the door. I could see the room was in disarray as the door swung open. There was a desk turned over on the floor and a hole in the plaster and lathe wall near the floor, behind where the desk had once been situated. The wallpaper had been torn and there was some white lace stuck in the lathe of the hole in the wall. There were plaster and wood fragments all over the floor. The contents of the desk were also strewn about. Papers and letters were everywhere.

As the door opened further, I saw a very young boy on the floor bleeding heavily from the neck clasping a letter opener in his hand. He was in the clutches of death and taking his last gasps of breath as I saw him lying there, on the floor. He had brown hair and had been wearing a cap that was now on the floor just above his head. He had on a white shirt half-stained with blood, and a black bow around his neck and a brown jacket with matching shorts and knee high socks. In taking in this sight I felt a hand grab and hold my left hand. It was the boy who had just died on the floor in front of me. He was standing where my coworker had been standing. As he held my hand, the boy began to tell me about the events that had transpired.

I looked down at him standing there as he held my hand and I listened intently. He could not have been older than five – seven years old. He told me that he had been playing with his little sister, who I assume must have been a baby. He said there was an accident and his sister had died. He tried to hide what he had done by taking her body up to the attic and dropping it down the hole in the floor that ran around the attic and made up the vacant space in the walls below. His father had discovered this and, in a fit of rage and emotion, punched a hole in the wall to retrieve his daughter. The boy said he was so afraid and felt so bad about what he had done that he took the letter opener from the floor and cut his neck because he couldn't live with what he had done. He told me he had seen this done with animals—they cut their neck and the animal would bleed out and die. So, he did this to himself. He insisted that what happened with his sister was an accident and that he never meant to hurt her.

When I woke up I tried to understand what I had just seen. It was perhaps the previous life of my coworker. He was the little boy. I was curious to find out how I could have seen such a thing. I consulted the books by the Yogi Publication Society for answers. I found the answer in a book called *Practical Psychomancy and Crystal Gazing*. In it is described something called the Akashic records. The Akashic records are recorded in the fabric of space-time in the same way light travels through the universe. It seems a bit out there but it makes sense if you think about it.

When we look up at the night sky we see all of these points of light. Some are very distant stars. The light leaving some of those stars that we are witnessing here on Earth, left that star long ago. This is where we get the term light-year. It's a measure of the distance light travels through space in one year. So, if we say a star is 50 light-years away what this means is that light leaving that star takes 50 years before it is visible on Earth. It is in this way that, if you were able to see from Earth, the surface of a planet orbiting that star 50 light-years away, you would be witnessing events on the surface of that planet which occurred 50 years ago. It could be more or less depending on how many light-years away the planet is. The movie *Interstellar* is based on this principle. Also, as I sit and write this I have read accounts of the Nazi "Bell" which some believe was some type of craft, but I have also read accounts that the "Bell" was a technological device that displayed events of the past.

I remember my father teaching me about the light leaving stars as a young boy. When he told me about this I thought that if you were to see a house on the surface of some planet, then in this same manner you should also be able to see what was happening inside that house as well. There would be light inside that house that would also be traveling through space. Little did I know how right I was in this thought, so many years ago. Around this time I tried to turn on the news and see what was going on in the world. I hadn't turned on my TV in many months. I could only take a few minutes of it before I just turned it off. I couldn't stand to watch it because I was seeing the world much more clearly. It was nauseating to watch the talking heads bicker about problems that they viewed as infinitely complex and unrelated. They weren't talking about how all of these problems were a result of our own fractured psyches manifesting physically in the world around us.

Every one of the talking heads was dancing around the clear solution; the singular cause of everything that is also its solution. The heads then began discussing a prominent figure in past political events and discussing what a great individual this was. In my mind, I saw this individual as a child. A child that was holding a giant oversized plastic wrench and walking to a plastic wall where there were giant oversized plastic bolts. I pictured this child then taking that wrench and turning those bolts as they spun freely in place within the plastic wall; turning his head to receive applause from his parents as to the greatness of his abilities. Yes, this is the extent of things in our society currently; having no true understanding of the meaning of a great man or woman.

A truly great man or woman would be speaking of things on a much grander scale; uniting the world in some greater cause such as automating the world's food supply. Uniting people behind huge projects that both make the planet a better place and constitute wholeness in the fractured psyches of the general public. Simplifying and streamlining production through mechanization in such a way that work becomes nearly effortless. But instead, we argue constantly about how much money a human life is, or is not, worth. Who among us will be the haves and who will be the have nots in a giant game of house in the land of ignorance and make-believe? Children at play living in their every emotion, acting out their every whim and shallow desire rather than working together to accomplish enormous leaps forward for the greater good of all humanity. It's madness and incredibly short-sighted.

I began to think about people who I had personally viewed as inspirational but none of the common names came to mind. One person I admired was not anyone who was famous. I thought of this story when I was dangling on the edge of the cliff; when I let go and fell into the abyss. I was home sick from middle school one day, flipping through the channels and stopped on a daytime talk show. For some reason I decided to watch it. The host was interviewing a woman whose husband and child were killed in a car accident. They were hit head-on by a woman who was drunk out of her mind around 9 am on a weekday. The woman who lost her family was describing that she initially reacted with anger. But her thoughts quickly turned. She began to wonder what was happening in this woman's life that she was drunk out of her mind by 9 am on a weekday.

The woman who lost her family reached out to the woman who had caused their death as she sat in jail. She began to help the woman in jail. After her release, she was invited to stay in the home of the woman who's family she killed. The woman who lost her family explained that she could have remained bitter, she could have continued to hate this woman, but in doing so she would be a part of the problem and not the solution. In getting to know the woman who had taken her family, she learned that she had been an alcoholic for many years; she had been sexually abused and was never taught that she had any value as a human being. The woman who caused the accident was brought out on stage and explained how grateful she was that this woman she had so wronged had now saved her life.

This is an example of greatness. People who were able to exercise immense mental and emotional control to the point they would forgive anything. To face something difficult or awful head-on—without reservation or judgment—with clarity of mind, and without fear. I knew the importance of this at a very young age and it always stuck with me. Mabel Collins explains this in *When the Sun Moves Northward*:

> *Most often the right and power to enter are won by conquering a feeling of justifiable resentment, of resentment against actual wrong. The surrender must be a profound one, made in the sanctuary of the spirit, and must be absolute, covering not merely a single instance of injustice or wrongdoing, but all instances of injustice or wrongdoing. Then arise in the heart the first words of the great song of life, which belong to the Feast of Love, the Feast of the Soul. Litany:*
>
> I. *Love is the only King; The only Ruler The Only Creator.*
>
> II. *Hate and Satan one; rebel, anarchist, destroyer.*
>
> III. *Love's action is what men call charity.*
>
> IV. *The action of hatred is known as malice.*
>
> V. *Love has only one punishment for the sinner, and that is forgiveness.*
>
> VI. *To live according to the law of love is a hundred thousand times harder than to live according to the law of hatred; to this great effort I pledge myself. To live according to the law of love means the ac-*

ceptance of every evil as a good. By that acceptance, if it is done in the spirit of love, the evil becomes good. It is to the conversion of evil into good in our natures, in the nature of others, and in the affairs of life, that we devote ourselves. Henceforth we do not avoid evil, we love it and transform it. By loving it we make ourselves a part of the creative principle which is love.

About a week after the Akashic records experience, I was again awoken sometime in the night. I was lying on my left side facing the wall with my back to the door. I had the familiar feeling of being unable to move. I could feel a presence behind me. *What's this now?* I thought. I wasn't expecting visitors. I then felt a hand on my right shoulder. The hand pulled me backwards rolling me onto my back. I looked up at the face that was looking down at me; I could see this beings eyes blinking from behind his thick glasses.

The being began to run its hand through my hair and telepathically told me, "Don't be afraid."

"I'm not afraid," I thought back to him.

"Then come with me!" he said in a very cartoonishly happy and upbeat manner as he grabbed my hand, lifting me from the bed. I noticed that his hand appeared to have an oven mitt on it. He had a thumb opposing what seemed to be perhaps four fused fingers underneath his glove. Both of his hands looked like this. He was wearing a grey suit that covered everything but his face. His body shape and suit strongly resembled that of a tele-tubby. His legs were very short but it didn't matter because he didn't use them. He was floating. He had a large round head with large cheeks. He held my hand as he took me out of my room very quickly and down the stairs. I told him to wait because I thought I was going to trip down the stairs, but, as I kicked my legs to go down the stairs, I realized I was floating too, as he was still holding my hand. He took me into the kitchen and we waited by the back door for a few moments.

As we waited in the kitchen, I felt a bit embarrassed that I had reacted that way about going down the stairs. I remember a meme from a few years ago where a woman was holding a chihuahua as it swam in a pool. She lifted it out of the water and it was still kicking its legs; unaware that it was now up in the air and not in the water anymore. I assumed that this is what I looked like as I went down the stairs. As I waited there with him in the kitchen, I could see his breathing pattern was faster than ours. Two other beings came out of my roommate's room. They looked identical to the being that was holding my hand except they had red colored suits on. When they saw me in the kitchen they stopped.

One of them said, "WOAHHHH!"

The other said, "OHHHHH!" It was clear they were amazed to see me there for some reason. I know they were in there collecting DNA from my roommate. I got that sense from the devices they had in their hands. One of them was holding in its hand this thick grey device that resembled a railroad spike. Between its forearm and chest was a cup-sized grey container with a lid that he was putting on top of the cup. They both had the appearance of being made of pewter or something.

I waved at them and thought, "Hello." I felt that they were instantly more at ease with my presence.

One of them said in a cheerful manner, "Oh! Hello, friend!" They seemed so friendly, innocent, and childlike.

The four of us floated out the side door from the kitchen. In the driveway was a football shaped craft that lit up as we exited the house. The two red-suited beings flew quickly into the square opening in the craft. The grey-suited being took me to the end of the driveway. He looked both ways down the street. I assumed we would be crossing the street for some reason, but he quickly took me back toward the craft and said, "Let's go now!" I then understood he was looking for cars that could possibly see the craft take off.

I have only a vague memory of sitting with them on the craft having pleasant conversation. I remember the inside of the craft being a brilliant white. Two of the beings were seated in front of me around a small table; the third had his back to us. I assumed he was steering the craft. I could see he had his hands on some kind of console that seemed to have a few black knobs on the front of it. They were so friendly and I was so happy to be with them.

I remember one of them asking me why I was opening my mouth and exposing my teeth. I laughed and explained that's the way we express happiness. One of the beings tried to smile like me; lifting its hands to its face in an attempt to make its cheeks move back as mine did, but it didn't work and I laughed. I could feel that they also found this amusing. They were very happy to talk to me. I remember having some conversation about my roommate's dog, Velcro. She slept in the bed with my roommate at night. I remember that they commented how soft she was because of her fur, they thought she was beautiful, and they really enjoyed seeing her. I vaguely remember one of them commenting that she loved him very much; in reference to the love Velcro felt for my roommate.

The next memory I have is being dropped off back at the kitchen side door. I was standing at the door watching as the craft left. The door was open and two of them were waving at me from the open door as they said, "Goodbye friend!" I have some vague recollection of going back in and going back to bed.

I know this experience was no accident. It was by design just like all of the others. I fully understand what it meant and what I was supposed to understand about it. I only mention this at this point because, as I type this, I'm listening to Enigma's "Return to Innocence," which should give you some idea.

A few days later, I was at work and one of my coworkers pulled up an article he had seen on a major news network. It was about a guy who was recounting his horrible abduction experience he had a few decades earlier. He recalled being paralyzed by evil floating beings that were fat and had claws for hands that abducted him against his will in their egg shaped craft. At one point they asked him if he was going to behave. I laughed at the article as I recalled how friendly they were. "Well, it's all a matter of perception, I guess," I said. This coworker then joked that I must be an alien. He then began to enumerate all of the things that normal humans do; that I do not. He was just joking around but he was kinda right. There are a lot of differences between me and other people. I believe a lot of that stems from the qualities I have cultivated in myself. Qualities like attention, patience, mindfulness, will over desire, and selflessness. The biggest difference, I think, is the fact that I have a serious lack of a need for comfort.

In the days that followed, I thought a lot about all of the things that had happened to me. Why me and not someone else? My outlook on life was very different from those around me. It always had been. I always believed the way we lived was wrong. I never understood it, to be honest. People everywhere tend to have the "me first" attitude, but I always put myself last. I tend to help anyone that asks for my help. I've been told by some that I'm so kind that I'm a pushover, but I've never seen it this way. Some even falsely view me as highly ambitious because I'm a high-functioning individual capable of handling a heavy workload without complaint. I take on that heavy workload because I can, and I see work that needs to be done, so I do it. In doing so I have the thought that this work I do is for everyone else and not for me.

I remember reading in one of William Walker Atkinson books that people like us are this way. Others view it as a fault and that others could easily take advantage of us. I do things for others not because I am a pushover as others may perceive, but because I understand that I don't view these things as an inconvenience to me, and therefore, I don't suffer them as others do. I don't view my time and effort as being something so precious to me that I can't possibly give any to others. Most people believe that their time is so precious that if asked to give up a few minutes, it becomes infuriating to them. I know that the fact I have no such thoughts entering my head means that mentally I am much stronger than they are.

I recently ran into this situation with two coworkers. I saw how one of them was totally unwilling to help the other one simply because it would have been a very slight inconvenience to her. I help others because it's the right thing to do but not everyone is as strong as me. I can see how, throughout my life, I cultivated these qualities and many other traits that helped me arrive here. Cultivating patience was important to that end. I've realized that newfound mental abilities rest in these qualities. This was the point of my whole experience with these floating beings. To experience them on their level, as one of them.

I was not initially going to include this next experience in the book but I came to understand that I had to because it explains where the conception of heaven comes from. It is blatantly obvious to me in the works of other initiates, and I will explain this in the artwork of

Leonardo Da Vinci later in the book. In many abduction experiences, people talk about genetic manipulation via creating hybrids and so on and I am no different. I believe for most of our history they have been genetically manipulating our DNA. I've read experiencer stories in which they are told hybridization is for a very important purpose for humanity. If you recall, I experienced this at the outset with the blue-skinned female in my room. There have been many experiencers that have met their hybrid children and I also experienced this. But in doing so I was given a much deeper understanding of what that's all about.

    I woke up one night in an odd position with that familiar feeling of heaviness and the inability to move. I couldn't even open my eyes. I was laying on my stomach with my arms wrapped underneath me as though I was giving myself a giant hug. I was told to open my right hand, so I opened it. I could hear the floorboards creak right next to my bed. I then felt the mattress move under the weight of someone sitting on the edge of my bed and I could hear it's familiar creaking. Because of these familiar sounds, I knew I was in my room. I felt a small forearm placed in my hand. I could feel this small arm had a thicker skin that was like the blue females skin. I could feel down to a hand that was also small and its fingers were much longer and thinner than one would expect for a human baby. As the arm and hand were pulled away through my hand I felt what I could only describe as static electricity that seemed to envelop my hand.

While all of this was occurring, I heard a voice say, "So you can come back to us," while receiving several mental impressions. The first impression was the idea of particle entanglement. The second was the idea that after my body dies I will continue in the bloodline of this being who's hand I just felt. Oddly, I understood all of this completely. I had read in *Life Beyond Death* that when a person reincarnates, they will do so to their highest potential. It's your DNA that becomes the evidence of your new highest potential. This may also explain a bit about why abduction experiences seem to follow blood lines.

This brings me to Travis Walton and his experience. He encountered some beings, which looked very human. I believe the reason the beings looked so human is because they were in fact human. They are the initiates of ages past. This is also why I believe cultures all over the world have the idea of an afterlife or heaven—dwelling in the stars or dwelling with the gods. The experience I had and the explanation I was given are the reasons for this religious idea of heaven.

As I sit and write this, I am reminded of a Greek myth that I will explain in further detail later in the book. Ganymede was a mortal boy that Zeus fell in love with. He was said to be the loveliest born of all the mortals. Zeus sent his eagle to collect Ganymede and bring him to Olympus so he might be among the immortals. It was said he was so lovely that the gods stole him away for themselves.

The reason I wrote the above is that in one of my waking clairvoyant sessions, I had a follow up question as I was writing and still half asleep. I was told something that caused me to wonder who they are to us; what is the relationship that exists there? As soon as I wondered, my answer was this: "Progenitors." I didn't immediately know what the exact definition of progenitor was so I had to look it up the next day. Waking clairvoyance is something that I will explain in the next chapter when I began waking with the names of authors or ideas being repeated in my head.

Chapter Six
RETURN

On Monday, August 15, 2018, I felt my connection turn off. What shut off was the sense of unwavering peace and incredible joy. I felt it immediately in my shoulders and upper back. Suddenly there was tension in my shoulders. I knew the instant it happened. I consulted *Our Glorious Future* for answers. In *Our Glorious Future* by Mabel Collins, she states that in fact this can only be felt for a short time. I noticed this was also something that was stated in the *Homeric Hymn to Demeter*. When the goddess is interrupted from placing the boy in a fire every night, by the boy's mother, Demeter states that the boy will only be immortal for a short time.

At this point in my journey I had not yet read a book titled *When the Sun Moves Northward: The Way of Initiation* by Mabel Collins, but I feel as I write this book that I should share a bit of its insight into what was going on here. In *When the Sun Moves Northward,* Mabel Collins has a diagram illustration that explains the process up to this point. I've borrowed this idea and incorporated it into the artwork on the cover of the book. To understand the artwork on the cover you have to understand the art of Leonardo Da Vinci, which I will explain later.

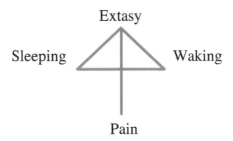

The Sign of the neophyte or newly planted one, the triangle, typifies the condition of sleeping and waking at the same time, and the mystic state of ecstasy which arises from this condition. Later on the cross comes within it, that new cross of higher suffering; the suffering in and with all humanity, the cross on which the Christos of man is continually crucified, as well as the Christ Himself.

That feeling of incredible, unwavering, peace, joy and calm was gone. This period can last months, or years; but it will end; just as Mabel Collins wrote. Having experienced this feeling even once gives you the knowledge on how you must lead the rest of your life, and marks the return in the hero's journey. As I sit and write this book, I do know that you can get this back if you decide to go through it again the next year, which I did do the following year. Mabel Collins also states that you can renew and expand your understanding on a yearly basis coinciding with initiation season, and as I sit and write this book I have found this to be the case. Let us not forget that when

Persephone returns from the underworld she is greeted by the goddess Hecate with many embraces. Hecate becomes Persephone's substitute queen. Persephone represents the human soul in this myth, which travels to the underworld and endures great pain. Upon its return, it is transformed. Hecate, with her many embraces, represents the new-found gifts. Hecate being the goddess of the night, moon, ghosts, and necromancy. At first, I was devastated with the fact that it had shut off. But after consulting *Our Glorious Future,* I understood. I knew that even though this feeling had shut off, I was still capable.

I decided to pick up the book I had started and not finished: *A Series of Lessons in Raja Yoga*. There was a reason I hadn't finished the last three chapters and I knew that. Everything happens for a reason. I wanted to possibly seek more answers there.

To understand what I found in the last three chapters of this book, it's important to understand how these books were put together. This book was originally a course broken up into its chapters. In other words, individuals would apply for this class by mail with William Walker Atkinson. He would then send course materials out to the students in chapters. He later threw this course material together into a book that he published. In the lessons of this book, specifically, in the last three chapters, he addresses some of the correspondence he had been receiving from his students. Atkinson purposefully left this in the book as a hint to readers that this book in particular was significant. His students are informing him that they are in immense pain. Because of this, he goes off on a bit of a tangent that he didn't intend but he felt he needed to address. Not only does he address the pain but also informs the students what they will receive on the other side. I will share with you the statements he makes in the last three chapters:

> *To realize just what we are offering to you, we would remind you of the old fairy tales of all races, in which there is to be found one or more tales telling of some poor cobbler, or tailor, or carpenter, as the case may be, who had by his good deeds, gained favor with the "brownies" or good fairies, who would come each night when the man and his family were asleep, and proceed to complete the work that the artisan had laid out for the morrow. The pieces of leather would be made into shoes; the cloth would be sewed into garments; the wood would be joined, and nailed together into boxes, chairs, benches and what not. But in each case the rough materials were prepared by the artisan himself during the day.*
>
> *Well, that is just what we are trying to introduce to you. A clan of mental brownies, loving and kindly disposed toward you, who are anxious and willing to help you in your work. All you have to do is to give them the proper materials, and tell them what you want done, and they will do the rest. But these mental brownies are a part of your own mentality, remember, and no alien and foreign entities, as some have imagined.*

He goes on to say:

If one lives on the plane of the race-thought, he is subject to its laws, for the law of cause and effect is in full operation on each plane of life. But when one raises himself above the race-thought, and on to the plane of the Recognition of the Real Self— The "I"— then does he extricate himself from the lower laws of cause and effect, and places himself on a higher plane of causation, in which he plays a much higher part. And so we are constantly reminding you that your tower of strength and refuge lies on the higher plane. But, nevertheless, we must deal with the things and laws of the lower plane, because very few who read these lessons are able to rest entirely upon the higher plane. The great majority of them have done no more than to lift themselves partially on to the higher plane, and they are consequently living on both planes, partly in each, the consequence being that there is a struggle between the conflicting laws of the two planes. The present stage is one of the hardest on the Path of Attainment, and resembles the birth-pains of the physical body. But you are being born into a higher plane, and the pain after becoming the most acute will begin to ease, and in the end will disappear, and then will come peace and calm. When the pain becomes the most acute, then be cheered with the certainty that you have reached the crisis of your new spiritual birth, and that you will soon gain peace. And then you will see that the peace and bliss will be worth all the pain and struggle. Be brave, fellow followers of The Path—Deliverance is nigh. Soon will come the Silence that follows the Storm. The pain that you are experiencing—ah, well do we know that you are experiencing the pain—is not punishment, but is a necessary part of your growth. All Life follows this plan—the pains of labor and birth ever precede the Deliverance. Such is Life—and Life is based upon Truth— and all is well with the world. We did not intend to speak of these things in this lesson, but as we write there comes to us a great cry for help and a word of encouragement and hope, from the Class which is taking this course of lessons, and we feel bound to respond as we have done. Peace be with you—one and all.

The above statement from Atkinson was profound and pure truth. It speaks to why this transformation is so difficult to describe. Transformation mimics life, possessing all of its parts: pain, birth, death, and rebirth. Ancient cultures knew this and incorporated it into myth. It is the hero's journey. For me it was real confirmation of what I had just been through. Atkinson and Collins wrote this series of books over 100 years ago that spoke directly to the experiences I was having. I wanted to know more about it so I could help people.

After reading this, I had a dream in which there was a man that I had a lengthy and detailed conversation with. He had a short salt and pepper beard, with more salt than pepper. He was stocky with a white glow to him. Because of this glow, I had, at the time, mistaken him for one of the light beings from the temple.

He spoke with me at some length about the human subconscious and human psychology. He stated that, "People can know something subconsciously without knowing it consciously." He said that when people know something subconsciously it will leave a conscious impression on their waking lives. He stated that the link between the two, pulling things from the subconscious into the conscious memory, can be accomplished through meditation and dreaming. He stated that the time in which most people do this is in the waking state from sleep. He stated that it would be important to keep a dream journal close to the bed as these moments of memory in the waking stages can be fleeting. They are the seconds where one is becoming conscious after sleep. He stated that pulling from the subconscious into the conscious memory is the goal.

He further explains that not only do you have a subconscious but that humans also have a collective subconscious. This means that as a race we all have some vague idea of the things that, "speak" to our subconscious. He used the example of this experience I had been having. How I was able to see the message of this new consciousness transformation everywhere…in art, music, books, theater, science… He explained that the reason I could see this is because these ideas are popular. They are popular because they "speak" to our collective subconscious; and all our conscious self knows is that we love this message, but consciously we don't understand why, we are left with only a conscious impression.

He explained that, subconsciously, we all know we must go through this change, and this is the reason we love works that speak to this message. This conversation was quite extensive. I asked questions and he answered them. He seemed to be wearing a metal band around his head with what looked like chain mail running over the top and down the back of his head; like he was a knight or something, and this struck me as odd. I woke that morning with the name Robert Moore running through my head over and over. So, I wrote down the things that this man had said to me along with the name Robert Moore. My intent was that I would start to look into these things after work.

I was amazed about hearing this voice while waking from sleep. Mabel Collins wrote about how she would also hear this and it's how she wrote *Light On The Path*. In *When the Sun Moves Northward* she writes the following:

> *I was in the state of consciousness known to the occultists of Southern India as **jagrat of swapna**, which is the consciousness of waking clairvoyance. Only a person ignorant of occultism could suppose that it was in any way possible to bring this knowledge to earth, except*

by the work of a disciple who had attained to this consciousness. In no state of unconsciousness of the scribe, by no overshadowing or control of the Master, can teaching of this absolute character be obtained. I committed to memory, in that state, the first lines of the ancient, mystic writing, now known to all students of occultism under the title of **Light On the Path**. *I brought it down into physical consciousness, and recorded it. I obeyed the order given to me, and, again and again, entering into a state of waking clairvoyance, returned to the chapel of light, bringing back the rules one by one, and writing them down, until I had obtained the whole.*

When I got home, I looked up the name Robert Moore. *Maybe he wrote some books,* I thought. I found a book by Dr. Robert L. Moore that seemed to fit. It's called *The Magician and the Analyst: The Archetype of the Magus in Occult Spirituality*. Dr. Robert Moore was a professor of psychoanalysis, culture, and spirituality in Chicago. He was also a Jungian psychoanalyst. Jungian psychology is named after its founder Dr. Carl Jung who was a Swiss psychiatrist that analyzed psychiatry through a prism that also involved anthropology, archaeology, philosophy, literature, and religious studies. Jung is considered the father of modern-day psychoanalysis. I was surprised to learn that not only had Carl Jung influenced Robert Moore but that he also influenced the writings of Joseph Campbell.

In Moore's book, *The Magician and the Analyst*, he states that he had, many years earlier, decided that he was going to look into why it was that so many young people were drawn to occult spirituality. He touched on initiation and how that relates to occult spirituality. Which led me to another one of his books called *The Archetype of Initiation: Sacred Space, Ritual Process, and Personal Transformation*. It was in reading this book that I began to understand the totality of my experiences.

As odd as it may seem... everything I had been through which resulted in this higher consciousness was in fact an initiation process. This was my big "ahhhh" moment. Up until this point I hadn't understood that. *The Kybalion* was written by the Three **Initiates**...now I got it. And I was supposed to know this, as well; otherwise I wouldn't have been reading that book.

One night, I was reading *The Archetype of Initiation* and got up to go to the restroom. I laid the book on my nightstand. When I came back and went to grab the book I noticed on the back cover was a picture of Dr. Robert Moore. He was a stocky looking man with a salt and pepper beard. This was the man I had seen in my dream. He was the one that taught me about human consciousness and psychology. I grabbed my laptop and did some research into him specifically. He died June 18, 2016. This is how he was able to communicate with me in my dreams. Robert Moore writes the following concerning transformation or initiation:

All discussions of the archetype of initiation start with the assumption that life is a series of transformations. As we Jungians use the word "transformation" it could be translated "initiation." In everyday life the word "initiation" usually makes us think of the initiation into fraternities and sororities and things like that, but initiation really refers to something that is part and parcel of the universal spiritual journey, the pilgrimage of human life. Initiation is the process of dying and being reborn. This archetype is so powerful in human life that it turns up in all parts of human experience, and once you have the eyes to see it, a lot of things that you have wondered about will begin to fall into place.

I understood what he meant by having the eyes to see it. I see it everywhere. For me, the most important lesson from *The Archetype of Initiation* was the process. Moore describes the symptoms of the onset of this process as not only consisting of depression but also of things like synchronicities, acting out, sexual promiscuity, the mid-life crisis, and so on. Carl Jung also talks about synchronicities. An example of this, in my case, was the day of coincidences I had when I drove to Patuxent River. The cultivation of attention in one's life will help them to recognize these synchronicities. Moore writes:

Maybe you are a young maiden and you are sitting by this nice little pond, and all of the sudden this ball rolls by, and it rolls down a hole. You go over there and look, and all of the sudden you find this passageway. Then the question becomes, "Will I or won't I go on and try to figure out what this is, and what it means?"

Campbell designates this kind of experience as "the call." It is a radical experience because the call is always a call to transformation, and contrary to commonly held romantic fantasies, it is always scary if it is real transformation.

Jungians talk a lot about the idea of synchronicity. "Isn't it interesting," Jungians always say, "how just about the time you thought there wasn't any hope, suddenly you run into this particular book? For example, Morton Kelsey, or John Sanford, or Carl Jung, or you meet someone personally." Of course, these things just happen and can easily be considered accidents. But they tell you something you need to know at the time.

Helpers appear along the way, but they cannot do the work. They just provide assistance, a little guidance. An elixir of life is usually gained, however, because there is something precious to be found here in this space. Mythology is just replete with this, and the New Testament is full of this. The pearl of great price is out here, or something like it, and you discover this treasure. If you are lucky and get the right help, and have the right amount of courage, then you try to return to the world outside the labyrinth, outside the cave with the treasure.

In *The Archetype of Initiation,* Moore describes the onset of transformation. Many people, when they reach a certain point in life, have done everything society tells them they need to do in order to be happy. They have the job, the cars, the house, and the kids, but often they find that something is lacking. After attaining these things; toiling day and night to fill the void within them; they step back to admire what they have accomplished for themselves. As they step back, the delight turns quickly into horror as they realize the void within them that they set out to fill 20 years ago, and haven't had much time to think about since, has grown more empty and cavernous: now a cave complex running deep through the soul. It's so powerful that it threatens to undo the hard work of the past 20 years.

Now it calls your name and beckons you to enter. Most will flee. They grasp at any distraction that comes along; a sports car, a new job, a bigger house, extramarital affairs, alcohol, drugs, trouble with the law; anything that will drown out the calls of the inner demons in the cavern. Moore describes these distractions as a searching behavior. The person is seeking the ritual elder that can show them how to turn this situation around and constitute wholeness within the psyche. In essence, the person is looking for someone or something, but they don't consciously know what or who that is, nor do they know why or what they are supposed to do. This is where Moore points out that in today's society there is a serious lack of these ritual elders. I have to inject here that the reason most people don't know about this transformation is that there is a simple concept that most people have not adopted. Forgiveness. It's such a simple word when spoken but it is quite another thing to adopt this as a philosophy. It is what separates the common man from the divine. Just as Mabel Collins states, the surrender must be absolute. It must cover not only a single instance of wrongdoing or injustice but all instances of injustice and wrongdoing.

Ritual elders should be known to everyone and available for easy access. The church and organized religion have always provided this in the past, but they no longer do. As it stands today, when someone starts to exhibit the symptoms, they are simply given a prescription for antidepressants, told that their emotions are not their own fault but merely a simple chemical imbalance in the brain, and sent on their way. This will almost always result in a failed initiation. They will begin to have experiences but never have any kind of leadership towards the correct knowledge, which could explain their vivid dreams or even the beings they see. It's tragic. Sometimes it appears that this person has just gone crazy. I believe the chemical imbalance in the brain is the cause of depression, but that imbalance is caused by your own negative thoughts; your inability or unwillingness to control the mind. The mind, just like anything else to do with the human body, must be manicured and looked after; it must be kept clean.

I found it interesting that Robert Moore writes about how one needs to "cook" for the appropriate amount of time. An experienced ritual elder would know when you're "done" or if you need to remain in the oven a bit longer. I believe this was the reason the small man appeared in my room and told me, "Don't give up, keep going." He knew I wasn't finished "cooking" yet.

During my return I had a small glimpse of the technology and it's mind-blowing. I also believe that they only permit us to see what they want us to see. The technology we see is not for them. I don't believe they need it. It's for us. I think the stuff we see is possibly ancient technology to them. It's just beyond our understanding. We see this tech that is just beyond us and we begin to wonder how we can create such a device.

As an example of this, I awoke in bed one night because I felt something placed on the back of my neck; once again I had the familiar heavy feeling. *What's going on?* I calmly thought. Instantly I could see what was happening from the perspective of the person standing over me. I could see a device that had been placed over me that ran the entire length of my body. I could hear what sounded like a whale song with higher and lower pitches. The device was a large screen that was lit in shades of blue light and I could see everything inside my body in real time. I watched as I could see my heart pumping blood through the individual veins. The device was zooming in and out on various organs in my body. The whale song makes me think it was sonic technology that would send these sounds out and the return would be interpreted as a real time image in this device.

I could see there was a floating metal sphere in my room. It was drifting around like a balloon and had some kind of a dull, red laser on it that appeared to be searching my room. It was looking around the room as though it were attached to an eyeball. The laser would change in intensity and in form as it was examining the room and scanning various objects. I felt the device removed from my neck as the sphere's light shut off and it left my field of vision. I felt two arms wrap around my chest under my arms. I heard a voice say, "Hold on; close your eyes." I didn't close them because everything happened so quickly. I immediately heard a loud bang and I was inside a tunnel of white light that was growing in intensity. It was disorienting and I lost consciousness.

When I woke up, I was not at home in bed. I was somewhere else. I opened my eyes and I was lying in the most comfortable bed I've ever been in. I looked down and there was a blanket over me made out of something I've never seen before. It was copper in color and seemed to be made out of loosely woven fabric with glitter or lights woven into it. It looked like it should feel course to the touch but it was incredibly soft. The bed I was laying in was made out of the same material. The lighting in the room was dim, and the wall I was facing also had a copper tinge to it. The wall looked like it was made of two-foot-high metal bands with bands of two-inch black material sandwiched between them. I was facing this wall and felt the urge to get up and look around, but a hand quickly passed by my peripheral vision and came to rest on the top of my forehead and a voice said, "Rest."

I was falling back asleep as I felt this being kiss me on the forehead like a mother caring for a sick child. I woke again later and was no longer facing the wall. The room was large and there was another bed on the other side of the room but it was empty. I didn't see anyone around. The banding I had seen earlier wrapped around the walls throughout the room and extended up to the domed ceiling. The banding on the walls seemed to continue into the corridors on either side of the room. The floor was black and highly polished like onyx or glass.

In between the beds there was a protrusion extending from the wall that was a bit taller than me. It had a silver metal dome with a brushed finish on top of it that looked like a lamp shade. The whole thing looked like a giant sleek lamp but it wasn't emitting any light. I expected the floor to be cold when I put my feet down on it, but it was the same temperature as the rest of the room. I was not afraid. I felt very welcome and at home there. I remember turning toward one of the doors to the room but that was the last thing I remember. I'm not sure what they did to me while I was there, but the day before, I know I wasn't feeling well. I had a mild headache and felt off. I feel like I was in this place for several days as I remember waking up several times and vaguely remember being given something to eat, but I awoke in my bed the next morning somehow.

Chapter Seven
THE PSYCHOLOGY OF TRANSFORMATION

Before I go on to describe some of the evidence-based revelations and experiences I had in the rest of my return, I wanted to take a chapter here to give you a synopsis of the psychology that leads to transformation and contact with what we now call the phenomenon.

The father of modern psychoanalysis Dr. Carl Jung rediscovered this psychology that has real physiological roots in the structures and hard wiring of the brain; specifically in the limbic system; which I will describe later in the chapter. I wanted to touch on this psychology because it will become apparent in the historical evidence from all over the world that was revealed to me in later chapters, and because this psychology can be applied to your own life; making you ripe for transformation.

I was directed to these books authored by Dr. Robert Moore because he was correct, not just because I had some correspondence with him after his death; none of that was just a coincidence. Unfortunately, some of Dr. Robert Moore's books are falling out of print. In one case I had to pay over $150 for one of his books and about $75 for another; this can't happen; these books cannot disappear. Despite the fact that I paid so much for them, I wrote in them, underlining important points, and took notes in their margins. I will do everything in my power to keep these books alive just as those that have come before me and kept alive the works of Ovid, Plato, Leonardo Da Vinci, Homer and countless others. In the beginning of this book I mentioned that I didn't want to rewrite the books I knew to be the true treasures of humanity and the works of Dr. Robert Moore are certainly among them.

In his book, *Facing the Dragon: Confronting Personal and Spiritual Grandiosity,* Dr. Robert Moore states that he called the book, *Facing the Dragon,* because the mythologic dragon or serpent has always symbolized the primordial evil that resides within us all as individuals. He also stated that he was going to write another book called *Riding the Dragon* as a sequel to *Facing the Dragon.* Unfortunately, he was diagnosed with dementia before he was able to write it. With his assistance I have endeavored to do that here; with this book, and in particular within this chapter.

Everything that I went through in the previous chapters was the last leg of a psychological transformation leading to a wholeness in the psyche; or a wholeness in the archetypal self as Moore and Jung would describe.

It may be that I will write another book concerning the subject of this chapter because there is certainly enough material for it, and I find a lot of the Jungian material I have read thus far to be incomplete, lacking, doesn't emphasize the right ideas, or is too difficult to understand. Moore also had this problem with a lot of Jungian material. Many authors on the topic will speak in very poetic and esoteric terms that seem nonsensical to the casual reader. My goal here is to explain this as plainly and simply as possible in order to help you understand why all of the events in the previous chapters happened to me and what it all means.

Ultimately, I want to get you to your own transformation. Getting to this transformation is hard enough without having to interpret an esoteric work by either a modern-day author or an author from antiquity. These concepts are fairly complex, and this chapter will be one that you will need to think about as you read, so please take your time with it and take notes if that helps you. I've found that the most valuable books I own are those in which I have underlined important points and taken notes within their margins. I would love nothing more than to see this book full of different colored highlights and notes all over its margins. In my opinion, books like that are made so much more valuable; because someone has applied that book to their own life and made it a part of their own experience.

In this chapter I will talk about some general concepts of Dr. Carl Jung, some of the concepts that Dr. Robert Moore built on within Jungian psychology, and I will add my own take on it. Throughout this chapter I will emphasis what I know to be important for the majority of people. They will be the concepts and ideas that are currently lacking in most of us while giving you a basic understanding of human psychology.

If you are already an experiencer, the ideas in this chapter will seem familiar to you as it is the thread that links all experiencers. If you are an experiencer who has not experienced consciousness, perhaps this may help guide you in your efforts of attainment. Further, it gives readers and experiencers alike the knowledge they need to begin educating themselves in order to help themselves and others, after all, it's not possible to help anyone if you don't fully understand what has happened to you. It will give you an understanding of what led you to your experiences and will give you the vocabulary to articulate your experiences to others in a way that makes clear, logical sense.

I'm about to use an analogy here that I hope will illustrate the human psyche. Earlier in the book I brought up the concept of mentalism from *The Kybalion* stating that the universe is mental, a mental creation. My question was: *How could anyone know that?*

What is true for the individual psyche is also true for humanity at large. What is true for humanity at large is true here on earth in nature. What is true here on earth in nature is true of the greater universe at large. It's like an onion. When you understand your own psyche you understand its layers; and you can easily comprehend how one layer leads to the next, and you can observe those same layers in the world and universe around you. You will see how one layer resembles the next, the correspondence from one layer to the next. If you understand yourself (know thyself) you can see how these layers of yourself and others extend out into the physical world around you and beyond. This means you will see structures that exist within your psyche and how you, and others, manifest those structures in the physical world through your actions and creations. Mabel Collins refers to this concept as well. She speaks of it in terms of "knowing the hearts of men."

If you don't "know thyself" then you stand within the center of the onion. You look out and you can see the outermost layer of the dried skin of the onion. You can come to the conclusion, that because you can't see the other layers in between, and have no idea they exist; that this layer I'm standing in is separate from myself which is separate from the skin I see out there, and none of it is related in any way because none of it has any resemblance of the other. This concept of the onion is what I'm about to describe to you in terms of psychology. This analogy of the onion explains why it is everyone doesn't know what I know. This analogy illustrates how the studying of these layers of the onion is something we have relegated and dismissed to the realm of philosophers and theologians; some of whom I will discuss in later chapters.

I've heard and read about experiencers referencing Dr. Carl Jung but I have not known any to have gone much farther than that. I even saw a Carl Jung book make an appearance in a show called *Project Blue Book* on the History Channel. It was the scene where a Soviet spy had broken into the home of Captain Quinn; the spy brushes her hand across a bookshelf and a book by Dr. Carl Jung. If one were attentive they would know that there are consultants for this show and they would understand that this scene was no accident. It was a hint.

Dr. Carl Jung, Dr. Robert Moore, Douglas Gillette, William Walker Atkinson, and Mabel Collins all wrote about these psychological concepts, this was actually just a modern day rediscovery of some very ancient ideas that can be seen physically in ancient structures around the world. Carl Jung was the psychologist that first rediscovered and popularized this idea that within the psyche there exist different archetypal structures or aspects of the psyche. Dr. Robert Moore, put his finger squarely on the psychology of transformation and, more broadly, on human psychology in general by building on, further developing, and condensing Dr. Carl Jung's theories. In this chapter I have condensed them even further to give you just a very basic understanding so that as you read the books I mention, you will already have an idea of what is being described more in depth. Dr. Robert Moore does ascribe to mostly the Jungian theory but he does borrow from other psychologists, such as Freud, where it makes sense; but in terms of the overarching theory, he aligns with those of Dr. Carl Jung.

Psychology is so elusive to most of us because we don't understand ourselves. What's the difference between a child that succeeds in school and one that struggles? What is the difference between the average person on the street and the violent criminal in prison? What is the difference between people with differing political views? What is hate, rage and anger? Why do we do the things we do? What is all of that? Many of us don't even bother to ask ourselves these questions because they seem like these incomprehensible, unknowable, complex social issues with no clear solution.

The answers to these questions are very simple and lie in some very simple qualities. It depends on the degree to which you have developed yourself as an introvert or an extrovert, the extent to which you have developed the will, and the extent to which you have cultivated attention, and discernment.

Jung's theories on human psychology start with the premise that humans have this collective unconscious or subconscious through which there is a level of correspondence with the rest of the human race. To access this consciousness one must constellate wholeness within their own psyche by correctly accessing the four main archetypal structures in the psyche in the correct proportions. This may sound like a daunting task, but so many of us are almost there already.

Why do I use the word constellate when I talk about these four archetypal structures? The answer can be seen in the ancient pyramids of the world and it is in fact the reason for these ancient structures; they are a representation of the human psyche. Robert Moore uses this structure to visualize the psyche. With each side of the pyramid representing one of the four archetypal structures. If you were to imagine your psyche on this structure, it would be represented by a dot on each side. The dot representing where you are. The idea here is to get each dot to the center of each triangle. Known to Buddhists as the middle road; and described in the Bible as being neither hot nor cold. From the center those dots have a straight shot to the top where they will converge with the subconscious. The pyramids of Egypt were tipped with a golden capstone. Gold because it never decays or dies. It is the path to immortality.

These archetypal structures, or aspects of the psyche, are only available to us through the subconscious. If we are given some understanding of these archetypal structures, we could approach them consciously rather than subconsciously or unconsciously. It is in doing this that we begin to constellate wholeness. The idea behind this wholeness is that you bring the subconscious to the forefront and begin to merge it with your conscious personality. You begin to experience the subconscious consciously. In doing so we can see how our lives, our social structures, and our society are an outward manifestation of the archetypal structures in the psyche. We manifest these archetypal structures through our actions that become physically manifest in the world around us.

Moore narrowed these archetypal structures down to four main structures which he developed more fully than Jung did. Jung did not understand the contents of the archetypal structures, so if you read books by Dr. Carl Jung I want you to keep this in mind. I don't dismiss his work because he describes a lot more than just these archetypal structures. The extent to which we are introverted or extroverted determines how you will relate to and manifest the energies of these archetypal structures in your daily life. Moore sometimes called this the God energy that burns fiercely within every individual. Moore states in several books that to touch this incredibly powerful God energy and not be completely destroyed by it is no small task. This experience is no joke, it is very real. It caused me to write this book, and it caused the ancients to move millions of tons of dirt, rock, and carved stone to manifest its beauty and dominance in the physical world.

Moore describes his interpretation of the archetypal structures in the *King, Warrior, Magician, Lover* series of books he co-authored with Douglas Gillette. Within each of our psyches are the archetype of the king, the warrior, the magician, and the lover; which I will explain more thoroughly later in the chapter. These archetypes and their contents are so powerful that when we don't deal with them consciously, they each manifest "shadows," or negative aspects of themselves, to appear in the psyche. The four archetypes operating in their fullness and the four shadows operating in their negative aspect comprise the eight-fold psyche.

We have to relate to these archetypal energies consciously or we put ourselves at risk of relating to them in sloppy ways with devastating consequences for ourselves and humanity as a whole. Just as with the rest of the body, we must keep these structures of the brain clean by approaching them consciously just as one would with any other organ in the body.

Introversion and extroversion, just like anything else, can be thought of as the two poles of the same thing. Opposites of each other resting at either end of a pole, and between them there is a whole spectrum or combination of the two. None of us is completely introverted or extroverted. The positive aspects of the archetypes operating in their fullness can be thought of as lying in the introverted part of the spectrum and the aspects of the archetypes operating in their negative aspect or shadow can be thought of as lying in the extroverted half of the spectrum. This concept is also what William Walker Atkinson means when he writes about turning your gaze inward.

Jung, in an interview, accurately explains the difference between an introvert and an extrovert; terms that he coined. Today when people speak of these terms we falsely believe an extrovert is outgoing, while an introvert keeps to themselves. We believe that to be an extrovert, to be outgoing, is a sign of success while the introvert never gets anywhere. Anything that you previously thought to define an introvert or an extrovert is likely incorrect.

In the interview, Jung explains that the extrovert pays little attention to the inner world, putting themselves at risk of living in the shadow archetypal energies in the mind. They are primarily influenced by the outside world. The extrovert concerns themselves with that which they perceive to be reality; that which they can touch, taste, smell, hear, and see. This is their universe. It is a universe of the physical senses; that which is tangible to them. They don't do much to restrain or train the psyche because, as far as they can tell, it has little to no effect on the world as they know it; falsely believing that the inner and outer world are completely unrelated. (Remember the onion.) Rather than understanding that the physical world, the society in which we live, is a physical manifestation of this inner world. As a result, the extrovert lives their lives from one emotion to the next rather than restraining and training the mind to regulate these emotions that belong to the inner world; a world that to them doesn't exist. They live more in the shadow, or negative energy, of the archetypes. Most importantly, the extrovert falsely believes that the inner world lies outside themselves. As a result, the inner emotions they feel such as hate, anger, rage, love, etc. are the result of actions acting upon them. They blame these actions and the resulting emotion on forces exterior to themselves.

The introvert is more in touch with the world within and is greatly influenced by it. They are aware of their emotions and perceptions because they can see how their emotions and perceptions will affect the outer world. They cultivate the inner qualities necessary in dealing with more delicate structures of the outer world. Mindful of how their inner world can damage the more delicate structures of the outer world. Cultivating the inner calmness necessary for such delicate tasks. For example, in tribal structures where men would go out and hunt, they would often sequester themselves from the rest of the tribe for a time before returning. They needed that time to wind down from the aggressiveness of the hunt. Their job was to bring back nourishment to the tribe and it was recognized that the aggressiveness of the hunt has its time and place; but has no healthy place within the greater civilized tribe.

Jung describes this inner world as one of moving images, or that which we would call fantasy. He states that fantasy is actually a type of reality. Jung states that it is so much a part of reality that if one man has a certain fantasy another may lose his life... or perhaps a bridge is built; the buildings all around us were at one point fantasy. They existed only in the fantasy of the architect who envisioned it. The psyche is a phenomenon that takes place in our bodies. So, the psyche must also be a quality of matter because our bodies are made of matter. And so we discover that this matter has another aspect... a psychic (of the mind) aspect.

The introvert, through what we would call fantasy, is observing another aspect of matter. A conscious aspect of matter. Jung states, this fantasy is not nothing. It is something; it exists. Jung then goes on to say that this is a very old idea; Democritus called this the spirit that is inserted into atoms. Jung then states that this is where we logically end up if we draw conclusions without prejudices. He says that the United States is extroverted as hell and implies that this is extremely unhealthy and dangerous. Jung says, God forbid, in a world of extroverts that something goes wrong with the psyche. Then they will find out just how real fantasy is in the form of the H-bomb; a bomb that was first conceived of in fantasy.

When one begins to act out and live in this shadow energy, Moore calls this grandiosity, which is a concept he tackles in his book *Facing the Dragon: Confronting Personal and Spiritual Grandiosity.*

In the integration of these archetypes in their fullness, one can constitute wholeness in the psyche, or wholeness in the archetypal self. In Jungian psychology, when one does work toward that end with their archetypal shadows, it is known as shadow work. When one is aware of these shadows, it becomes easier to control them because you will have some emotion pop up that you will recognize as the shadow of one of your archetypal energies and you will squash it.

In *Facing the Dragon,* Dr. Robert Moore says the following about Jung's theory:

> *Thus I came to realize that Jung was right about the quadrated psyche, that the four major configurations did, in fact, exist, though he had not understood the contents of the quadrants. At that time I had not studied the ancient Egyptian concept of the self, so I didn't know that the ancient Egyptians thought the self had an eightfold nature and that one of the eight was your physical body. I also did not realize that sexuality and embodiment, and both the positive and negative qualities of the lover, usually come out in bodily forms. It is kind of a shock when you realize that people 3,500 years ago had some of these things figured out better than we do today. At the same time, it served as a helpful confirmation to find out that some people in the ancient world also understood the eightfold structure of the archetypal Self, what Jung called the **double quaternio**. All these configurations exist with Jung's **coniunctio**, the inner sacred marriage of king and queen, and they are held in balance in the deep psyche, all*

symmetrically balanced in the deep archetypal Self of every individual.

Thinking about your emotions throughout the day is essential in leading to this experience of wholeness; examining those emotions, perceptions, and reactions that could have been handled better. It was something I did constantly throughout my life. There is a saying in the military: *"If you don't mind; then it doesn't matter."* Many in the military hate this saying for the same reason many people hate the idea of Stoicism; a concept that belongs to the archetypal lover. They misinterpret its meaning. Stoicism is the act of taking an object or emotion and breaking it down to its bare bones, stripping it of all of the pomp and circumstance we normally assign such things, to view it for what it truly is, rather than what we may perceive it to be. Marketing is a profession that is all about changing the perception of a thing; transforming it into an object that you cannot live without. Stoicism would be the reverse of marketing. People are unaware how to transmute their emotions and perceptions, so the only thing they can do is bottle them up; they have this conception that Stoicism is about bottling up emotions.

This bottling up is also the reason for the backlash of political correctness. When people are asked not to say certain things, or behave in a certain way, they find the only way they know how is to bottle it up; shoving it deep down inside themselves by brute force, rather than to simply not allow such nonsense into the psyche to begin with. This would be an example of how an extrovert deals with emotion. The introvert will seek the reason for this emotion within themselves, while the extrovert seeks the source of that emotion outside themselves. Through logic and reason, the introvert will begin to control their emotion and perception. They begin to train themselves to the point that if they don't want to be angry they won't be angry; they will kill out the emotion or perception before it even comes to fruition within the psyche.

In the extrovert the bottled up emotions eventually explode to the surface in the form of a backlash or an outburst, which is no better than the temper tantrum of a child. This inability to transmute emotion and perception leads to feelings of insecurity and feeling a lack of control.

Psychologically, if an individual can't control their own emotions, perceptions, and fantasy (the internal world) because they are an extrovert, they will set out to physically control the external world as the perceived source of that emotion. As an extrovert one believes that their emotions somehow are created outside themselves; so they set out to physically, and sometimes violently, control that inner universe they believe resides outside themselves. With the internal world in disarray they will seek physical control of their environment because they perceive that by controlling the exterior world they can thereby control the inner world. This is why the person who batters their spouse will have the opinion that: *"I wouldn't have to hit you if you didn't make me so angry."* As an extrovert you will set out to physically control the exterior irritants that make you angry in an attempt to not get angry. It becomes an outward physical manifestation of the archetypal energy; giving birth to a malignant narcissism within the psyche. This malignant narcissism that exists in the human consciousness manifests physically in the world around us every day. It's not only present in extreme behaviors such as spousal abuse but the same psychology is present in passive aggressive behavior as well. It manifests in our system of government, our laws, our economy and our wars. Playing out in destructive ways as the extrovert seeks to exert physical control over the universe rather than be in touch with it.

When one begins to project this outward control and malignant narcissism, because they are an extrovert; they begin to also look outside themselves for the structures of archetypal energy. We always have some awareness of these subconscious energies because they're always speaking to us on a subconscious level. Extroverts will look outside themselves for the king, the warrior, the magician, or the lover. The extrovert will act out the negative aspects of this archetypal energy in shadow form; while the introvert incorporates the positive qualities of these archetypal energies in their fullness into the conscious personality.

As an example of this archetypal energy's destructive capability, it can become particularly dangerous when you have large numbers of people who look outside themselves for archetypal energy, particularly when it comes to the hero myth. The subject of this book.

The hero myth, or hero's journey is an individual inner journey in which one could see themselves; in which one would realize they themselves are the hero; within themselves lies the Salvatore Mundi (the savior of the world) and the Axis Mundi (the center of the world). As an extrovert, you will still seek the archetype of the hero but you will seek that hero outside yourself. In projecting this outwardly rather than inwardly, you begin to find yourself in a very dangerous situation. This drives our motivation of placing people on pedestals and valorizing leaders. Jung said the following in an interview:

> ...*They are not conscious of the fact that while they live a conscious life; all the time a myth is played in the unconscious. A myth that extends over centuries; namely, archetypal ideas, a stream of archetypal ideas, that goes on through one individual through the centuries. It is like a continuous stream and that comes into the daylight in the great movements; in political movements, or spiritual movements.*
>
> *For instance, in the time before the reformation people dreamt of the great change; and thats the reason why such great transformations could be predicted. If somebody has been clever enough to see what was going on in peoples mind, in the unconscious mind; (they) would be able to predict it. For instance I have predicted the Nazi rising in Germany through the observation of my German patients. They had dreams in which the whole*

thing was anticipated, and with considerable detail. I was already absolutely certain in the years before Hitler... Well I could say in the year 1919 I was sure that something was threatening in Germany; something very big and very catastrophic; and I only knew it through the observation of the unconscious... Psychologists really should look out for these things, but they prefer to think that I am a profit. HA!...

The interviewer then goes on to ask Jung if Hitler was fulfilling the projection of the archetypal father figure in the minds of the German people. Jung replies:

(Hitler) I couldn't possibly explain that well complicated fact... Hitler... It is too complicated. He is a Hero figure; and a Hero figure is far more important... He was a hero in the German myth; and mind you a religious hero; he was a savior. He was meant to be a savior, that is why they put his photo up on the altars... He's just a Hero myth...

In understanding this psychology of the myth that plays in the subconscious, as Jung states, I understood that this is why I could look up the things that were happening to me in terms of mythology because consciousness speaks to us in these archetypal and symbolic ways. Once I looked up the mythology of the symbols I was seeing, I began to make sense of the symbolism. This is also why so many abduction experiences, vivid dreams, and sleep paralysis experiences seem like so much nonsense. These experiences are not speaking to the conscious self; they are speaking to the subconscious in an attempt to bring it to the surface.

The beings associated with the phenomenon practice something that I would call subconscious basing. Where they exist entirely in the subconscious mind. This does not mean that you lose a sense of individuality; you are still an individual but you are much more in tune with the whole. It is on this level that we are all alike. This level is where concepts like remote viewing and telepathy are possible. The more we are in touch with the subconscious the more we can remember of our dreams, the more we can recall of our experiences with other centers of consciousness that we come into contact with on the mental plane. They are so in tune with this other aspect of matter that I believe they can remote view themselves here on the physical plane in which we could begin to see a physical form; but if we were to reach out to it, the seemingly solid form will just fade away. They can close their eyes onboard a ship in our solar systems asteroid belt; instantly transporting themselves behind me. Reading as I type this out on my laptop; and whispering suggestions. They can enter a nuclear missile silo and physically flip switches or push buttons. They can visualize what wires lead where and instantly understand its electrical schematics. To them this is child's play. You have to understand that they have at least ten million years on us in terms of the development of these abilities. I would even go so far as to say that we would not be here were it not for them. But I'll get into that later in the book.

Some may say, and I know because I have had this argument many times, "If all this is true why can't you demonstrate this for me here and now? Why can't you tell me what I'm thinking? Why can't you read my mind or communicate with me telepathically?" The answer is that that these skills are just that. You have to work at and develop these abilities. Nobody is a surgeon or a rocket scientist right out of the womb. At times these things have happened for me; but that doesn't mean I can replicate it at will if I don't understand how I did it. It has happened enough for me that I know its factual, and I think there is a balance in the mind that is just the right mixture of concentration, intent, will, and desire that will cause this to fall in place; but there's no way I can just do it whenever I feel like it. A doctor has to go to elementary school, high school, get an undergraduate degree, get a graduate degree, then obtain a doctorate before they can call themselves a doctor. So I'm a bit baffled that people would think these types of mental abilities would just be immediate. No ability or skill anyone has ever had just happened. It requires training and effort to do it really well.

One of the reasons I know I had to write this book was because I understand the psychology and mythology involved with transformation in a way that many people do not; but they need to. They need to because if they don't do the psychological work necessary, they won't ever be able to constitute this wholeness within the psyche.

When you start to examine human history, religion, and mythology through the prism of the facts laid out in this book, it begins to make cohesive sense. You begin to see throughout history where we have projected our archetypal energy. You can see these projections in our social structures and everyday interactions with people. The extrovert will project all of their archetypal energy out there in the world. Moore writes the following in his book, *Facing the Dragon* concerning the extroverted projection of archetypal energy:

> *To the extent that you refuse to acknowledge the enemy within you, then emotionally you must project it somewhere else. In Jungian terms, you refuse to admit, "Yes, I have a shadow, and it is part of my problem, and it is part of your problem, and I am trying to deal with it the best I can." One of the borderline dynamics that results is that you have to expel your badness onto someone else. You can do a whole psychology of religious tribalism by looking at people who deny the badness within themselves and try to put it all out there on other people. That is one of the key dynamics in how the archetype of spiritual warfare operates.*

The Four Archetypes of the Psyche

It is necessary to understand the contents of the four main archetypal structures. These four archetypal structures together compose the hero or savior in the psyche. I'm going to give you a synopsis of each and emphasize their most important qualities both in their fullness and shadow so you can begin to understand where you are with a bit of advice on how to constitute them in their wholeness within the psyche. All of these archetypes depend on and reach into one another in order to constellate wholeness.

The king, operating in its fullness within the psyche is the central archetype. It embodies also the feminine equivalent in the queen. It is order, stability, and organization. It is upon this archetype that the other three depend. It is the center around which everything is structured. It organizes and structures the psyche through discernment. The king makes good decisions based on being able to distinguish one thing from another. Discernment may seem fairly unremarkable but it's incredibly important. I'm not talking about the ability to distinguish between a mouse and an elephant; that's easy. I'm talking about the type of discernment necessary for transformation. The ability to distinguish between the finer points; the ability to distinguish between the two poles of an emotion. The two polar opposites are pretty easy but as you step out of center you need to be able to understand and clearly define where that center is. This takes work. I would liken it to temperature. If your body temperature is 98.6 degrees, and this temperature defines the center, then it would be necessary to distinguish the difference between a glass of water that is 98.5 degrees or 98.7 degrees.

The king acts as the primary archetype that sets the groundwork in the psyche for the transition from childhood psychology to adulthood; although there are people who never make it this far. I see it in people every day. I think we all know adults that act like children.

We see this represented in how their body language and facial expressions strongly resemble that of an angry toddler with childish displays of anger and fear. This type of discernment seems pretty straight forward but it's difficult for many people to discern what emotions are appropriate or justified based on perception.

The king polices the mind and enforces order. I also think of the will and desire as being qualities inherent in this archetype. The king and queen are not shadows of each other but co-rulers in the psyche. They must be balanced. Someone operating in the fullness of the king and queen will appear to have a structured life and will have the outward manifestation of being well put together, just, and fair. They will be sure and decisive with a great deal of confidence and an incredible amount of self-reliance. A child that is transitioning into adult psychology is beginning to make the desire subservient to the will in the psyche. They are starting to understand that they cannot act out their every emotion.

The two poles of the shadow king are the tyrant and the weakling. The tyrant rules his kingdom through fear and intimidation while the weakling is impotent and unable to make good decisions. The weakling and the tyrant cannot rule from a position of power and strength because they are enslaved by their own inner demons.

The warrior operating in fullness is energetic motivation. It is an offensive state of mind rather than defensive. The warrior is courageous. It gets after and confronts the issues of life head-on. It is alertness and mindfulness. The warrior is confrontational about the inner problems. The warrior commits to transpersonal causes or some greater cause than himself. The warrior doesn't mind work, be it physical labor or cerebral. He commits to the work and provides the motivation to accomplish tasks. The warrior will have a strong sense of loyalty and duty. The warrior lives life according to ideals like freedom, fairness, loyalty, and justice. The warrior will insist on these ideals within himself or herself because these are inner qualities despite what others may think.

The shadow warrior poles are the sadist and the masochist. The shadow warrior is outwardly destructive and cruel while possessing an outward hatred of people he perceives as weak; attacking the vulnerable. In terms of the warrior and the onion analogy, we can see that physical war falls in the realm of the shadow warrior. It is a sadomasochistic endeavor with no winners. Nobody ever wins a war contrary to what others may have you believe.

Today we continue to fight the Civil War which has morphed into a seemingly different issue as we come to terms with the systemic racism that has persisted since. "No justice no peace," is our battle cry. We can have no peace because there is no justice, and we can have no justice because there continue to be problems that make peace impossible. When externalized by the extrovert the shadow warrior energy becomes a paradox from which there is no solution and no escape. Too often we confuse justice and revenge. Revenge is born of the rage that exists in the externalized shadow warrior energy rather than the internalized energy of the warrior operating in its fullness.

When operating in its fullness, warrior energy can affect the type of change in the psyche that is so eloquently captured in Dylan Thomas's poem *Do Not Go Gentle Into That Good Night*. The introverted energy of the warrior becomes the courage, insistence, and the persistence to remain engaged in battle during the most difficult of internal struggles.

Peace and justice do not exists in the physical world because within most of us they do not exist in the internal world. These qualities exist within us and we manifest their existence, or lack thereof, in the physical world. There is no crown made of justice that anyone can place on your head. There is no blanket made of peace that anyone can wrap themselves in. We cannot legislate them into existence in the physical world. Peace and justice are discovered within one's self and when you find peace you will know the meaning of justice. In the inner journey, you discover the ultimate form of justice in the physical world is forgiveness, just as is stated by Mabel Collins.

The really great part about the qualities of the warrior and all the other archetypes operating in their fullness is that things are changing in the physical world. It is a symptom that things are changing in the inner world of many of us. These struggles in the physical world are symptoms of the constellation of the archetypal energy in its fullness. Some of our founding fathers were no doubt aware of this archetypal energy in the psyche. In our founding documents they asserted that all men are created equal in a time when there was anything but equality. They left us a treasure map in these documents. Just like peace and justice they left us an ideal, a path to perfection that we have been battling to live up to ever since. Reaching constantly for that ideal that lay just beyond our grasp.

If we want to strengthen our inner warrior we have to face life head-on. We all know people in our lives that have every excuse as to why they can't accomplish something. No longer can you be a person with excuses. We can no longer be lazy about life. If some task finds you, then you must do it with haste. Excuses and procrastination are for the shadow. We must commit ourselves and see that commitment through. We must do these things not only in the outer world but in the inner world as well. We cannot shy away from work that must be done, be it cerebral or physical; building the inner endurance, persistence, and insistence needed for navigating life and ultimately transformation.

The magician, in its fullness, is insightful, reflective, inventive, and calm. The magician contemplates. It seeks wisdom and knowledge. Ultimately it seeks the knowledge that is beyond human cognition. It comprehends things that are hidden to most people. It seeks the deeper meaning of things. The magician is the shaman, healer, or restorer. Whenever we put a lot of thought into life, we are accessing the magician. The magician energy is manifested strongly in scientists who develop technology or cure disease.

The shadow magician is a passive aggressive manipulator. When confronted with their manipulation they turn into the "innocent one" exclaiming, "Who me? No…" He will use knowledge as a weapon and hides the truth. The shadow magician is a manipulative, controlling, liar.

To cultivate the magician in its fullness requires a great deal of thought and requires aspects of the lover and warrior. It is the magician that contemplates life's experiences and seeks to learn from them; be it an encounter with a stranger, a documentary, a movie, or any of life's difficulties it is the magician that seeks the lesson in everything. The magician asks in situations big and small, *"What did I learn from this?"* The magician then applies knowledge to solve problems and work out solutions. When confronted with something that seems out of the ordinary the magician seeks to understand it. In transformation it is the magician that accepts and embraces new ideas about the nature of reality. The magician will seek to understand this new reality and embrace it rather than run from it.

The lover in its fullness is full of empathy and forgiveness. It has the ability to put itself in the shoes of others. The lover is artistic and **creative**. The lover is sensual about its experience of life and willing to push the boundaries of what is socially acceptable. Moore states that musicians are often mainlining the lover energy. This can also be why we see so much about this transformation within our cultures; the creative types are tapping into this energy of the collective subconscious.

The shadow lover is an addict who overindulges, which is another trait we see in the artistic types. They are always imagining the grass is greener on the other side and are endlessly restless because they are never satisfied.

I'm going to spend a bit more time here on the lover because I believe in terms of Jungian psychology it is, even today, misunderstood and grossly underestimated in terms of its central importance in the four archetypes. When we think of the lover archetype in terms of transformation and myth, we need to understand that love is creation.

We learn in *The Kybalion* that there are other planes of existence. On the physical plane, love manifests as sex and generates life. On the mental planes, love generates and creates as well. It generates thought; creative thought. So any type of generative thought is a quality of the lover archetype. This makes the lover operating in its fullness extremely important because the lover is a regulator of the other archetypes, through creativity in the mind. You could almost view it as a type of pressure release valve of archetypal energy. Without the lover operating in fullness, transformation is impossible because it is the mechanism that allows the other archetypes to operate in their fullness. Because the lover is creativity in the mind, the lover operating in its fullness becomes the interpreter of the physical and inner world. It is your perception of reality. The other archetypes act on that perception. This is why stoicism was so important in ancient cultures.

An example of this regulation within the archetype of the lover is that, through creativity, one can begin to imagine themselves in someone else shoes. You're cultivating empathy when you can creatively imagine how you would feel in those shoes. Another example of this regulatory mechanism is the idea of taking a situation that others would view as bad and transmuting that situation into a win for yourself. In my own life I can see how I used it. I no longer view things through the perception of success or failure. I didn't view life experiences as being pleasurable or painful. I didn't care if I was at home or at work; it was all the same to me.

In another illustration of this type of thought; I had recently taken my truck into the shop for repairs. It was crowded in the waiting room, so I sat and began reading my book. I honestly have no idea how long I was waiting but when the service staff called me back to the desk, they told me they were going to give me a discount because I was the only one that wasn't complaining about the wait. The fact was that if I weren't at this service center sitting reading my book, I would have been at home reading the same book. So what did it matter if I were at home doing that or in this waiting room? It didn't matter; so there was nothing to complain about. Some may say it's a matter of comfort; but the need for comfort has to go. I'm not some baby that needs to be swaddled. When one perceives that they "need" comfort, they automatically limit their own field of vision and possibility within the human experience. In doing so, you create this box that is comfort, and you will not venture beyond that box.

I was at a point in life that if I wasn't learning from what I was doing then it wasn't worth my time. I viewed learning not as work but it was enjoyable to me. The more intense and seeming difficult the situation was, the more I embraced it. It is through this creativity of mind that we are able to learn valuable lessons in life which result in the cultivation of wisdom, giving birth to the magician operating in its fullness. This creative regulation is the most important quality of the lover operating in its fullness.

I didn't understand the importance of the creativity of mind and that it was a quality of the lover until I was reading other myths and works from ancient Greece. I had read the *Homeric Hymns* and saw the lover archetype present in all of them, but I didn't understand why.

We can see the qualities of the archetypal lover represented in Greek mythology. The Greek god Eros was said to be the god of love and he had a consort, or wife, named Psyche. To the ancient Greeks, Psyche was the goddess of the soul. She was a mortal woman that became immortal when she married Eros. In the mythology, Eros falls in love with Psyche and she with him, but he never permits Psyche to see his physical form. Whenever they are together, it is in darkness. Eros was said to be an extremely beautiful man. Psyche's sisters are skeptical when they find out that she's never seen him. They insist she can't know if he's beautiful because she can't see him; he could be hideous for all she knows. In this mythology the lesson is to see beauty where others cannot. To view beauty as the introvert views beauty, to be blind to the concept of an "undesirable experience" that others would find too difficult or too boring to waste their time on.

The Roman equivalent to Eros is Cupid. Roman artwork depicts Cupid as a blindfolded baby. It speaks to the childlike innocence of seeing the beauty in everything and being blind to the experiences of life that others would find undesirable. Some may say that they don't want undesirable experiences; and to that I say; you should not. You should not view ANY work or experience as undesirable. The reason Cupid was depicted as a child is because, as you adopt this philosophy of learning from experience and approaching difficulties without reservation or judgement, you become almost childlike. You become the Japanese proverbial principle of see no evil, hear no evil, speak no evil.

This concept of Eros or love is discussed in Plato's *Symposium* and can be seen physically at the ancient Greek temple to Dionysus. Since eros was thought of as erotic love, the temple to Dionysus had stone carved phalluses in the complex, but understand that these are symbols of creation in the physical world and the temple is all about the type of creation in the mind necessary for transformation. The complex is situated on the island of Delos. The island is fairly barren and rocky making it undesirable and unwelcoming; yet it was incredibly important in Greek culture for that very reasons. Despite its inhospitable setting, it is the site of the temple to Dionysus, and was said to be the island where the goddess Leto gave birth to Apollo. There are many authors who have written about the dichotomy of Apollo and Dionysus. The island of Delos is the place where the lover in the psyche is born. It is a lesson in psychology. It speaks to the fact that an appreciation of beauty is born of terrible hardship and it takes a special kind of mind to view those hardships to be as beautiful as they are awful. To view hardships as gifts that should be welcomed with open arms. When life gives you lemons, you make lemonade; as the saying goes.

There was an oracle at Delphi that ordered the purification of the island of Delos. All bodies buried on the island were removed. She declared that there could no longer be physical death or birth that would take place on the island because she understood all of this to be mental. She wanted to highlight the mental rather than the physical.

When the public would come to consult the oracle at Delphi on matters of life, the oracle would often respond with questions or a riddle. She did this to get the public thinking along these psychological lines. The public would travel from all over to Delphi seeking the council of the oracle. They would enter a dark smoke-filled room where the oracle was seated on a tall tripod throne with a priest standing beside her who would be her interpreter. She was said to speak in "tongues" but I don't believe this was the case. Upon further examination of this situation, I believe the oracles were foreigners and can make a case that they were born and trained outside Greece; my money would be on Egypt. I believe this because of the works of Plutarch who was a priest at the Temple of Delphi and I'll get into that later.

Plato, in his work *Symposium*, tells the story of a dinner party with several guests. One of the guests in attendance is Socrates, who was Plato's teacher. It is decided that the dinner will be dedicated to Eros; the Greek god of love, and that each of the guests will make a speech about Eros. It is decided that Socrates will go last as his speech is sure to outdo the others.

Many scholars view *Symposium* to be Plato's finest work. I think it's absolutely amazing on so many levels. It's a psychological masterpiece. When it comes time for Socrates' speech, he begins to tell the story of a dialogue he had with a woman named Diotima. He describes her as an oracle and I would presume an oracle at the Temple of Delphi. Socrates states that Diotima is the one who taught him about love. In the dialogue between Socrates and Diotima, she walks him through a logical thought process as to the true nature of love: what it is, why people seek it, and how it is the path to the Eleusinian Mysteries. She describes how the extrovert looks for love versus how the introvert looks for love. Socrates poses the question of why it is so few actually seek birth in beauty (the end state of the Eleusinian Mysteries). She states that all seek birth in beauty but the difference is that some men are pregnant of body and they will seek to lie with a woman and generate; while other men are pregnant of soul and they generate the things that are proper for the soul to generate; mental qualities; virtue and wisdom.

The dialogue touches on the same ideas Robert Moore does when he discusses the fact that if we were to examine our possessions, these objects we view as extensions of ourselves, we would see where we are lacking. For instance, you may enter someone's home and see a collection of symbols of the warrior, lover, king, or magician. It would become obvious that the individual needs to cultivate the real qualities of those archetypes represented in their collection. These things are also clear to people like me that can see these layers of the onion.

When Socrates finishes his speech the guests are awed by his brilliance but this isn't the end of the story because there is a knock at the door. It is one of Socrates' former pupils, the last dinner guest, who has arrived late and drunk. The last guest is described as being accompanied by a flutist and crowned with garlands. (Dionysus is often depicted this way.) The last guest is informed of the speeches to Eros and begins his own speech on Eros. He begins speaking about his admiration for his old teacher, Socrates, whom he so admires. He speaks about the wonderful inner qualities Socrates possesses; comparing these qualities to golden statues of the gods that lie in his core. He speaks about how desperate he was to impress his old teacher, and how his adoration of Socrates was never reciprocated, no matter how hard he tried. There was nothing he could do to earn the affection of Socrates. He implies that Socrates is so strong and pure that all anyone could do in his presence is want to become a better man. *Symposium* is really a summation of this entire chapter.

The last guest's speech encapsulates everything Socrates stated in his own speech and also describes Socrates as a person living the archetypes in their fullness. The preceding speeches by other guests also support the final two speeches. They deal with the concepts discussed in this chapter. Some of *Symposium* remains a mystery to many scholars because it is so complex. There is a speech by one guest that was said to be a comedian of his time but his speech is not comedic. I believe Plato did this so as to hide the true interpretation of this speech. It actually deals with the concept of duality which is something I refer to as polarity: the natural dualistic nature of all things. The thing I really love about *Symposium* is that through these speeches it shows the progression of the lover from beginning to end. It illustrates the progression from the simplest of understanding to the more complex and much deeper understanding of the lover archetype.

The lover makes an appearance in Genesis. Genesis 1:3

And God said let there be light: and there was light.

God uses the power of the spoken word to creatively speak reality into existence. And it is through these same means that man can participate in creation. Genesis 2:19.

And out of the ground the Lord God formed every beast of the field, and every fowl of the air; and brought them unto Adam to see what he would call them: and whatsoever Adam called every living creature, that was the name thereof.

And so we see that Adam begins participating in creation. He decides what his reality will be. He decides what he will allow to have power over him. He decides his mood and his actions.

Keep in mind that the archetypes as I have described them here are a very abbreviated synopsis of the four archetypes, there have been whole books written on each of these archetypes alone, and I would encourage you to read them for a more comprehensive understanding. The series of books by Robert Moore and Douglas Gillette on the topic of these archetypes; are brilliant. Throughout the series they bring up various myths and I would encourage you to read those myths and understand their lessons.

Because the balancing of these archetypes can be a bit tricky, the books by Robert Moore and Douglas Gillette are the only ones I would recommend at this time. Moore points out that a psychologist can receive training as a Jungian analyst and get an idea of what constitutes the four archetypes, but, unless you have been through this transformation, the archetypes' contents can be a bit of a mystery to you.

If there is one issue I have with Robert Moore's books it's that they talk about all of this in terms of the male psyche. I don't think the female psyche is any different in terms of these basic concepts.

We can either live these four archetypes in their fullness or we can live the shadows of these archetypes or some combination of the two, but we also project these archetypes or their shadows onto other people or things as extroverts. A glaring example of this projection, and one that Moore uses because it's so obvious, is codependency in a relationship. Let's say this relationship is between a man and a woman just for sake of clarity and differentiation, but it could be a same-sex relationship; it doesn't really matter. You may have a man within a relationship that is lacking in the lover, while the woman has incorporated this into the psyche. He then allows this woman to hold that energy for him. He projects that aspect of himself onto her. Within that same relationship you may have a woman who is lacking the warrior. So, she projects that aspect of herself onto him so he can hold it for her. He doesn't need to be the lover because she is, and she doesn't need to be the warrior because he is. Too often this is a perfect match made in hell.

We've all heard couples talk about how they complete each other. Nobody should be completing anyone. We should be complete in ourselves. Where things go right in this situation is that this doesn't have to be dysfunctional. We often are attracted to others that have cultivated qualities we have not cultivated within ourselves. This is what attraction is. In this way you can begin to cultivate within yourself the qualities that attracted you to that person. You become those qualities in observing how that person has cultivated them. Often, after you do this, you find that attraction begin to wane. You've cultivated within yourself the qualities that you once sought in that other person and the marriage falls apart. You are no longer projecting yourself onto that person.

Where things start to get really ugly is where we start to see this type of attraction projection not in the archetype of fullness but in the projection of the shadow. Things can get equally ugly when one or the other partner, or both, decides they will no longer hold that archetypal energy for the other. They may decide to withhold that archetypal energy from the other in an act of manipulation or control over the other.

A very important point here that I need to share, because it's something that is only realized when one goes through this process and constitutes this wholeness, is that when we project these archetypes onto others, rather than incorporating them into our own psyche, we become attached to that person or thing. That person or thing becomes an extension of your own psyche. In other words, someone finds a quality they lack in someone else. They keep that person around and under some level of control, perhaps as a boyfriend, girlfriend, or spouse. Rather than incorporate that quality within themselves, they control that quality in someone else as an extension of themselves. When that aspect of the self is ripped away or withheld, it hurts because it's tearing the psyche. This is an important part of Buddhism: ridding one's self of attachments. By not projecting these pieces of yourself on other people or things, you rid yourself of these attachments. This is also why in the mythology of the birth of Apollo, his mother Leto, gives birth to him on an island with no attachment to the earth; the island of Delos.

When this wholeness is beginning to be constituted in the mind, you will crave simplicity. You will no longer project these pieces of yourself onto other people and things. Because of this, you no longer are drawn to people and possessions in the same way. I found that I was very unimpressed with others and had a hard time feeling attachments to them. Some would say this is the result of some form of mental illness or another but they're wrong. I was unable to feel these attachments because I couldn't find positive qualities in others that I hadn't already mastered. The result was that I was very unimpressed. Living like a monk becomes desirable, as you will begin to see possessions as burdensome. The large house that has to be cleaned and dusted suddenly isn't as appealing anymore. The expensive sports car with all of its maintenance becomes more nuisance than it is enjoyable. The simpler life is the better. You won't need to fill your life with external symbols of the archetypal structures so "stuff" becomes undesirable. This is also the reason people like Jesus and Buddha are said to lead the lives of simple men, but you can't just throw yourself into a simple life and expect things will fall into place; you need to do the psychological work necessary.

There is a Netflix show called *Messiah* that illustrates archetypal energy perfectly. In the show, there is a man that people begin to follow because they believe he is the Messiah. It illustrates how people begin to project the energy of the savior, or hero, on him. There is a scene in one episode where a prostitute is sent to his hotel room in an effort to discredit him. He refuses her advances. As she becomes more desperate she starts grabbing at him and says, "I just want to be close to you." He refuses her yet again and tells her, "You don't know how to be close." He then goes on to explain why she doesn't know how to be close, how she doesn't even have any comprehension of what that means. There's all this archetypal energy flying all over in this scene and the one they call Messiah refuses to hold any of it for any of the parties involved.

Religions throughout the world have lists a mile long of "thou shalt nots" and tell you what qualities make up a "good person." They all have this ideal of what constitutes a good person. It just so happens that this ideal often will mimic what you become when you constitute this wholeness in the psyche. This is where the world's religions fail us. They don't teach us about this psychology that leads to this ideal. Instead, they often simply say it is enough to just believe. Just believing is not going to help you psychologically.

As Moore points out, the question is not whether you possess the archetypal shadows but where are they hidden? We all have them. The problem is that most people are unaware that any of this exists; so, what ends up happening as we live in these archetypal energies is that we put ourselves at risk of living the shadow or negative aspect of the energy in our everyday lives. When we live these shadows, our lives become outwardly destructive and chaotic. The more you live in the shadow, the more outwardly destructive and chaotic your life becomes.

What we see in the above is the idea that people instinctively do this. They project their shadow energies on the "other." The other becomes the scapegoat for our archetypal energies whether the scapegoats are immigrants, Jews, homosexuals, men, or women we project our primordial evil on that group; making that group hold these destructive shadow archetypal energies for the rest of us. As Moore points out, in these types of conflicts, you have that group of people project their own shadow right back. So, you end up with a brave soldier on one side of a conflict fighting a brave soldier on the other side and they're both fighting the same archetypal projection. When introverted, the archetypal energy of the subconscious sets out to destroy perceptions and emotions that are not in line with it. When extroverted, this energy becomes the destruction of the other; or anything that is different from itself. Extroverts will see the qualities in others that must be destroyed but they won't see those qualities within themselves because they have their gaze turned externally. They become blind to themselves and their own flaws.

We project this hatred of the "other" rather than face the fact that hatred comes from within us. It is this projection that causes us to drop bombs on one another. Rather than understanding that the only thing we should ever be dropping on people is aid and assistance; nobody can ever hate you for that. I want you to understand how powerful the archetypal energies are so you can begin to wrap your mind around the dire nature of our current predicament. It is much easier to massacre men, women, and children than it is to come to terms with the archetypal energies within ourselves. Think for a moment about the implications of this in an age of nuclear weaponry, political polarization, economic collapse, and pandemics. This political polarization is in fact an archetypal projection.

My favorite modern-day transformation myth has to be the *Wizard of Oz*; because it speaks directly to the psychology that leads to the transformation. It concerns the constitution of wholeness within the psyche. Frank Baum was a student of theosophy, just like Mabel Collins, and knew what he had written was a masterpiece. He supposedly framed what remains of the pencil he used to scratch it out on paper. And just like Mabel Collins, he was familiar with the path. Follow the yellow brick road; follow the golden road to immortality; to a land that exists somewhere over the rainbow. Suddenly the words to "Somewhere Over the Rainbow" take on a whole new meaning that has actual roots in a much deeper reality.

Dorothy embarks on a journey of discovery where she incorporates the archetypes of the psyche into her conscious personality; she kills the wicked witch, representing the shadows, through a cleansing process, a baptism, throwing a bucket of water on her to wash away the evil. Dorothy incorporates the king, warrior, lover, and magician. The Scarecrow finds his brain, the Cowardly Lion finds courage, the Tin Man finds his heart, and she learns that magic resides within herself. She was the magician she needed all along and possessed the power to go home at any time, but she never knew this until she constituted wholeness within herself.

My advice along these lines is to introspect. Just be alone with your thoughts and your emotional pain. Let go of your fears. Let yourself confront your own emotions head on. Take ownership of your emotions. Your emotions and perceptions are yours. If you become angry it is because you allowed that to happen. Can you imagine a world where everyone was practicing this type of mental control, where everyone has taken maturity to this next level? You suffer what you choose to suffer. At that point we would all collectively decide we will no longer suffer anything.

This is a hard pill to swallow but one that the Greeks and Romans understood and it's the reason they practiced Stoicism, which, as I stated earlier, is a quality of the lover operating in its fullness. Suffering is a choice. It's all in your head. It is your own choice no matter what your lot in life. Nobody is ever a victim of circumstances; you are only ever a victim of yourself through your emotions and your own perceptions. Never forget that your outer life is a manifestation of your inner self. The truth of all of this psychology lies hidden in plain sight all around us. We can see the most successful people among us have cultivated patience and attention; inner qualities, while our prisons are full of the most outwardly violent among us. Those who pay little attention to the inner world, limiting their existence, it is a life of living from one emotion to the next; acting out emotions physically on the physical plane. This type of manifestation too is polar. There are the extremes of the peaceful monk and the violent murderer in our society; but between those poles there is a whole combination of people in between.

I found that the integration of these archetypes was enabled by the practice of Stoicism. Stoicism was practiced in ancient Greece and Rome, it was all about the transmutation of perception and emotion; many people would do well to study and incorporate Stoicism in their everyday lives. The difficult truth of your own emotions is that you could be locked away in prison, in a concentration camp even. In these circumstances it would be very difficult to not fall victim to your emotions. But something people need to understand is that the soul or consciousness is the real you; the "I," is immortal and needs nothing to survive. This consciousness is all about control of the illusory emotions and perceptions described by Mabel Collins as the pairs of opposites in *When the Sun Moves Northward* and the shadow polls by Robert Moore.

Seeing things for what they truly are is key in the psychology of transformation. In doing so you are able to learn from every situation. You learn that regret is unrealized success. The same is true for failure. Regret and failure exist only in the mind and are only present in the absence of some learned lesson. It becomes difficult to view a situation as a failure or regrettable if you learned a valuable lesson from it. Therefore, you should be thankful you had the experience; if not, then you wouldn't have learned your valuable lesson. It's really a matter of finding the will to identify the positive aspect of any situation. There are great books by Seneca, who was a Roman philosopher, and Marcus Aurelius, who was a Roman emperor, on the subject of Stoicism. If you Google the definition there are two listed and both are correct but the second is more complete:

1. *the endurance of pain or hardship without the display of feelings and without complaint.*

2. *an ancient Greek school of philosophy founded at Athens by Zeno of Citium. The school taught that virtue, the highest good, is*

based on knowledge; the wise live in harmony with the divine Reason (also identified with Fate and Providence) that governs nature, and are indifferent to the vicissitudes of fortune and to pleasure and pain.

So, it's not that you are able to endure without the display of hardship or complaint; it is that you are **indifferent** to those hardships in the first place. This theme is present in Plato's *Symposium* as well. The last dinner guest describes the ability of Socrates to endure great hardship without so much as a thought to its difficulty and with no thought to his own well-being.

If one begins to exercise the will, one begins to become mentally stronger. In an earlier chapter I stated that I had adopted a philosophy that forced me to become stronger in this way. If the thought ever occurred to me that I don't want to do that right now or, I'll do it later; I took this as my cue that I needed to accomplish this task immediately. In other words, don't procrastinate. Procrastination is for the weak of mind. In becoming stronger you find it much easier to accomplish tasks. In the above definition, you can seemingly do things that may be very painful, emotional, and difficult. Some weak-willed onlooker may look at you and observe your lack of difficulty in doing something that would have been very difficult or impossible for them to do; to them it may almost seem magical. They may even think you are suppressing this difficulty by brute force, bottling it up and stuffing it deep down inside; because it's the only way they know how to do such things.

A strong will allows you to begin to master your own mind; you decide what thoughts enter your mind and what thoughts do not. Stoicism is the practice of doing this. Stoicism, is the study of the true nature of a thing. The thing is stripped of all its illusion, and assigned a status based on its bare bones. Remember that the strong will belongs to the king archetype; the central archetype upon which all of the other archetypes depend. It is the archetype that allows the psyche to transition from childhood psychology to adult psychology. The reason for this is the maturing of the psyche as the will begins to become stronger than desire. To some extent, many of us have done this and perceive ourselves to be mature adults. But you can and should take this maturity many steps farther than you currently have.

Plutarch, who was an initiate of the Mysteries of Apollo, and a priest at the Temple of Delphi, wrote a long stoic letter to his wife upon the death of their young daughter. He told her that the Mysteries had given them the knowledge that death was not final, and that at this time they should conduct themselves in a manner befitting that knowledge. He warns against mental indulgences in sadness and grief. Comparing it to the excesses of pleasure and desire. He urges her to remember that she must exhibit mental control. He reminds his wife of Aesop's words about the god Grief. When Grief asked Zeus for recognition among the gods, Zeus granted that he be recognized only by people who deliberately wanted to acknowledge Grief. Plutarch tells his wife that things like grief imprison the mind. In this letter, Plutarch writes truth, he urges the middle road as the Buddhists would say. He does so because he knows how imperative mental control is and how important it is to rest always on love and happiness rather than allowing lower emotions to rule the mind.

Marcus Aurelius wrote *Meditations* and was a graduate of the Roman Mysteries which were said to be similar to the Greek Mysteries. *Meditations* were bits of insight the emperor wrote to himself, and today, provide a glimpse into the practice of Stoicism; or the practice of the transmutation of human emotion and perception. These little bits of inner wisdom are similar to ideas I was hearing from others I know to have found this consciousness. In reading through *Meditations,* I can see some of the ideas I had adopted in my own life. Stoicism is not something I was aware of before all of this began, I viewed my way of life as simplification. I naturally adopted this philosophy as a way to be ruled by reason and logic rather than by my lower emotions and warped perceptions. It was something I did on my own and didn't attribute it to any ancient philosophy.

Just to give you an example of how this works, in *Meditations*, Marcus Aurelius writes about his throne. He ponders the difference between a throne and a stool. He comes to the conclusion that they are no different; a throne is just a stool that has been covered in fabric. This practice is even apparent in the *Homeric Hymn to Demeter*. The lady of Eleusis offers Demeter her splendid chair, but the immortal and stoic goddess Demeter refuses the chair and opts to sit on a stool instead. Marcus Aurelius applies this same philosophy to his royal wardrobe. His royal purple garments are nothing more than the same wool everyone else wears, but they're dyed purple with the blood of dead sea crustaceans making them dirty and even undesirable in a way.

Likewise, this can be done with human emotion as well. It becomes an analysis of the emotions you feel, and the cause of those emotions within yourself. With human emotion it becomes difficult because you have to look at your situation objectively. For instance, if some situation causes you to become angry. You would step back and dissect the situation. Was this a situation that was within your control? If it was not, then feeling any emotion about the situation is an unjustified expenditure of energy. Therefore, when this situation comes around again, rather than getting angry and possibly bottling that anger up, you simply choose not to feel that emotion because it's not productive. If the situation that caused you to become angry was within your control, then you need to think about why, and examine if anger was justified; in doing so you should find that it almost never is justified. Perhaps the anger was due to misunderstanding and born of frustration. How could that be handled differently? So, when you see someone gloating and sitting on their throne, you don't become jealous; you feel sorry for them because they can't see that throne for what it truly is—a stool covered in fabric. When the masses are incited to anger and violence over some issue or another; you will see this as destructive rather than constructive; and remain unmoved.

There were many other great philosophers who wrote about these concepts of Stoicism as well as the idea of the immortality of the soul. These were thoughtful men who pondered things that they had some awareness of. Being graduates of the mysteries allowed them to do this. Today, we dismiss the writings we consider to be "spiritual" in nature yet we embrace the lessons of the writings that teach psychological lessons. We do this because we have no understanding of this "spiritual" aspect of the universe. It's not spiritual. It's fact. It is a factual aspect of the reality of our universe that was previously unknown and unavailable to us. As Jung points out, it is an aspect of matter that can be seen scientifically in the double-slit experiment.

Plato wrote about and pondered these issues in the *Allegory of the Cave*. In Plato's *Allegory of the Cave* it is clear to me he is describing the difference between an initiate and a non-initiate. I feel his pain in this story because describing all of this to someone who has never experienced it can be difficult. I often won't bother because to do this is to live-action role-play Plato's *Allegory of the Cave*. I will help those who know there's something to all of this but I won't argue with someone that isn't even dealing in reality, because they will get there eventually. We all will. I have cultivated a great deal of patience over the past ten million years so a few hundred or thousand more isn't going to break me.

Until one has known reality for themselves, they can't possibly even begin to comprehend, debate, and ponder its intricacies or finer aspects. In *Allegory of the Cave,* Plato uses "shadow people" as an example. In this story there are several people chained down in a cave so all they can see is the cave wall in front of them. They see shadows on the cave wall of people in passing. Because it is all they know, the chained people believe the shadows to be gods and have no comprehension that the shadows are just projections. Given what I know and understand, I find this story intriguing on so many different levels. There is the whole aspect of the shadow on the wall as a manifestation of an actual person which I will address when I discuss Spinoza in the next chapter. Also, people have always seen shadow people in sleep paralysis experiences such as mine and they have no understanding that there is a much deeper and greater reality to them. This speaks to the brilliance of the story told in *Allegory of the Cave*. It speaks to the experience as something someone must know for themselves.

It's difficult for someone to leave the cave and experience a new aspect of reality, then return to the cave and try to convince others of this reality they have no comprehension of. Not to mention the brilliance of using the cave which represents transformation. I also think that shadow people were incorporated into the *Hymn to Demeter*, where Demeter wanders the earth in a dark cloak with a veil over her face visiting various cities. Perhaps this was a hint that this tall dark figure visiting you at night is divine in origin. A hint that it is the goddess Demeter in the search for her daughter Persephone, or the human soul. These myths are engrained in the human subconscious, so the experiences we would classify as high strangeness or paranormal are designed to speak to the subconscious. They don't make sense in the context of the conscious self for that reason.

In this book I have written about having a clean and disciplined mind, but what does it mean to have a clean and disciplined mind? It means being constantly introspective and mindful of your emotions. It is not enough to simply bottle them up or suppress them. You have to decide that they will no longer enter the mind and you will no longer be enslaved by them. When things are going wrong in life, it's never anyone else's fault. It is in these times that you must turn that gaze inward to discover what's wrong. When one becomes introspective there are many things that begin to happen within the psyche. As you begin to do this mental work you will find that you begin to have a flat affect. You will seemingly lose interest in things that seem to delight others. You will no longer be so easily manipulated.

I began to see how others were using my own emotions as a weapon against me, so I began to really control them. I noticed the things I liked could also be used and manipulated by others to move me. I didn't enjoy the idea that others could hold these things over my head to manipulate me. I decided to reign that in as well. I knew it wasn't enough to suppress my enjoyment of any particular thing, I had to not enjoy it. The way I did that was to think about how that thing could be used to move me. In my mind, it made that thing very unenjoyable to me. I could see how that thing was imprisoning my own mind as I was a slave to that thing. I know what you're thinking… as you read this… you think how awful it sounds. I know it seems antithetical but in doing this work I found I was much happier. I could choose to be happy rather that giving that power to others who would decide my mood. I was known as someone who was smiling a lot because I was genuinely happy. When others would try to manipulate my mood, I would recognize it right away and simply ignore it and smile or laugh at them. I began to have a rather flat affect and had no opinion on most things that had no real substance. In high school, a friend of mine got me a button to put on my backpack. It said, "vaguely dissatisfied with everything." It's not that I had a vague dissatisfaction; I was simply indifferent to many things.

    I will say that I began to feel a deep depression slithering its way into my life when transformation was upon me. I knew something was wrong but I didn't know what. I guess I first noticed it as I stood shaving in the hospital mirror. I had been doing this type of mental yoga for so long and to such an extreme that I was unmoved by the possibility of my own death even. There were some people who had come to visit me while I was in the hospital, but I thought it was unnecessary. I didn't need anyone there because I wasn't afraid. I had taken on this philosophy that I would embrace any task that came my way; and I had done so to such an extent that there wasn't really anything that intimidated me. The prospect of my own death was no different. I instinctually had no reaction to the situation. I was indifferent. It was then that the depression crept in. I didn't know where it was coming from and I couldn't control it. I knew myself very well so there was nothing I could attribute it to. In transferring to a new duty station I had found I was considerably less busy. I no longer had the real estate keeping me busy after work and I no longer had all of the other heavy duties that would keep me occupied. I think maybe it was a matter of not having the distractions of work. Suddenly, I had much more time to think.

Early in life, I also recognized that the people and things I was drawn to were people that possessed qualities I wanted to possess. So, I incorporated those qualities in myself; allowing for the archetypal energy to begin constellating within my psyche. I could not have done this without a great deal of introverted thought and analysis.

I bring this up because I worry that there are many on this path that will begin to wonder what's wrong with them; just as I did. I can assure you there is nothing wrong with you; on the contrary, you are beginning to become more in touch with the forces that govern the universe.

There is a trend happening lately with living simply. People are moving out of their large homes and finding comfort in tiny houses. They're inexpensive so you are no longer in debt to some bank for the rest of your life, and their size makes it possible to do away with all but what you absolutely need. When I see trends like this it makes me hopeful.

In the beginning of this book, I eluded to the subject of this chapter when I mentioned the conversation I had with some of the junior sailors at work. "If you don't enjoy anything then the Navy can't take anything from you, in fact nobody can," I said. It was shocking to hear it come out of my mouth because it wasn't the type of advice that people normally give to one another, but it was true. In my quest for simplicity I had rid myself of what seemed like enjoyment; yet I found an inner, unwavering happiness in that: a form of freedom that most people will never know in this lifetime. If there are comforts around, I can appreciate them but I don't need, or particularly want them. At the time my depression began sinking in, I didn't understand that this was a result of the wholeness I was beginning to incorporate into my psyche, and I find it alarming that today's psychologists would likely have told me I was very sick.

I recognized how, throughout my life, I had been helpful toward others and also recognized how difficult it was for others to have this same level of enthusiasm toward their fellow man. At the time, I wondered if I was a pushover; or if I was being taken advantage of. Was I wrong in doing this? Were others correct in their unwillingness to help others? I have since learned that I was correct. And when I began to read about this psychology in the world's religions and mythology, I began to actually understand the answers to these questions.

I recently read an article about a group of Silicon Valley billionaires that were living like monks. The article expressed how silly this was but I saw the truth of it. They are clearly looking for this consciousness. Just like Steve Jobs, who dropped out of college after he read a book called *Cosmic Consciousness* and moved to India to study under a guru. When he returned from India he started Apple.

My hope for these billionaires is that they find what they are looking for. Christianity has the same struggle with this that I think these billionaires are facing. We know where this transformation ends up. We all have this image of the holy man that lives like a monk and wants for nothing; the Buddha and Christ figure. That box is well defined. How you evolve into that is not as understood. So many religions around the world define the box and encourage their followers to fit themselves into it with a laundry list of "thou shalt nots." There is the box; now make yourself fit; but it doesn't work that way. Often the consequences of this type of activity are disastrous. You need to recognize where you're lacking the king, warrior, lover, or magician. Perhaps you lack the cultivation of attention, patience or discernment.

My experiences in the navy taught me a very important lesson that these billionaires are trying to learn. I noticed that dropping everything in my life was very difficult. Giving up comforts and attachments to go out to sea where there was none of that. I noticed that I was having difficulty with work, I was distracted by the attachments. The only way to move forward was to surrender the attachments. If there was ever anything that I felt I couldn't do without, I knew I was becoming too attached to it and I would let it go. When we encounter such situations in life, most of us have a tendency to double down. We double down on the attachments and overindulge which is a quality of the shadow lover.

We will go out shopping, for anything; to distract ourselves from being alone with ourselves. Projecting ourselves on all of our stuff. We concern ourselves, deeply, with the thoughts and actions of others. When we are alone, our mind begins to wonder and it will eventually turn inward. People will look to others for their "happiness," they falsely believe as an extrovert that someone else is responsible for their happiness because the distraction that person brings to you forces your gaze in an outward direction. This relationship makes you feel better, the inner pain begins to subside and you begin to become codependent. The psychology of this is very interesting. Robert Moore says the following concerning these kinds of toxic relationships.

> *For example, when you fall in love with someone and do not have any understanding of these dynamics, it can become an overwhelming possession. I get people coming in saying, "I just cannot live without this person. If they leave me, I will die." It is as if you just met Astarte, the Phoenician goddess of fertility, or Isis, the goddess of the Egyptians, and you are mesmerized as one of her servants, and suddenly your autonomy and your initiative are gone, and your sense of self-worth is gone. You see this constantly in both sexes. This is an overwhelming idealizing projection of externalized grandiose energy, or god-energy.*

I was recently speaking to someone about a breakup. She told me that she had recently called her ex looking for closure. I explained to her that closure, just like happiness, is not something someone can give you; it is something you find within yourself. One will only ever find closure when they move above and beyond the thing that causes so much angst, when you stop projecting the archetypal self on this individual. I explained that the relationship she seeks is one born of the lower emotions. She seeks lust and not love. Many people can't tell the difference. Love is absolute and unconditional. When two people become involved and they decide to date exclusively, this becomes the first condition, the first mechanism of control over each other, it is born of the lower emotions and it is not love. When this is recognized, that is your closure.

Sex is something that often gets distorted. Sex is amoral. Before you get all worked up about that, let me explain that I'm not implying the argument that this is about the creation of life. It doesn't matter if we are talking about a heterosexual relationship or homosexual. This is also where Plato's eros comes into play. It's important to let sex be exactly what it is; the creativity of love. We tend to want to put all of this window dressing around it in the form of emotions like shame, guilt, jealousy, acknowledgment, and manipulation that doesn't need to be there. In doing so we make it something that it isn't.

If you were to become jealous when a significant other cheated on you, then you'd be projecting and therefore attached. I understand that this may be very difficult to accept. You are projecting yourself and you are seeking to control that perceived aspect of the self as an extrovert. I believe this is also what Plato was getting at in the *Symposium* where he implies that love is the road to the Eleusinian Mysteries. In addition to being about the transmutation of emotion and perception, a relationship also serves as a kind of litmus test to see where you stand on love. It will tell you if you feel a need to control your spouse, it will tell you if you know the difference between lust and love, It tells you what you're projecting and how much.

In terms of myself, I have a bit of difficulty understanding the shadow projection of the "love" that most people feel for one another. In the past, before my transformation, I didn't understand the need some people felt to be in a relationship. I was not comfortable giving power over myself to someone else. I now understand what all of that was. I was very unimpressed with others because they hadn't constituted wholeness as I had. I felt whole within myself and therefore did not need to seek that wholeness in others. I was seeking nothing more than friendship.

Before I joined the Navy I had a relationship. It was the same ex that the being in my room had projected. This ex told me that I frightened them which left me a bit puzzled. I was speechless, in fact, because I didn't understand that. I certainly have never been one to resort to violence or even raise my voice. I now think I understand what was happening there. I didn't have that handle on my back that we can grab in relationships to manipulate one another. It's rare that someone wouldn't have that handle. So, I could see how being involved with someone you can't manipulate in any way might be a little frightening. To be involved with someone that is more whole than you are, so you have no archetypal energy you can hold over them, could be psychologically shocking. With anyone else you would always be able to gauge where you stand and what that person is thinking through a manipulation of archetypal energy. But not with me. I often will recognize manipulations of this sort and won't play into it.

In a Jungian sub on Reddit, I ran into a post from a guy who had been doing shadow work. He posted that his wife had told him that she "hated that he was doing this." He asked people why his wife would "hate" his self-improvement efforts. I responded and explained to him that she hated it because he was getting rid of that emotional handle on his back that she could grab and use to manipulate him.

Whether you are heterosexual, homosexual, bisexual or anything else it doesn't matter. Whatever your preference is just don't make sex and relationships something they're not. I will say that I have been all over the spectrum at different times in my life, so I know it doesn't matter if you're bisexual, heterosexual, or homosexual. Plato's *Symposium* seems to imply that homosexuality is preferred when it comes to consciousness but I can't say that for sure; all I can say is that sexual preference is not something that we should feel weird about. The only thing that is important is that you understand it doesn't matter. Perhaps this is why some ancient native American cultures encouraged their children to have homosexual relationships; and why homosexuality was viewed as a sign of divinity.

In this chapter, I have given you a lot to think about. It's very important that within this process you cultivate patience with yourself. When one is patient with themselves they are patient with others.

If something you are doing isn't working, don't go immediately to anger. You should instead seek to understand why this thing you are doing isn't working. Take a step back and figure it out. Anger and frustration get you nowhere. These emotions will cause you to give up. Giving up is the worst possible outcome. If you give up when things become difficult then you are in no way ready for this transformation.

Apply this philosophy to your emotions, to your finances, to your everyday lives and you will begin to make more logical decisions rather than emotional ones. The desire will become subservient to the will rather than being ruled by it. Your strengthening will, your confidence, and your patience will begin to feed off of one another. As you begin doing this, you may want to throw in some exercises in cultivating attention. As you clean objects, begin examining them. What is the object made of? How is it fastened together? Was it made in a mold? Why does this particular thing get dirtier than anything else? I tend to do this because I find it entertaining and it cultivates attention.

Physiology of Transformation

There exists also a physiological aspect of this psychology. There is a treasure trove of information on the physiology of all of this in the fall 2020 edition of *Popular Science* magazine. I don't want to rewrite the contents of that issue here but if you read it you will see the parallels with this book. I can't agree with all of the scientific conclusions reached because some of those conclusions are reached under the assumption that consciousness is produced by the brain rather than the brain operating as a consciousness receiver and transmitter. The fact of the matter is that any and all psychological ailments have their roots in this transformation in one way or another. Many in the field of psychology will disagree because they don't know what they're doing. They would claim that one's behavior will change as a result of a change in brain chemistry but, most of the time, the reverse is actually true. A person's brain chemistry will begin to change as a result of behavior, perception, and false ideas. These things will compound and get worse if the behavior isn't addressed. I would say that the chemical imbalance acts as a type of consciousness dampener and keeps you locked in a delusional reality.

Psychology believes that behavior is the hardest thing for an individual to change. It is said that an individual is "set in their ways." The reason human behavior is difficult to alter is because, as a race, we have not empowered ourselves with the simple psychological tools to enable us to cultivate the necessary characteristics to easily correct behavior. In cultivating the will, it becomes easier to face life head-on allowing for transformative experiences. I noticed these changes in myself when my brother died. I had allowed myself to fall into this state of grief. As a result of that there were all these other mental traits that began to snowball. I recognized it at work one day. I was walking across the flight deck and there was a group of people standing around to my right. They all began laughing all at the same time. I immediately became angry because I perceived that they were laughing at me. It bothered me, not because I perceived that they were laughing at me but because this isn't who I was before. I was always very outgoing. I never had any problem talking to people I didn't know and I loved laughing at myself. The old me would have walked up and asked what was so funny. Not in an aggressive way but because I wanted to laugh too. I recognized this and immediately began correcting it.

Robert Moore states that any type of life-changing experience has the potential to be transformative and I have since seen the truth of this. I have read a lot about this type of experience taking place in addiction treatment facilities. To demonstrate the intensity of this transformative experience, I would encourage readers to watch an episode of *This Is Life with Lisa Ling.* There is an episode titled "Benzos," in which patients are shown "coming down" off benzodiazepines. There were several people shown shivering and crying while their teeth are chattering. Although I wasn't on benzos, this is exactly the same kind of pain I experienced with the same intensity, for months. With the right ritual elder in these situations, one can become transformed. Without it, one will return to the underworld year after year just as in the *Homeric Hymn to Demeter* states.

I find it interesting that epilepsy can be treated with benzodiazepines because they effect the same area of the brain; the limbic system. I don't think the fact that this pain of transformation resembling benzo withdrawal is an accident. I think it means that these drugs effect the same region of the brain responsible for the four archetypal structures within the limbic system. Even Moore points this out as do many people that have been through this process. René Descartes was a philosopher and stated that the pineal gland was the seat of the human soul. This gland is part of the limbic system in the brain. If you were to do some research on the limbic system, you would discover that it is known as the seat of human emotion. If you were to research what types of emotions the limbic system is responsible for, you will clearly see the four archetypes taking shape in these emotions.

When I was in the thick of these experiences, I often had dizzy spells that seemed to originate from the center of my brain. At times, I felt as though there was a vibrating cellphone within the center of my head; within this limbic system. At times I would get these dizzy spells while walking through corridors at work and I would have to grab a chair rail on the wall to steady myself. If we examine this system and what it does in the brain, everything I have said about the psychology of transformation begins to make sense.

Science tells us that this region of the brain is responsible for our emotions, behavior, long-term memory, and motivation. These would be the lover, king, magician and warrior respectively. This region of the brain is responsible for posture as well. I mention posture because as I stated in the last chapter, I felt the connection shut off, and I felt it immediately in my shoulders and back. My posture was different when I was connected. It was much more upright, balanced, and natural. The limbic system is thought to be the oldest and most primitive part of the brain because it is also responsible for many unconscious functions of the body like automatic vegetative control. What I believe is happening within this transformation or initiation is that we begin consciously accessing and controlling this region of the brain and getting it to function in an integrated proper way. This is where I believe neurology, psychology, medicine, and spirituality merge. I was reading a scientific article the other day where some scientists discovered that taking DMT causes the cells in the limbic system to vibrate at the same frequency and this is what is responsible for out of body experiences.

The reason medicine will be involved is because of the fact that this area of the brain is responsible for quite a bit of involuntary function. There is an episode of a podcast I have listened to called *Where Is My Mind* that I will introduce you to in the next chapter when I discuss consciousness and the scientific work being done to that end. In one of the episodes they discuss a woman who had cancer. She was beginning to experience organ failure because the cancer had spread to stage four. She had weeks to days left to live. She was in and out of consciousness. In a dream she saw a being that told her why she had cancer. It had to do with her mental state and her perceptions. She decided she would turn that around. In so doing, her immune system began attacking the cancer and she recovered.

I used to think that all religious ritual was nonsense but I'm starting to rethink this because I think the ritual may have its roots in the physiology of this transformation. I believe there is some ritual that has roots in vibration.

There are rituals performed that may seem to be nonsense but are truly transformative, if they are not taken out of context. Vibration is everything. As *The Kybalion* states: "Everything is in vibratory motion." As early man, we would perform ceremonies with rhythmic dancing and drum-beating. Vibration, is what was essential about those ceremonies and rituals. Vibration has everything to do with mental development. I've read many ancient sources that imply music is incredibly important to this transformation. It's why the temple priests at the Temple to Demeter hired musicians to play around the clock during initiation into the Mysteries; and it's the reason I listened to so much music during my own experience. I don't know the scientific reason or explanation for this yet but I know it to be the case.

The other day, while thinking about this, I was watching a TED talk with a sleep scientist named Dan Gartenberg. He explains how listening to a certain sound, while you are in the reparative stage of sleep, also known as deep sleep, can contribute to better mental health. When he played the sound, I recognized it immediately. It sounded like waves washing up on the shore, but it sounded like those waves were made of sand. It reminded me of a certain bear that my mother would place in my crib at night. She told me about this when I was older, and the bear was still around years later when she would place it in the crib with my younger brother. The bear had a knob on the front. When you turn the knob it would turn on a recording of my mother's heartbeat that would play continuously. This was the sound Gartenberg played in the TED talk. It was not just the sound of the beat you might hear with a stethoscope; it was the internal sound of the beat with the rushing blood. It's what the heartbeat sounds like to the fetus within the mother's body. I believe this had a positive effect on the growth, development of my brain, and mental health. Just as the music I listened to during my transformation aided the changes in my brain later in life. There are some who would say this was just a comforting sound, but I think there's much more to it. It makes me wonder if Alzheimer's or dementia could be treated with vibratory therapies. There is clearly something to vibration and the brain, and I think it would be smart for science to explore that connection.

I would like to end this chapter on psychology with a few final thoughts. So much of what I have written about in this book will be dismissed as spiritual woo woo. People will dismiss it as such because they have never experienced it, but I will tell you that anyone who does this psychological work will find consciousness.

One of the questions I get asked most often is: "Are there evil aliens?" I would hope that after reading this chapter you would recognize the absurdity of this question, but I'll explain it, nonetheless. This question itself is a shadow projection. We project our badness. We assume that they would behave toward us as we do towards them. If you're looking for bad aliens, we are it. Their mission here is to get us to realize this. They are in touch with consciousness and therefore could not be considered evil. The ability to communicate through consciousness would preclude you from being harmful. People insist on this evil alien theory because of the bad experiences. You have to understand that in doing things you would consider evil, they are pointing out *your* flaws. Perhaps they frighten you because they are aware you have not yet rid yourself of fear. They know this so they're trying to get you to understand this as well. In this same vein a child that wants to have ice cream for dinner may perceive their parent, who won't let them do that, as evil. So, in frightening you they're showing you that this fear you hold on to is not ok. In hanging on to it you put yourself at its mercy. You are controlled by that fear rather than by your own disciplined mind. In this consciousness control of the mind is essential because the mind manifests what you will it to, and you can read into that statement whatever you like.

    As a child, I used to observe all of this psychology at work in people around me. There was no way I could articulate it as I do now but I could see it. I could observe how the extrovert would become very frustrated with some delicate repair to something. The inability to perform the delicate task would frustrate them. The frustration would turn into anger and rage that would cause them to give up either by walking away or throwing the delicate thing into the garbage. If you were to try to have a primate construct a circuit board, they would possess neither the steadiness of hand nor the patience to complete such a task. They concern themselves mostly with food; an external reward for a job well done. They still very much rely on the externalized senses.

The same could be said of our situation. I would hope one would recognize that the extreme technological advancement that these beings possess and display, that has not destroyed them as it would us, would also imply a maturity above and beyond our own. By accessing consciousness we become closer to them, but in comparison, when we access consciousness we are still just babies to them. Babies that are only just now after ten million years beginning to say our first words and take our first steps.

For those who doubt any of this and how powerful these psychological structures are, I would challenge them to look around. Our economy is a perfect illustration. It is based on the shadow aspects of the psyche, it encourages and is based on greed and hoarding. Markets swing wildly based on human emotion. The answers to our current predicament with concern to the pandemic is clear. We shut down the economy because we value human life over the almighty dollar. But we find we can't do that because when we do this people are laid off leading to chaos, abject poverty, and starvation.

Money has value because we believe it does. We could decide tomorrow that we no longer believe that. Our economics are a prison that we have constructed in our own minds. Such prisoners we are to our own minds, and the constructs we have built in them, that it manifests the very real possibility of starvation and death in the physical world; limiting us as a race in scope and possibility.

It reminds me of a movie I saw many years ago called *The Mouse that Roared*. In the movie there is a group of POWs that have been captured in a war with a friendly country. As they are being led away, one of the POWs insists on his rights under the Geneva Convention. He insists that he has the right to a regulation-sized cell with a regulation-sized bed and regulation meals. His captors tell him, "Well, if you insist..." The scene cuts away to him eating porridge from a tin bowl with a spoon within his tiny cell as patriotic music plays, while the other POWs are shown enjoying a long table full of food in a plush banquet hall. We all do this to some extent. We have this idea in our head about how something will happen and we will insist that this is the way it needs to happen; even though an alternative we can't envision may be far better for us.

Although it is funny, this bit of the film does illustrate how we become prisoners of the ideas we cling to in our own minds.

So too with our economy. Money is nothing more than a control mechanism we exert over each other. This virus has done a very good job of exposing what's wrong with our way of life. It's almost forcing us into a situation where we begin to manufacture only what is absolutely essential. A situation where everyone doesn't have to work. It's forcing us to be alone and isolated from one another. It's forcing free time. In this free time people are forced to deal with these inner issues; suddenly they are confronted with the reality that a black man died because he used a counterfeit 20 dollar bill. We are confronted with the reality that his life was worth 20 dollars. Some may say he was drunk, mentally ill and combative but to that I say I don't care. Life is worth more than 20 dollars; there is no way you can toss this situation that would have any possibility of justifying its outcome.

It is in this same way that we gaze on our possessions at this time. We may look at that pineapple made of glass beads and wire that sits up on a shelf and does absolutely nothing. We realize we don't need that trinket because it becomes a much more personal question. Is it worth the life of someone I know to have this trinket? Is it worth the worker's life that they should go to work and make this worthless trinket? Is it worth the lives of the people at that manufacturer that work in bookkeeping, the employees that clean the factory, or the life of my own family member that went out to a retail center and bought it for me as a gift? No... Suddenly you're faced with the facts... that worthless trinket on the shelf that once looked so pretty up there now has a body count that makes you want to vomit; and it becomes one of the ugliest things you've ever seen. Suddenly you're also faced with the reality that not only do you not need that now but you never needed it. Now, it sits there mocking you; standing proudly on the shelf as a testament to your juvenile idea of reality and morality.

We are also faced with the fact that prisoners are being released from prison due to corona virus concerns and it begs the question: If they can be released from prison because of a virus, why were they in there at all? In this country we have corporations that own prisons and lobby lawmakers. Lawmakers that make it very easy for someone to find themselves in prison. More prisoners make more money for the system unless they're sick, then you'll have to pay for healthcare.

The question really becomes do we care for each other or don't we?

If the answer is that we care about our shadow economy more than we care for each other, then be prepared to take a few steps back because everything is going to fall apart. If the answer is that we will care for one another, then we can begin building a world more conducive to that. I have some fantastic ideas on a way forward that I have seen in my dreams since this whole thing began.

In deciding we will keep this economy we are gambling that there will be a vaccine for this virus. There's no guarantee that will be the case and we shouldn't be afraid to envision a way forward that fundamentally changes the way we live our lives. Let's seize this opportunity to correct all of the societal deficiencies this virus has made glaringly obvious. I am in no way implying that this will be easy, but I do know it will only be as difficult as we decide it will be.

As we look at the death of many things we used to enjoy, such as movie theaters, bars, sporting events, and dining in a restaurant, we can accept the new realities staring us in the face or we can double down. We can take a lesson from a few lines of the multileveled truths that lie on the sacred pages of that great gift to humanity; the Bhagavad Gita:

(They) are but finite things of the moment - and not the Real Man at all. They perish as all finite things perish. Let them perish. Up, O Prince of Pandu, knowing these things, prepare to fight!

I ran into this psychology in my own life because I happened to be doing all the right things. I can see how all the world's religions and mythologies throughout human history have been attempting to describe the psychology and the transformation it leads to. I approached this with a great deal of caution. I approached this in the same manner I would have working in Naval intelligence, which I did for 16 years. I let the facts lead me. I had no preconceived beliefs about any of this and because of that I now understand. I'm writing this book to help you understand it because I am confident that I am correct. The reason for my confidence resides in the rest of the book. In the chapters that follow, I will be pointing out historical evidence that supports what I experienced. More importantly, I'm going to tell you how I came to this evidence through consciousness.

I want to leave you with some a final thought and some videos to watch. In my experiences I have found that actors and comedians are often ripe to experience consciousness. Their success in their profession is due to the cultivation of attention. They're so attentive that they can pick up on subtle nuance that makes them good at what they do. If there is any doubt about that I would like you to go to YouTube and watch Jim Carrey's commencement address at the 2014 MUM graduation. There are other videos in which Jim Carrey talks about depression. Finally I would like you to listen to Charlie Chaplin's final speech from a movie he did in 1940 called *The Great Dictator* because it is, in my opinion, one of the greatest speeches ever written.

Too often throughout history we have chosen to destroy ourselves at moments such as these rather than seize the day; *carpe diem* is the slogan. Today, we stare down the barrel of a shotgun blast in the form of economic collapse, a global pandemic, and civil unrest; we find ourselves on the edge of an abyss between two great fires. Which fire will we choose? Destruction is certain and so is great change; but the nature of that destruction and the resulting change is up to us.

So what does all that mean? It means pushing yourself beyond the point where you are now. We look upon the world around us with all of its uncertainty, violence, and instability. Everything boils down to individual decisions. Individual decisions where emotions get the better of us. We have to, as individuals, begin to live the archetypes in their fullness. Leonardo Da Vinci's *Vitruvian Man* depicts this fact. It shows a man with perfect proportions in two different positions. Within the crucifixion, he touches the square which represents the profane material world. The circle is never ending; it is infinite. Through man in his perfect proportions, all opposites are brought to center and all paradoxes are reconciled. Man can then rise above the crucifixion and become infinite. Within man the circle is squared. Within man lies the bridge between the profane and the divine.

Chapter Eight
MODERN AND ANCIENT EVIDENCE

The next two chapters will essentially be a continuation of chapter six, "Return." I was led through modern and ancient evidence of transformation in cultures around the world. In order to truly understand this transformation, we need to understand what consciousness is. Then you will understand how this evidence of transformation I was led through would even be possible or how anything in this book is possible. I will also give you an idea of how this evidence presented itself to me, because just as William Walker Atkinson states, I was introduced to kindly mental brownies that are a part of my own mentality and aided me in the research for this book.

In the *Kybalion* there is mention of something called the Law of Attraction. The following chapters are a demonstration of this. In the beginning of my journey I set out to understand what this was all about. I wanted to do this so I could help humanity in some way. I had been doing the psychological work outlined in the last chapter. My strong will and balanced desire mixed with intent and expectation brought me some of the evidence I needed to write this book. I attracted these things to myself. It is in this same manner that you can do many things in terms of mental ability. You may already be accessing these abilities and don't realize it.

Consciousness

One morning, after I had finished reading Robert Moore's books, I woke with two names in my head: Steven Nadler and Dean Koontz. Dean Koontz was a complete mystery to me. He wrote a ton of science fiction; so many books that I didn't know what I was supposed to read. I decided I would look first at the books Steven Nadler wrote and I put Dean Koontz on the back burner.

Steven Nadler wrote a couple of books regarding the philosopher Spinoza. Baruch Spinoza was a Portuguese Jew living in Holland during the 17th century. In a book called *Spinoza's Heresy: Immortality and the Jewish Mind,* Nadler lays out a compelling case that Spinoza's views on the human soul or consciousness were in fact the reason for his cherem or excommunication from the Jewish church, in which Spinoza was declared a heretic. His views on the human soul being more in keeping with everything that I now know to be correct.

Steven Nadler wrote another book concerning Baruch Spinoza's and René Descartes' philosophies called *Heretics*. It's more a book for young adults because it's put together in the style of a comic book but it's an entertaining read. In reading *Spinoza's Heresy,* I was delighted that Nadler does a wonderful job of laying out Spinoza's views in a simple and objective way. In my opinion, no philosopher that I have read yet has more completely and thoroughly hit the nail on the head than Spinoza about what consciousness is.

Spinoza believed that the universe consists of a singular consciousness from which everything flows, to include all knowledge in space and time. Everything that exists flows from the source. Everything that exists, exists as an extension of this singular consciousness. There exist infinite extensions with infinite attributes. Spinoza believed that it was possible to understand and comprehend these extensions and their attributes through what he describes as *adequate knowledge* formed through an organized thought process that reveals certain essential natures of the eternal or the singular consciousness.

There are three different types of knowledge that compose what he calls adequate knowledge. He believed that the first type of knowledge consists of knowledge based on random experiences that form inadequate ideas, perhaps something akin to observation. The second kind of knowledge would be the apprehension of truths through reason, also known as deductive reasoning. The third kind of knowledge is intuition. It was his belief that one could begin to view the nature of a thing through this type of thought process. Then, using deductive logic and reasoning, begin to understand certain attributes of its eternal nature. Finally, applying the intuition, you begin to form adequate knowledge of the thing, which "synthesizes into a metaphysical truth—an essence (of God). It thereby generates a deep yet casual understanding of a thing, that is, an 'internal' knowledge of its essence. Such an internal essential knowledge situates the thing immediately and timelessly in relation to the eternal principles of nature that generated and govern it."

When I first read this I was shocked that the nail had been so squarely hit on the head by Spinoza. "Yes, that's it!" I exclaimed as I read. When I first came into this consciousness, I remembered that kind of awe I was in. I was looking on the world as though it were new and I'd never seen it before. I was constantly observing things I didn't know were possible, stopping me dead in my tracks several times a day, as I thought, *What is that?!!* I would literally be able to feel universal forces at work in any given situation I was observing. It could be as simple as hearing two people talking in which I would literally feel a tug as their emotions began to create a vortex around them that I could feel as it pulled and spun. Because of this connection, I had some idea of where situations were going and how they would end through an observation of these forces that I was unaware of before. Steven Nadler writes the following in response to this.

> *Spinoza's conception of adequate knowledge reveals an unrivaled optimism in the cognitive powers of the human being. Not even Descartes believed that we could know all of nature and its innermost secrets with the degree of depth and certainty that Spinoza thought possible.*

But it is possible. These concepts are a bit difficult to conceptualize, but the easiest way I can explain is that since the universe is in fact a singular consciousness, it also resides within you. The way to begin understanding the external universe is through that internal piece of the universal consciousness that resides within yourself. I noticed I could feel universal forces moving and working all around me, I could sense them affecting everything around me but not interacting with me anymore. I would liken it to walking through the bottom of a canyon of flowing water, but I existed in a bubble where the water would just bend around me, whipping about in every direction, acting on and in everything around me, but I remained untouched in the bubble. I know this seems strange but it's the only way I can describe it.

When you are able to tap into this within yourself, then that which is seemingly external to you can be comprehended internally, which could be thought of as a type of expanded intuition. It's more than just intuition, because we all have our gut feelings about something, but I would liken this to the gut knowing. This intuition is more than just the conscious impression most of us feel in describing intuition, and it crosses into the threshold of a conscious knowing, because it is so much more powerful in this awakened state. This speaks to the psychological difference between the extrovert and the introvert. I think the cultivation of attention is particularly useful here. I think this is partially what Carl Jung means when he talks about observing the subconscious.

I understand this may sound a bit out there but it makes sense to me. How would the beings I saw have been aware that I was about to go through this transformation? The answer is that they live in this expanded reality and they can therefore sense these universal forces in a way we cannot. When we meditate and ask for assistance, they sense that too. It's a strange thing but I can assure you it's very real. I had a sense of this one day as I stood in the kitchen. I felt a presence behind me. I could sense another center of consciousness. I turned around and there was a praying mantis on the wall above the back door. I could sense he was dying. I held my finger in front of him and asked him to climb on. He did. I took him outside and held him up to a branch on the bush just outside the back door. I told him to climb onto the branch and he did. I saw him again several months after that and he had grown much larger.

My whole life I've been attentive and, therefore, constantly observant; the knowledge one gains through observation of the world around them is incredibly underestimated. Because I was curious and observant, I was able to accumulate a great deal of general knowledge. When one becomes connected to the universal consciousness, you can easily begin to observe it operating within its infinite extensions and infinite attributes just as Spinoza claims. You will observe how it works and manifests and how our fractured psyches play into that. Because you can perceive connections others do not, seemingly complex and seemingly unrelated problems become very simple. Because of that I can understand how discovering this as a race, you could reach a technological zero point rather quickly. Consciousness is really the key to everything we don't yet understand about ourselves and the physics of the universe.

Spinoza believed that an individual's consciousness is recycled upon death. That same consciousness is reborn with only the knowledge one has gained of the eternal. This knowledge of the eternal will stay with you as an impression, or that which we call instinct; and I can see that this is correct. I had actually reached the same conclusion before I read anything to do with Spinoza. This transformation becomes a significant event in this knowledge of the eternal, because never before in the life of your consciousness have you been able to comprehend such a vast amount of eternal knowledge. So, when this consciousness is spoken of in terms of the attainment of immortality it's not that you were not immortal before, it simply means that this is the first time you were consciously aware of this fact.

What Spinoza, Jung, and Moore are all describing here is the subconscious. Most of us don't experience the subconscious consciously, and this is the heart of the problem. We instead are left with impressions and "gut feelings," but when you bring the subconscious to the fore and begin to experience it consciously, things become more obvious and clear. Religions would describe the subconscious as the human soul. Atkinson describes it as the "I."

In William Walker Atkinson's book *The Crucible of Modern Thought*, Atkinson adds this quote:

> *Sir Monier Williams says: "Indeed, if I may be allowed the anachronism, the Hindus were Spinozites more than two thousand years before the existence of Spinoza; and Darwinians many centuries before Darwin; and Evolutionists many centuries before the doctrine of Evolution had been accepted by the scientists of our*

time, and before any word like 'Evolution' existed in any language of the world."

Of course, we know this goes back much farther than that, based on human mythology and archeological evidence from around the world. In his writings titled *Ethics,* Spinoza goes a step farther with all of this and he once again hits the nail on the head, Nadler writes:

> *At one point in the* **Ethics** *Spinoza suggests that someone who has undergone a radical change in consciousness has,* ***ipso facto****, undergone a radical change in personhood. 'Sometimes a man undergoes such changes that I should hardly have said he was the same man.'*

Spinoza's idea of heaven is not the traditional view; he thought the traditional conception of the endless feast was nonsense. In Spinoza's conceptualization of what is to come, he claimed that there was no endless feast, no riches beyond belief. In other words, one grows out of what we currently call the human condition. After passing beyond these things, one would have no use for an endless feast with a bottomless glass of booze and a pocket full of diamonds. In transcending the human condition, one moves past the want to exercise power over others, a characteristic of the psychological shadows, one begins to recognize that this serves no purpose.

As immortal beings, no one of us is "better" than any other and there isn't a single one of us that doesn't have value. It is understood that living simply, not wasting labor manufacturing items that serve no utilitarian purpose, everyone wearing the same clothing made from the same durable yet incredibly comfortable utilitarian and nontoxic fabric, doing what we consider work 24 hours a day is the direction in which we must go. Disagreements become severely diminished as we all would understand what all of this is and what we must do. Having no possessions that are your own personal property because everything that exists, exists for the use of everyone, technology and knowledge belong to everyone. If there were any inventions ever conceived of, they were conceived of first by the ONE; the singular consciousness for use by all or they would not exist, so the idea of a patent vanishes as well. Everything that plagues the human race is washed away.

Spinoza understood that this idea of eternal peace and freedom results from the ultimate surrender of everything that keeps it from happening. He understood that this idealized conception of heaven is something you cannot have unless you can create it here and now because if you can't create it, then you don't get to have it, because you won't be able to keep it. Spinoza knew that at the threshold of the kingdom of heaven you must surrender that which people believe to be themselves; greed, fear, possessions, and hate have no seat at that table. He knew, just as many others have always known, that it was all psychological; while also knowing that this truth was so profound that it formed the basis of all the world's religions.

Spinoza writes that he's somewhat uncomfortable talking about certain concepts of the eternal because he doesn't want to give fuel to the fires of organized religion, which he viewed as keeping people locked in an endless cycle of hope and fear, hindering this inner change. I would agree. The Christian view that sins cover the soul and don't allow it to shine through, I believe is correct within the psychological work I outlined in the last chapter. The modern Christian view of what sin is; is completely wrong. Many of the current Christian teachings as to what is sin belong to the shadow and are born out of a want for control over its practitioners. Spinoza was also reluctant to document what happens when someone reaches this transformation and their physical body dies, but I have no such apprehension. He was worried that if he revealed this he would feed into the religious idea of "heaven," but he did know that it was important to live in this type of thought, also known as eternal thought.

Mabel Collins writes about living in the eternal. What she means by this is getting rid of the old mindset. Living, instead, with a mindset composed of the psychology I wrote about in the last chapter, living the list in *Light On the Path,* or at least getting as close to that as we can on a daily basis; applying the principles to our lives. If you examine the books I mention, you can almost imagine how someone who is immortal would in fact naturally adopt the qualities outlined by Mabel Collins in *Light On the Path* because they are also the attributes one begins to acquire as they live the four archetypes of the psyche operating in their fullness.

Living in the eternal is something we all need to start doing. The Renaissance was an example of a time in which there were some who were doing this. The Renaissance was a time of rebirth. If you really studied the Renaissance you will find these same concepts from *Mabel Collins, William Walker Atkinson, Carl Jung, and Robert Moore* etched in the history of the Renaissance. It was a movement that was described by Carl Jung as a time when the subconscious archetypes were becoming integrated into the conscious psyche.

It's important that we remember there exists a connected subconscious through which the ones who are living in the eternal are able to influence the larger population, pushing humanity forward. Therefore, this process of transformation—with its darkness, pain, and uncertainty within the individual—is also true of the greater whole of humanity. We need to keep this in mind as we push forward in a polarized society that is dealing with a pandemic, economic collapse, and civil unrest; as humanity fights to resist "The Call," like the alcoholic who picks up the bottle to shield himself from the painful, blinding inner light. The drug addict who doses to do the same; so too does the rest of humanity double down on old ideas, serving themselves a glass or dose of anger and hate, lest they too be consumed by the pain of this inner light.

Spinoza was someone just like myself that had found consciousness. Some would say his views were his own and he was just a philosopher, but science does in fact have something to say about consciousness. It's so new that not a lot of people are aware of it yet and the science is coming from some very reputable scientists. Just as I woke mornings with the names Robert Moore, Steven Nadler, and Dean Koontz in my head; I woke another morning with the name Mark Gober in my head.

Despite the blowback they receive, there are scientists studying consciousness. Mark Gober is an excellent source for this science. Gober wrote a book called *An End to Upside Down Thinking: Dispelling the Myth That the Brain Produces Consciousness, and the Implications for Everyday Life*; he also has an excellent podcast called *Where Is My Mind*. In the podcast, he interviews scientists that are working on the consciousness issue to include a Nobel Laureate in physics, Dr. Brian Josephson, and other PhDs from various scientific fields. The main argument Gober is making is that consciousness is non-local or not produced by the brain. This scientific work supports the theory of the singular universal consciousness of which we are extensions, just as Spinoza suggests. Gober states in episode one of his podcast that, in science, this problem is referred to as "the Hard Problem of Consciousness." *Science Magazine* listed this as the number two question remaining in all of science. The number one question was, "What is the universe made of?" The answer to both of these questions is the same.

In the podcast one of the female scientists working on the consciousness issue describes a conversation with a colleague. The colleague told her that she didn't care what evidence was presented; she was simply never going to believe it. The scientist replied, "Well, you can continue practicing religion, and I'm going to continue practicing science." The facts and evidence point to non-local consciousness. In experiments conducted by these scientists, where results in the 25% range would speak to chance, and consistently the results are in and above the 38% range; it's scientifically significant. Some of these scientists have also studied savants. People who, from some accidental bump on the head, can suddenly play the piano without ever having taken a single lesson. The implication being that the bump on the head caused some damage to the brain; damage that resulted in some consciousness damper in the brain to stop functioning.

I love when someone pulls out that stale, old, dusty Carl Sagan quote, "Extraordinary claims require extraordinary evidence." What nonsense! It's really the kind of garbage statement that has no place in science. Science is about data, numbers, facts, and specific measurable thresholds. Within this statement there is none of that. What is the measurable threshold where ordinary crosses into extraordinary? Can you imagine applying this statement to aerospace engineering? Well, I've put extraordinary joints in the wings of this aircraft... Let's fill the rocket with an extraordinary amount of an extraordinary fuel... What does extraordinary mean? It means that, as a scientist, you hold up this statement, stick your head in the sand, and continue to practice what you believe, which is religion not science.

In writing about the scientific work, I listened once more to the first episode of the *Where is My Mind* podcast. I became incredibly emotional at the end listening to a doctor who was involved in one of the case studies describe "waking up on the other side with the light." I know it well because I have seen it for myself. It took me back to the descriptions of William Walker Atkinson in his book *The Life Beyond Death,* Mabel Collins' descriptions in *Our Glorious Future*; and my own experiences. It is a reminder to me that people will be able to put together PowerPoint presentations complete with graphs and statistics where they can point to various changes and hard evidence; but this is not a substitute for the experience. An experience reserved for only the purist of souls. The only way to truly know it is for one's self, because to experience consciousness for one's self is undeniable and that is the ultimate evidence.

To experience this Nirvana or Enlightenment; to witness events you didn't think it possible to witness; to know anything you want to know by simply wondering about it and it gets placed in your lap wrapped in a nice little bow. To constantly pick up your phone seconds before it rings, a text message comes through, or an email arrives in your inbox; is the ultimate proof. To me it is a truth I experience proof of every day, all-day. To me it has become an absolute certainty. To wake in the morning hearing a statement of some future event and then see that event actually play out in your waking life. Most things I hear, pertaining to future events, concern me personally and are for me to deal with, most of which have concerned the content of this book. I think about some of these things and can see how someone with a weak mind could be driven into a state of absolute terror and panic by them, but I am grateful for them.

If you're still a bit skeptical, I would encourage you to look at what Mark Gober has put together about the scientific work being done on consciousness, because the evidence the scientists have compiled is compelling.

I'm going to add something here because it is time for science to look at consciousness. What I'm about to write here may be dangerous for me personally and perhaps I shouldn't; as if this book itself isn't... During the onset of my experiences, I approached someone who, I knew, would know about these things and who's name I'm afraid I will never mention. I was in a unique position to be able to speak to people that the general public does not have access to. If this person wishes to step out of the shadows, they may reveal themselves and I will confirm their identity, but not until then. I approached this person and became quite emotional during the onset of my experiences. I was terrified about what was happening to me. I described how I was an atheist and these books I was reading described people like me as the threads through which humanity clings to the divine. I was hysterical, *"What the fuck does that mean?!! I have absolutely no comprehension of what the fuck that even means!!"* I said as I was crying, hyperventilating, and trembling with fear. I now know that it means this connection to consciousness. This person calmly stated, while eating some French fries, *"Well, there are things about the universe that may seem a bit out there, but we are discovering that they are quite natural."* This actually occurred just days after the small man in my room woke me and told me not to give up, to keep going.

Constellations in the Sky

This may be a bit too in the weeds for most readers, but to understand transformation which is described as a cycle of death and rebirth, or death and resurrection, that pervades mythology, religion, and our physical environment, it is important to understand what is happening with various constellations in the sky at various times of the year. With this understanding, it is possible to interpret religious texts, artwork, or any other works by previous initiates. Often when myths and stories were written down they described the positions of various constellations in the sky during the season of initiation. The Book of Revelation in the Bible is something that Christianity and theologians alike have struggled to understand. I am going to walk you through it and reveal its original intended meaning. It is a meaning that would be impossible to extract unless you have experienced consciousness through initiation.

If you would like to follow along, there is software for your computer or phone that will illustrate the movements of the constellations in the sky on certain dates and times. I like the software I downloaded for free on my phone called Sky View. It allows you to change dates and times while holding your phone up to the sky and view the sky on your screen as it would be seen on that date and time.

One of the reasons I decided to go so deep in the weeds here is because, through this description, one can interpret that the world's religions are describing initiation. Using the mythology of the sky as evidence, we can see that all religions are the same. The only difference is that they describe the initiation, that happens at the same time of year, using different characters and different stories. In all of these stories the constellations and the time of year are all exactly the same. Everyone from the Babylonians and the native cultures of the American continents to the Abrahamic religions and the ancient Egyptians; all exactly the same.

Many would consider ancient cultures around the world to be primitive and ignorant, yet they all had advanced knowledge when it came to astronomy. The knowledge they possessed was so advanced they even knew where constellations were positioned in the daytime sky. Their gods and heroes were represented by the various constellations in the sky. When interpreting these myths we have to look at the hero or god in the myth and see where its corresponding constellation is in relation to the rising sun in the east. Most of the major myths concern the time of year that particular constellation is rising in the east with the sun; either directly behind the sun, or around the sun.

Throughout the year, the sun eclipses 13 constellations in this way. This path of the sun is known as the ecliptic because the sun eclipses these 13 constellations throughout the year. This is where we get the different signs of the zodiac. With the signs of the zodiac, however, the signs are split up into 12 evenly-spaced chunks of the year so the zodiac doesn't always match the actual ecliptic because some constellations are larger and some smaller, so it may take more or less than a month for the sun to travel through each of the 13 different constellations. The zodiac only consists of 12 constellations because it excludes the constellation Ophiuchus, the serpent bearer, as the sun passes through a small part of his leg. To the ancient Greeks this constellation represented the god Apollo as he wrestled with a giant snake at Delphi.

The constellations in the sky seem to move faster than the sun. What I mean by this is: If you were able to take a picture of the horizon at sunrise every morning with the constellations around the sun and behind it visible, and then flip through those pictures to create an animation of this, you would see the sun moving across the horizon as the ecliptic constellations rise behind it; one after the other.

To give you a quick example of the mythology playing out in the sky; there is a Greek myth that illustrates this. When the Titans ruled the earth as the gods their king was Cronos. Cronos had many children to include Zeus, but he ate them as they were born because he was told one of them would usurp him. His son Zeus forced him to vomit up his children one by one when Zeus usurped him and imprisoned the titans. This vomiting up of his children would be illustrated in the sky as the sun vomiting up these constellations, and it tells the story of how Zeus became king of the gods on Olympus.

The winter solstice is a very special time of year celebrated around the world, and if you truly understand what this time of year really means, it becomes particularly moving and deeply personal.

The ancient Egyptians viewed the winter solstice as the birth or resurrection of the sun. In her book, *When the Sun Moves Northward: The Way of Initiation,* Mabel Collins says the following about the ancients and their view of the winter solstice.

> *The difference of climate in the various parts of the earth does not affect the religions of the world in their universal acceptance of the month of January as the season of the return of the light of the world... Man's spiritual being is indissolubly associated with this little child, this lightbringer, and as the disciple attains psychic consciousness he becomes aware of the mystic recurrence of that miracle which is described in the religions as birth, death, and resurrection.*

To understand the title of this book by Mabel Collins, *When the Sun Moves Northward: The Way of Initiation*, you need to understand what it means for the sun to move northward. As the sun rises on the horizon every morning it is either slightly more north or south of where it rose the day before depending on the time of year. On the winter solstice, the sun begins moving northward across the horizon, reversing its southerly track across the horizon. On the summer solstice, it begins moving south across the horizon, reversing its previously northward track. In between the solstices we have the equinoxes as the midpoint between the solstices.

During the equinoxes the sun rises due east and sets due west. When the sun begins moving northward after the winter solstice it is reborn and when it moves south it is old and dying, in terms of mythology.

The really special thing about the equinoxes is not only does the autumnal equinox mark the time of the beginning of the initiation where the initiates receive their bearings, in knowing who and what they are, but it will also literally give you bearings to the four cardinal directions of the earth because on this day the sun rises due east.

Orion is a special constellation and on the autumnal equinox he is the figure in the Bible seen in the beginning of the book of revelation with seven stars in his hand and surrounded by seven candlesticks. The book says he holds the keys to hell and death; and the following description will help you to understand what this means.

On the evening before the autumnal equinox Orion's belt is rising nearly due east. This would be taking place on September 21st around 11:59 P.M. His belt is rising at about the place on the horizon where the sun will rise in the morning; pointing the way to the spot on the horizon where the sun will rise the next day on the autumnal equinox; due east. The constellation Orion is surrounded by 12 stars known as the winter circle. To Orion's side is the constellation Taurus which contains the Pleiades also known as the seven sisters. This is why some cultures also carefully tracked the Pleiades. This concept with the constellation Orion is the reason that some South American sun gods are depicted with three boxes on their belt such as the depiction on the Sun Gate at Tiwanaku.

Hell and death being marked by the autumnal equinox, as it marks the beginning of initiation, and the constellation Orion points the way. In Revelation, this figure is described as being girt about the paps with a golden girdle; we would know this as the belt of Orion. He is described to have feet that were like bronze and had been burned in a fire; this would be the fire of initiation. The same fire Demeter places Demophon in every night to burn like a log. During the solstices, there appears to be a three-day period during which the point on the horizon where the sun rises appears to remain stationary. After three days, the sun appears to begin reversing its previous path along the horizon. This is why during the Roman Saturnalia festivals, celebrated during the winter solstice, there was a celebration of reversals. Slaves were waited on by their masters. Men and women would swap clothing. In general, it was a lot of debauchery and anything that could be reversed during the festivities would be reversed. The Roman philosopher Porphyry associated the feeling of freedom of the Saturnalia festival as being "symbolic of the freeing of souls into immortality." This is also the reason that following his death and burial, Jesus was resurrected after three days. In death and resurrection myths there are references to three-day periods for exactly the reasons listed above.

Also apparent in these death and resurrection myths may be a mention to the four directions of the earth, represented by four gods, angels, or stars. This is a reference to the time of the beginning of initiation on the autumnal equinox where the sunrise will give you an east-west bearings; 90 degrees off that east-west line will give you your north-south bearings.

Currently, scholars interpret stories in ancient mythology as death of living things in the winter and rebirth in spring; everything to do with crops, but you have to remember that the psyche is inseparable from the rest of the universe and so we also have these cycles of death and resurrection within ourselves. The reason these myths often refer to the harvest is not because of the harvesting of crops in the autumn but rather because it marked the beginning of the harvesting of souls.

Physicians are aware of the depression that settles in around this time of year and call it seasonal effective disorder. This time of year, for us as humans, is about the death and resurrection of the human psyche. The proof of this exists in warm climates, such as South and Central America, where crops can be planted year-round yet we see these same myths and temples aligned to the equinoxes and solstices within native cultures.

Book of Revelation

I want to preface this by letting you know right now that I do not endorse the Bible nor do I endorse any organized religion. I view them as nothing more than a vehicle to separate you from your money. If asked whether you should enter a church or a casino I would tell you to go to the casino. At least at the casino there is an opportunity that you may come out richer than when you entered. I can't say the same thing about a "holy" structure of any kind. The Book of Revelation is nothing more than a description of the process of initiation using constellations in the sky to indicate the time of year, and accompanying stories that teach psychological lessons.

I decided to revisit the Book of Revelation with fresh eyes. I knew Christianity didn't understand it, and I knew it was going to have something to do with this transformation because of the "Happy Camp" experience in Jacques Vallée's book. In reading the King James version of the Book of Revelation, it became clear the book was describing transformation and that was apparent from the beginning of the book.

John sees a figure in the beginning of the book. The figure holds in his right hand seven stars. I believe this to be a representation of the constellation Orion. The figure tells John he has the keys to hell and death. At this point in the book we can see that we are in the early morning hours on September 22nd. This refers to the constellation Orion pointing the way to the spot on the horizon where the sun will rise due east. This figure is described as having feet that had been burned in a furnace; meaning that this figure has also been through initiation and is pointing the way. The figure then tells John, "To him that overcometh will I grant to sit with me in my throne, even as I also overcame, and am set down with my Father in his throne." I take this to mean that the throne is in fact for you the reader. He also says that to him that overcometh will he give to eat of the tree of life. Eating of the tree of life is referred to in Genesis as the attainment of immortality. It is the same immortality discussed in the Bhagavad Gita and numerous other religious book around the world.

The figure then talks about patience and suffering while not suffering the things that come your way. This part of the book concerns the psychology of transformation.

The figure then states that if you overcome, you will not be hurt of the second death. The implication being that overcoming the first death (the transformation) one will not then suffer the physical death of the body. They will have gained immortality.

Next, John is taken in Spirit (astral projection) to heaven where he sees a throne. This imagery of the throne is twofold. It concerns the symbolism that this is an internal process to the individual while secondly describing the throne as the sun in the sky.

Around the throne are 24 seats on which 24 elders are seated. The imagery of the throne surrounded by these elders becomes apparent. If one were to visualize 24 elders sitting around a throne you would think of them as being hunched over. They would visually appear curved and white; as they are described as wearing white robes. The throne represents the human heart and the elders represent the 24 human ribs. This is a signal that everything to follow is an internal process within an individual. It describes the inner light. The sun produces light that illuminates the earth; and the inner light illuminates the universe. The inner light is being equated with the illumination given off by the sun.

I think this symbolism of the 24 elders is several fold. Revelation does little more than to describe the right time of year and has little in the way of what will be happening. I have another theory that I'm working on with this symbolism. There are several heroic mythological stories written that are composed of 24 books. There are the *Orphic Rhapsodies* which are lost to history and only exist in fragments. The *Odyssey* and the *Iliad* by Homer are two others. So we may be looking at the fact that Revelation is describing the time of year but hinting that it would be paired with tales of the hero's journey to explain what happens this time of year.

It also became apparent that there wasn't anything in Revelation that didn't relate to the human mythology of the sky. As the story proceeds we are introduced to the throne as the path of the sun. The throne is enveloped in a glow or rainbow; indicative of sunrise. At this point in the story it is sunrise on the autumnal equinox; September 22nd at about 6:15 A.M. John describes the one seated on the throne as like a jasper stone and before the throne is a sea of glass. I believe this to be a description of a green flash that occurs before a sunrise or after a sunset, the sea of glass would be the mirage effect seen on the horizon.

Next, there are the four beasts surrounding the throne. These beasts or constellations have represented transformation in ancient human mythology since at least the time of the Babylonians. The beasts are full of eyes pointed outward and inward. This symbolism also speaks to the psychology of having eyes to see inward as well as outward. The lion represented by Leo; the calf is Ursa Minor having a star called Pherkad derived from the Arabic "calf." The beast with the face of a man is Centaurus; the eagle is Aquila. These four constellations flank the path of the sun from the autumnal equinox through the winter solstice.

John then sees a book in the right hand of the one on the throne, which is sealed with seven seals. A call goes out as to who is worthy to open the book. The lion steps up and opens the book. He leads the way as the constellation Leo precedes the rising sun in the east on the autumnal equinox.

This could also be the reason for the veneration of the jaguar in South America, and the sphinx in Egypt.

If you were to look at this in the sky, you would see the sun within these four constellations. But the really intriguing thing is that there are three other constellations inside this box in the sky. They are Virgo, Bootes, and Hercules. Virgo represents Persephone to the Greeks while Bootes is the son of Demeter; who is known as the shepherd; which could also be associated with or represent Dionysus. According to ancient myth, these individuals are all initiates.

The story takes another turn. After the lion opens the book but the one worthy of taking the book out of the hands of the one that sits on the throne is the lamb that has been slain. The lamb now stands in the middle of the four beasts. In the sky this is represented as the constellation Bootes (the shepherd) who is rising on the horizon to the north of the sun in October. The idea of a shepherd of men is an old one, proof of that can be seen as far back as ancient Egypt. Egyptian pharos are depicted and buried with crossed arms holding shepherding tools in their hands which is symbolic of their roles as shepherds of men.

The shepherd is the one who can open the book, as he has been "slain." In other words, one who has been through this process and understands it can act as your ritual elder, and interpret the book.

After the book is opened, there come the horsemen. Now that we have framed the path of the sun from the autumnal equinox to the winter solstice; we walk the constellations in the path of the sun with the horseman from the autumnal equinox to the winter solstice. First there is the one with the bow which is indicative of Orion on the autumnal equinox. Next, there is the one with the great sword referring to the constellation Virgo. To the Greeks, this constellation represented the goddesses Demeter or Persephone; the destroyer and bringer of death. Virgo is being eclipsed by the rising sun in September through Octoberish. One of the stars in Virgo holds to this tradition in that its name is Spica which is Latin for ear of grain and is eclipsed by the sun around October. Persephone is often depicted holding ears of grain representing her role in the harvest of souls. At this point in the book, there is a hint given to the reader of this truth in the following quote; a tip of the hat to the Mysteries of Greece and Rome in Revelation 6:6:

> *And I heard a voice in the midst of the four beasts say, A measure of wheat for a penny, and three measures of barley for a penny; and see thou hurt not the oil and the wine.*

The reference to wine is indicative of the other greater Mysteries involving Dionysus. He was the god of wine, fertility, madness, religious ecstasy, and theater; he was sometimes called Bacchus. Those who participated in his mysteries were said to become possessed by the god himself; thereby experiencing liberation.

In some ancient early Greek texts, Dionysus was also identified as the son of Demeter and showed humanity how to cultivate grapes for wine and, in some myths, showed women how to make olive oil and wine with just the touch of a finger. The above quote from the Bible is advising the reader to ensure they don't damage the gifts given by the archetypal lover and archetypal warrior because they are so crucial in getting through the process of transformation. But is also indicative that the sun at this point in the story is eclipsing the ears of grain in Virgo's hand on sunrise around mid-October. As this is happening, Bootes or Dionysus is rising on the horizon to the north of the sun.

You need the lover to transmute the pain and emotion of the process and you need the inner warrior to stay engaged in the fight.

In the ruins of Pompeii there is a villa of some wealthy resident that today is known as the villa of the mysteries. This villa is named such because there is a room within it that contains mural frescos depicting a young woman as she journeys through the Dionysian Mysteries. The corner images in the room depict a winged divine entity whipping the young female initiate with a whiplash across her bare back; a physical depiction of the inner pain of initiation. The last panel shows the young woman as a tower of strength and radiant beauty.

The next constellation and horseman in Revelation heading toward the winter solstice is the scales in the form of the constellation Libra which is eclipsed by the sun in November. Followed by death in the form of the constellation Scorpius and the winter solstice in December.

In cultures throughout the world, the constellation Scorpius was a part of a much larger constellation. Scorpius was one of the feet of the constellation Ophiuchus or Serpens (the serpent bearer). It's a constellation of a man wrestling with a large snake. In other cultures he is depicted as a woman with snakes for legs, or a half human-half serpent. It fits for this time of year. The winter solstice marking death and the time when initiates are wrestling with the primordial evil within.

The next events in the Book of Revelation 6, I believe are very important to understand because it is not interpreted correctly in modern-day Christianity. Its meaning has been lost over time.

9 And when he had opened the fifth seal, I saw under the altar the souls of them that were slain for the word of God, and for the testimony which they held:

10 And they cried with a loud voice, saying, How long, O Lord, holy and true, dost thou not judge and avenge our blood on them that dwell on the earth?

11 And white robes were given unto every one of them; and it was said unto them, that they should rest yet for a little season, until their fellowservants also and their brethren, that should be killed as they were, should be fulfilled.

12 And I beheld when he had opened the sixth seal, and, lo, there was a great earthquake; and the sun became black as sackcloth of hair, and the moon became as blood;

13 And the stars of heaven fell unto the earth, even as a fig tree casteth her untimely figs, when she is shaken of a mighty wind.

14 And the heaven departed as a scroll when it is rolled together; and every mountain and island were moved out of their places.

15 And the kings of the earth, and the great men, and the rich men, and the chief captains, and the mighty men, and every bondman, and every free man, hid themselves in the dens and in the rocks of the mountains;

16 *And said to the mountains and rocks, Fall on us, and hide us from the face of him that sitteth on the throne, and from the wrath of the Lamb:*

17 *For the great day of his wrath is come; and who shall be able to stand?*

In 9 and 10 of the above excerpt, we see the people who have died that in life went through the transformation, asking when this process will be complete. Which is also a subject of one of Plutarch's essays titled *On God's Slowness to Punish*. In 11 they are told that the process will be complete when everyone on the earth has transformed as they were transformed.

In 12 there is a reference to the moon. It refers to a blood moon which occurs when the earth blocks the sunlight from reaching the moon's surface. In ancient times, the moons cycle of life was a month long. Every month the moon was born again, which is also a theme present in the *Homeric Hymn to Hermes*. The full moon representing the midlife of the moon. During the blood moon there is a death that occurs midlife as the earth temporarily blocks the light of the sun. It's a representation of transformation in the night sky. It represents the painful death and resurrection or initiation that happens within a person's lifetime.

In 13 there is a very interesting occurrence. There is a reference to untimely figs and stars falling from heaven. This reference is interesting because of the mythology of the fig and fig tree. It is a symbol of death and rebirth in cultures around the world, but I believe this could be a reference to a myth involving the god Apollo. In the myth, Apollo sends his crow out with a cup to fetch some water. The crow is distracted from his mission when he comes across a fig tree. The crow waits in the tree three days until the figs are ripe. The crow, on his way back, picks up a water snake as the excuse for why he was so late. Apollo was upset by this lie and cast the crow, snake, and cup into the sky in the form of the constellations Corvus as the crow, Crater as the cup, and Hydra as the snake. Every year during the summer solstice there is a meteor shower within the constellation Corvus. These constellations have been symbols of this process since the time of the Babylonians because they flank the rising sun to the south from the autumnal equinox to the winter solstice. By the time of the winter solstice, they rise in the night sky on the horizon before sunrise.

14 speaks to the fact that everything becomes clear after the transformation. You will see the universe for what it is. 15, 16 and 17 speak to the rest of humanity going through the transformation, heading for the caves which represent transformation or the underworld in human mythology.

When we begin to view Christianity's symbolism as it pertains to human mythology and the sky, we begin to see that Revelation is describing the internal, individual process of transformation that is described by all the world's religions. Other religions use different stories to describe the same thing; they're all describing initiation.

As further evidence in Revelations, there are beings unleashed on humanity with the power to hurt men five months; again, the pain of transformation and initiation. It was fairly acute for about five months. They are the same beings referred to in Genesis as the cherubim that keep the way of the tree of life. In Revelation, the king of these creatures who hurt men is named Apollyon. Apollo of course is the king because he is the constellation Orion that points the way to the beginning of initiation. Later in Revelation there is a reference to the four angels of the four corners of the earth, which is also a reference to the four cardinal directions that can be determined on the equinox. There is also an angel that gives John a book and he is told to eat the book which makes his belly bitter, speaking to the knowledge being a hard pill to swallow. Much in the same way I encountered Coldplay's "Hymn for the Weekend" early in my experiences. Eating the book or drinking from the cup are all metaphors for the attainment of knowledge.

Another bit of important Christian symbolism is the cross and the crucifixion of Christ. In *When the Sun Moves Northward*, Mabel Collins sheds light on the mythology of the cross and the crucifixion of Christ. The cross is represented in most religions. It represents the great burden of mankind. The pain and suffering of the human race crucified by what Mabel Collins calls the pairs of opposites and which William Walker Atkinson calls polarity. When she refers to the pairs of opposites, what she's referring to is the fractured human psyche living in the shadows of the four archetypes of the psyche. The pairs of opposites represent that which man currently has not the strength within him to transmute. So, there man remains, nailed to the cross in the crucifixion.

Many, perhaps, in speaking of the pair of opposites would use the example of love and hate as being two opposites, and even *The Kybalion* makes this mistake, but I'm a stickler for semantics. Love and hate are not opposites of each other. Lust and hate are opposites on the same pole. Love has no opposite because it is unconditional and therefore no opposite could ever exist. Love simply IS. Love is what you find as you come to center. It IS the center; as described by Diotima to Socrates in Plato's *Symposium*. Mabel Collins says the following in *When the Sun Moves Northward* about this symbolism.

> *It is by the conquest of the lower self in the intense experiences of love and grief, joy and anguish, effort and disaster, success and failure, that the miracle of transmutation is effected in man's nature. There is no other way, for the path leads through human life to the life beyond it. When one separates himself from humanity, he leaves the path, for he turns aside, and his steps must be retraced. For the purpose of experiencing human emotions and learning from them, do the spirits of men descend into matter and become crucified in time and space. This is the meaning of the time-old symbol of the*

Cross, which appeared first without the Figure, symbolizing the mystery of creation, time and space, and all the conditions of material life, having been made ready. Then the Figure appears, entering consciously upon its suffering in the experience of life within the limitations of the pairs of opposites. As the Svastika, the Cross is found on Chaldean bricks; in ancient Egypt it appeared in the ansated form; the Spanish conquerors of Mexico found it used there, and designated "The Tree of Our Life;" it has been discovered on the backs of the gigantic statues found on the submerged continent in the mid-Pacific Ocean; it is the oldest symbol in India. The Egyptian deities carried the ansated Cross as a symbol of the god in man; with the Figure came the idea of the Deity suffering as man, and suffering consciously, enduring the crucifixion which is man's lot, for love of man.

Those who live through their human life with the sole object of obtaining pleasure and avoiding pain, refusing to take the step of acquiring self-control, not only retrace their course until they can follow it rightly, but find experience more and more intensified, the torture more defined and acute. For man, if he will not learn, must be taught. Through incarnation after incarnation the unwilling students are compelled to learn, by severity of trial and misfortune.

In Plato's *Symposium*, Diotima stated that love lies halfway between ignorance and wisdom. When Socrates asked if love was a god or a mortal, she states that love is neither; love is a daimon (a demiurge) and lies in the middle of the two as an intermediary between the divine and the mortals.

In human mythology, death, resurrection and transformation has always been represented in the form of the underworld, hell, or a cave. Probably because for most of the history of humanity that is where this transformation took place, in caves. The cave paintings of early man are evidence of this. In fact there is an ancient relative of Homo sapiens called the Homo naledi that was burying their dead in South African caves around 100,000 years ago. I believe this indicates a knowledge of something after death. If you would like to know what happens deep in the darkness of a cave, just look up accounts of miners and cave explorers that found themselves trapped. Early man was aware of this.

I believe it is a mistake to view all of this only through the prism of a single religion or mythology. It is usually found residing in the myths surrounding mystery schools. We see it in the Greek mythology of Demeter and her daughter Persephone, and Apollo. In ancient Egypt, we can see this with Isis and Osiris. The Hindus find this in the mythology surrounding Shiva and Kali.

*** Ancient Evidence/Greek Mythology ***
and the Homeric Hymns

When all of this began I had a hard time understanding mythology until I had completed the process. The only reason I became aware of this cycle of death and rebirth is because of a vision I had. It was in this vision I became aware of the *Homeric Hymn to Demeter* and it's also the reason I included it in the beginning of this book.

I was meditating one evening before I went to bed, when suddenly I had a vision in the meditation. It lasted for only a few seconds. It was the image of a forest that was so vivid; it was like looking at a photograph. It was unlike any forest I had ever seen and was incredibly beautiful. The trees had white bark with black spots on the trunks and yellow leaves. It was the beginning of autumn as some of the yellow leaves were falling to the ground. It was the kind of vivid imagery I receive in meditation that I understood to be significant. I wasn't sure what it meant. I wasn't even sure how I was going to figure it out because I didn't know what kind of trees these were. Was it the location that was significant? Was it the trees? I didn't know. I was actually busy writing the first draft of this book at the time and had been water fasting for two weeks. Several days had passed and I hadn't looked into it yet.

A week later, as I was working on this book, I glanced at my phone because I had received one of these messages about what was trending on Reddit. I seem to get them at least once a day. When I opened up the notice from Reddit, I got my first lead. It was a photograph that was taken in Crested Butte, Colorado that someone had posted in the earthporn sub. I could see the trees from my meditation session in the photograph. I set the book aside and began to research. I looked up Crested Butte, Colorado and came to the town's web page. I read that the area is known for its trees, specifically, the quaking aspen.

It took me over a month to figure out what it meant. In reading about this particular tree, it was clear to me that this tree represents humanity. This led me to several books that I found to be useful, but I knew there was more. It didn't FEEL like I had my answer yet. I was seeing this tree in all kinds of spiritual art and books. I knew there was something deeper here. I started looking up the aspen in terms of human mythology and didn't find anything. I knew I had to incorporate this into the book somehow, but I wasn't sure what it was I was supposed to incorporate.

One day it occurs to me that the aspen is a poplar tree. It was then that I began looking up the mythology of the poplar tree. This led me to the Greek mythology of Persephone and her poplar groves outside the entrance to the underworld. It was another "aha moment" for me as I read that this myth was associated with the Greek Mysteries in the form of *The Homeric Hymn to Demeter*. It was the myth that was central to The Eleusinian Mysteries in ancient Greece. I began researching the mysteries and I quickly learned that the ancient

Greeks were in fact conducting these consciousness initiations themselves and that the myth represented everything I had been through. It became clear that Persephone represents the human soul. The hymn's author did this because he knew that it is the soul or subconscious that begins the initiation as it calls out to be set free.

Persephone's mother, Demeter, represents our ritual elder. In the myth, Demeter puts a small boy in a fire to burn away his mortal soul thereby transforming him into an immortal god. She is the keeper of the process. The initiation is a painful process and this is the reason that fire is used in the myth. Fire always represents immortality in myth for this reason; because it is the fire that consumes the gross and reveals the immortal. It is the conscious self that must make the choice to remain in this painful state and see it through to the end.

The Greek Mysteries were incredibly important in ancient Greece and began around September or October, according to some sources the date varied as it began with the harvest moon. The Mysteries began in this month with a water purification ritual. We can see evidence in the hymn as to what time of year this is. In the myth, Demeter wanders the earth for nine days and on the dawn of the 10th day she is met by Hecate, who comes to Demeter with a torch in her hand. In the myth, Hecate is a representation of the constellation Orion. Hecate is the goddess of witchcraft and necromancy which I believe also symbolizes the gifts of the initiate upon their return. This is the reason Persephone is greeted by Hecate with many embraces upon her return from the underworld.

As Demeter sits on a stool in the presence of the Lady of Eleusis, an old woman named Iambe starts making jokes with Demeter and turns her mood in another direction. The hymn then states that Iambe became a part of the rites of Demeter. Iambe represents music and vibration. Iambe is of course the root of iambic pentameter which is a term used in music and poetry having to do with rhythm. The priests of the mysteries hired musicians to play music around the clock during initiation. The music that was played probably consisted of these 33 Homeric hymns.

Iambe, also known as Baubo, is depicted as a headless nude female goddess in ancient Greece. There were figurines of this goddess found buried in the ruins of the Temple to Demeter in Eleusis. You can't see her head of course because it's blurred out just as in my own experience with the blue being in my room. This phenomenon can also be seen in the headless gods depicted in the stone columns at Gobekli Tepe.

Further, when Demeter decides to reveal herself and casts off her disguise, she gives off a light that is described as being like lightning that illuminates the entire palace. It occurred to me that the lightning bolt analogy, and the divine light description, was similar to what I had seen behind the being that stood over me in my bed. In ancient Greece, I could see how they would equate that with the same kind of light produced by a lightning bolt. As the being in my room stood over me, she radiated this light to the point that it illuminated my entire room which morphed into rays of light extending from the head.

Gobekli Tepe clearly holds this same type of symbolism. There are clear north, south, east, west lines. On column 43 there is a rather primitive depiction of Aquila holding the rising sun with the constellation Scorpio under it. Perhaps this was a winter solstice depiction. The other carved creatures above the scorpion on the column would make up Ophiuchus. On the winter solstice, December 21st 2020 at roughly 7:30 am, you can see Cygnus and Aquila rising to the north of the sun on the eastern horizon and Scorpius to the south. I later read that Graham Hancock also has this opinion. But, I figured out, that the constellations have shifted in the past 12,000 years. 12,000 years ago, this was a depiction of sunrise on the autumnal equinox.

If you need evidence of this you can load software on your computer that will allow you to enter a date for 12,000 years ago. This would also account for how they were able to build these structures with east-west alignments. In fact, there would not have been any other way for them to determine east and west. Not only are we forced to rethink the history of humanity, because this site is around 12,000 years old, but we are also forced to acknowledge that this civilization that built these monoliths also had advanced knowledge of astronomy. There it is; carved in stone; a scene of the constellations rising in the east behind the sun on the autumnal equinox. You would not be able to predict what constellations would be behind the sun, because you can't see them, unless you had advanced knowledge of astronomy. It's clear to me that they were practicing these same initiatory mysteries there.

In ancient Greece, there was a lot of knowledge that had to be transferred to the would-be initiates. Initiates were not present at any of the winter celebrations. In fact, I read in some ancient sources that initiates returned to their families in the spring. There was no ceremony where they all left the temple together because the path is different for everyone and they returned individually one by one. Indicating that there was an awareness of the amount of time one needs to "cook," as Robert Moore describes. Initiates were said to return to their families very changed people and unafraid of death. Humanity has practiced these transformation initiations in one form or another for a very long time. I would argue that ancestors of early man were practicing these initiations in caves over 100,000 years ago. Many of the depictions of "space men" that ancient alien theorists point to are not depictions of a being with a helmet; they were attempting to depict the rays of golden light emanating from the head.

There are 33 *Homeric Hymns*. The significance of this number was not lost on me. It is a number that is seen in freemasonry today and I believe goes back much farther. I found, in looking up information about the Eleusinian Mysteries, that there were lesser mysteries the initiates had to graduate from first before continuing to the greater mysteries. The *Hymns* are filled with symbolism and teach the qualities I found in *Light On the Path* and the psychology taught by Carl Jung and Robert Moore. The key to the lesser mysteries lies in the other *Hymns*. All of Greek mythology, in fact, teaches the cultivation of the qualities in the psyche necessary for transformation. The difficulty lies in interpreting them correctly. Which is the challenge for all ancient religious texts, and that's why they are so grossly misinterpreted. They really can't be interpreted correctly by someone who hasn't been through the process.

The *Homeric Hymn to Hermes* is a perfect example of the psychology involved. In the hymn, Hermes is depicted as a baby who does wrong against Apollo. When confronted, Hermes lies about what he's done. Claiming that it could not have been him because he's just an innocent little baby. Which we know is the shadow magician as the "innocent one." Apollo and Hermes take their feud to Zeus who tells them that they must go forth with one mind and solve their problems. Hermes then makes amends with Apollo and shows Apollo how to make beautiful music as a depiction not only of the lover in transformation psychology but also the magician operating in fullness. Hermes teaches Apollo how to make the music for himself rather than hoard the knowledge.

While researching the story of Demeter, I came across mythology concerning the same story in the Sumerian epic poem of *Inanna's Descent into the Underworld*. In it, Inanna enters the underworld where she must pass through seven gates. She had arrived in her finest clothing and jewelry. Each time she passes through a gate, she must remove an article of clothing. Until finally, she has passed through seven gates where she stands naked and vulnerable in the underworld.

Inanna's sister and queen of the dead, Ereshkigal, passes judgment on Inanna killing her and hanging her dead rotting body on a hook in the underworld. Inanna is eventually freed from the underworld and resurrected after three days and three nights. There is much more to this myth in the *Epic of Gilgamesh* where it is revealed that Inanna was visiting the underworld to pay her respects for Ereshkigal's slain husband who was a bull. Inanna is the one who was responsible for the death of her sister's husband and therefore Inanna arrives at the gates of the underworld as the shadow magician, a trickster, and the innocent one. And so we can see Jungian psychology at work in this myth. Inanna slays the beast within and descends into the underworld. She is then extinguished completely and resurrected after three days.

There are many Jungians who point to both *Inanna's Decent* and the *Homeric Hymn to Demeter* as ancient representations of Jungian archetypal ideas. Many critics say this doesn't hold water because the last few lines of *Inanna's Decent* sings the holy praises of Ereshkigal. The critics don't understand why Inanna is not the one who is praised. The answer is simple. Ereshkigal is the one who initiates Inanna into this higher consciousness through the constitution of wholeness. Being Inanna's sister makes Ereshkigal just another aspect of Inanna herself.

Ereshkigal can be thought of as representing the human soul, killing out the shadow or bad self. If you recall the words of the goddess Demeter when she is discovered by the boy's mother as she is burning Demophon in a fire: "silly mortal, unable to tell good fortune from bad." Just because something is painful doesn't mean it won't end up being the biggest blessing you've ever received. It's the lesson of approaching pain and pleasure as the same thing. Nobody runs from a perceived pleasurable experience, and they shouldn't run from a perceived painful one either; you should view them equally. Those same critics also fail to understand what happens in the psyche once this wholeness is constituted. This is not a joke, I'm talking about knowing the true nature of the universe for yourself; I'm talking about profound mental abilities that will develop and prove this truth to you on a daily basis, I'm talking about immortality.

But, alas, here we are in 2020. The ancient Greeks and Egyptians knew the earth was a sphere and they knew its circumference, and yet; today there are still those who think the earth is flat. Just as there were those who knew about initiation back then. So, mankind continues to languish by the severity of trial and misfortune. Falsely believing that it is our technology that will get us to the stars. It is not our technology or our understanding of technology that will ever get us there. Some of us are there now; because it has everything to do with consciousness. Just like Dorothy in the *Wizard of Oz,* we have to understand we have the power to go home at any time. I can tell you that if we think we can reverse engineer their craft and attempt to leave this place; it won't be permitted; not without the consciousness to accompany that technology.

Since these ancient myths were first written long ago, there have been a great number of other writings published on any number of topics that are no longer in print today. One needs to really think about why that is. The reason is that they are kept alive; preserved by those of us that understand their importance, and those of us that love the way these stories speak to us. These works serve as a reminder that this experience has always been known to us; it serves as proof that everybody all over the world throughout time has not been wrong.

The Renaissance

Francesco Petrarca is said to be the father of the Italian Renaissance. He inspired this through his works. He was an avid reader of ancient knowledge and literature; translating many of those works for public consumption. It's clear to me he understood all of this as an initiate. He was living in Italy and knew there was a treasure trove of knowledge in Roman and Greek mythology that was close at hand. He believed that scientific knowledge did not preclude the existence of God and insisted that we were given our minds to use them to their fullest. It was the Renaissance that brought us the wonderful works of Leonardo Da Vinci, Michelangelo and many others whose art reflects the topics of this book.

Although the Renaissance was a period of rebirth, there was eventually a swing in the opposite direction. It is the swing of the pendulum described in *The Kybalion* as the principle of rhythm. And so the pendulum swings, as it has for the past ten million years, powering the wheel of human evolution. That clock of human mortal existence losing momentum as we "come to center" with inner peace and strength; until that day when the pendulum will stop as the fires of initiation burn through the last of us, and the pendulum is reduced to ashes.

Nadler says the following concerning the views of Spinoza on the above.

> *Spinoza suggests that it may even be a desirable state of affairs. He makes it fairly clear that the more adequate ideas two minds have, the more they 'agree with each other.' This is the road to social peace and political well-being.*

The rebirth in humanity and expression during the renaissance delivered mankind some of my favorite paintings. I thought it appropriate to discuss my two favorites by a fellow initiate; *Salvator Mundi* and *The Adoration of the Maji* both by Leonardo Da Vinci. Both of these paintings, when interpreted correctly, depict transformation and initiation in an art form, and accurately depict the truth of what people are now calling the phenomenon.

His paintings depict what happened to him, what happened to me, and what has happened to so many others. Da Vinci's depictions of Christ are linked with the Greek mythologic figure Ganymede. Zeus is constantly falling in love with various humans. One human is Ganymede (the wine pourer). Ganymede is abducted by Zeus to be the wine pourer of the gods on Olympus. Zeus dispatches the eagle Aquila to bring Ganymede to dwell with the gods. Zeus then places them in the sky. Homer writes of this myth in the *Iliad* from the Lattimore translation:

> (*Ganymedes*) *was the loveliest born of the race of mortals, and therefore the Gods caught him away to themselves, to be Zeus' wine pourer, for the sake of his beauty, so he might be among the immortals.*

Zeus fell in love with him for his beauty. But to truly understand the myth, one has to understand the meaning of the name Ganymede. Greek philosophers had pointed out its root meaning, ganu "taking pleasure" and med "mind," having the meaning of something like "beautiful mind."

In Da Vinci's *Salvator Mundi* (savior of the world) Da Vinci depicts Christ in his true representation: as that of the sacred pattern of death and resurrection, or as the pattern of transformation. In this particular painting Christ is shown as the resurrection but also as the Greek Ganymede and the constellation Aquarius (the water pourer). Christ is depicted holding in his left hand a globus cruciger. Normally a globus cruciger is a globe with a cross on top of it, but this one seems to be missing the cross, or is it? If one were to look closer at the globe in this painting you will see three dots within the globe. These three dots represent an asterism, or a collection of constellations in the sky, in what we call the summer triangle. Within the summer triangle rest the constellations; Cygnus the swan, which is comprised of the Northern Cross; Aquila, the eagle, and Lyra, the harp. Therefore, the cross lies within the globe in the form of the Northern Cross. In this painting, the star closest to the hand of Christ would be a where Aquila is in this asterism. This asterism is rising to the north of the rising sun on the morning of the winter solstice (the resurrection of the sun).

Da Vinci left a hint in his painting that this is the correct interpretation of the three dots. The hint is in Christ's clothing. First off, the fold in his robe as it passes behind the globe, and the three dots, happens to coincide with the milky way as it passes through the summer triangle. Within the globe he has reversed the summer triangle as one would naturally see the reverse image in a solid glass sphere, but it is the only thing he reversed within the globe. The second hint is that the Northern Cross in the globe, as it would rest within the depiction of the summer triangle, corresponds to the same angle of the belting across the chest of Christ. On this belting is a woven pattern representing unity and eternity in Islamic design.

Not only is Da Vinci depicting Jesus but he's also depicting a much deeper truth here in depicting Jesus as the mythological figure, Ganymede, or the constellation Aquarius. To the Greeks, the constellation Aquarius represented Ganymede the wine pourer; the mortal that the God's stole away to themselves, for the love of his pure and beautiful mind, to dwell among them on Olympus. Zeus sent an eagle (the constellation Aquila) to grab Ganymede (the constellation Aquarius) from the earth. So if we were to watch the rising sun on the eastern horizon and the constellations that surround it from the winter solstice to the vernal equinox, we would see Zeus's Eagle rising to the north of the sun parallel with the sun on the winter solstice. As we head toward the vernal equinox in March we see the eagle lifting Ganymede up into the sky and across the rising sun. Where Ganymede, or Jesus, temporarily becomes the sun, illuminating the world with his knowledge and Devine light. Da Vinci used this symbolism in the painting to represent the resurrection of the sun as this time also coincides with the rebirth of the human psyche within transformation. The really special hint involving Aquarius and the vernal equinox, left to us by Da Vinci, in this painting is… I'll leave that to the readers to figure out. I can't have all the fun. This hint is so subtle yet so obvious. And so we see Christ as Da Vinci did, as the yearly pattern of death and resurrection in the human psyche.

Some may say, "Well that's going too far with this interpretation," some may say that it is outrageous that I would link something like what we currently call alien abduction with such a painting, but this is not the only painting where Da Vinci depicts Jesus as the constellation Aquarius or Ganymede. The *Last Supper* is another one; and that depiction is much more obvious. So obvious that it can't be argued.

This is an interpretation of the *Last Supper* you won't find anywhere else because I've never heard anyone explain it this way. Some have come close but they're a bit off. It may be helpful to pull up images of these paintings as well as star charts as you read the descriptions. The 13 people around the table represent the 13 constellations on the ecliptic path of the sun. We can start with Jesus in the center of the *Last Supper* as the constellation Aquarius. If you examine the posture and positioning of Jesus in the painting, you can see that his posture matches the form of the constellation Aquarius.

To his right there is a large V-shaped gap. This is also a hint that we can see matches the constellation Pisces which is to the right of Aquarius just as depicted in the painting. Pisces is represented by two fish jumping out of the water in opposing directions forming the V. Next to Pisces is Aries followed by Taurus, then Gemini as the twins with the two hands held up, followed by Cancer, then Leo at the end of the table.

To the left of Jesus, or Aquarius, we have Capricorn pointing upward above just as the horn of Capricorn points up with its horn but also a hint that all of this is in the sky. Next are Sagittarius, Ophiuchus, Scorpio, Libra and finally Virgo at the end of the table. The gestures, body language, and clothing of the people around the table hold the shapes of these constellations.

I read an account of Da Vinci as he painted the *Last Supper* in that he was very concerned with the placement and gestures of the apostles. He would sometimes only come in and paint a hand in a day. The reason he did this is because he intended to depict Jesus as Aquarius or Ganymede and he didn't want to be seen using star charts to complete the painting. I think in his time such a thing could have caused him a great deal of trouble. But he really wanted to make sure his true depiction of the story of Christ came through in the painting. He depicts Christ in his true form as an allegory for transformation;

Christ as Ganymede, the one who had gone through transformation and who the gods stole away to themselves through the process of initiation.

There are four groupings of constellations that are separated by either an equinox or a solstice representing the four seasons. These constellations are placed next to each other in the painting, as they are in the night sky. Above the gap between Jesus and the person to his right, there is a square lantern hanging on the wall as another hint at the true interpretation of the painting; representing the square of Pegasus.

My other favorite painting plays into these same ideas but also more plainly plays into the initiation aspect. *Adoration of the Magi* was never finished by Da Vinci. People can say what they want about the historical reasons for this but I happen to know this was by design. He never intended to finish it. Insofar as Da Vinci was concerned it was finished. This painting is much more complex than *Salvator Mundi* as it depicts the entire cycle of initiation. The painting, if taken at face value, is a representation of the three kings that have come bearing gifts of gold, frankincense, and myrrh for Christ; the son of God. It depicts the birth of the sun; which we have learned has a much deeper meaning. Christ is seated on his mother Mary's lap. It's such a beautiful painting. Unlike a photograph, a painting cannot include anything accidental. Everything in the painting has meaning. It could be argued that this is also a representation of the Book of Revelation which is why he never finished it; as this is an ongoing process; it's never finished.

    Let's start with some of the subtle yet very telling hidden symbolism in the *Adoration of the Maji*. Just above Christ and Mary there are two trees in the background. On the ground between these two trees there is a rabbit. This represents the two legs of the constellation Orion, in the tree trunks, with the constellation Lepus at his feet. It accurately portrays these two constellations as they are in the night sky. The foliage on the trees is angled to form Orion's angled belt. So, we see in the trees the death occurring with the autumnal equinox, and beneath it on Mary's lap is the resurrection; the child and light bringer; the sun reborn. If you remember, the winter solstice to the ancient Egyptians represented the birth of the sun. If we follow the line of Orion's belt to the star Sirius, we come to a man in the crowd with his finger pointed up toward the sky. Just above him there is the construction of an ancient Egyptian temple on some ruins in the upper left corner of the painting. We know it's an ancient Egyptian temple because of the columns with lotus flower caps.

    Also, at the base of the two trees there is a woman holding her hands up on a rock as though she is gesturing the opening of a cave. Next to her there is a woman pointing up toward the opening of a cave in the upper right corner of the painting. We can see Da Vinci sketched a mammoth on the wall to its entrance as though it were drawn by the initiates of early man.

My favorite part about this painting has to be walking through it from right to left. In the bottom right there is a man distracted by something and he's looking off the canvas at it; perhaps some synchronicity. He is enveloped in death and darkness just as the goddess Persephone is distracted as she gazes upon the narcissus flower. He then enters the chaos of the cave of transformation, through the winter solstice, to the temple of ancient knowledge, until finally he exits the initiation. He now stands at the bottom left corner of the painting a wise man; a philosopher who has found consciousness; wrapped in deep contemplation of the nature of all things.

The same could be said of the kings kneeling before Christ with their gifts of symbolic immortality. The king at the bottom right is dying and appears grotesquely skeletal. He then becomes a seeker as there is a figure just above him that appears to be seeking. He then is leaning in just above Mary's right shoulder; weak from the tears and pain of initiation. Beneath him he is then depicted looking at his own reflection in a puddle on the ground. Finally at the feet of the philosopher he is reborn; a young man glowing with inner light. Every figure in this painting tells a part of the story of this initiation. I feel like I could write a book on the different characters in this single painting. When one begins to equate the biblical story of the kings following the star to the birth of the sun with the ancient Egyptian idea of the death and resurrection of the sun, this painting begins to make a lot of sense. It speaks to the fact that wise men follow the death and resurrection of the sun; they follow the pattern. Even Christianity begins to make more sense when you are able to see the truth of this painting. There are some that interpret this painting as depicting the death of the pagan religions and the birth of Christianity but to take that view would be to accept that the only traditional Christian depiction in this painting is Christ on Mary's lap; if that is the case then why bother with the detail of all the other stuff. Da Vinci is equating the truth of Christianity with the truth of the pagan religions. He knew it was all the same, just as I do.

The reason this is the time of year when initiation is performed is because it is in keeping with the vibration of the universe. Just as one can breathe with the vibration of their body so too can you initiate with the vibration of the living, breathing, conscious universe. It is the time of year where death crosses the threshold to rebirth. Vegetation that had been dying will soon begin to come back to life. So, it is also true of the human psyche. When I look at these paintings, they bring tears to my eyes because I understand them as they were intended to be understood. The most important thing revealed in these paintings is the very real process of transformation, which is misunderstood and grossly misinterpreted throughout the world; but above and beyond all of that, these paintings are beautiful.

I included Mabel Collins' interpretation of the crucifixion. The triangle representing the womb of rebirth on the cover of this book. The song "Ave Maria" is based on this truth. Jesus could be described as our pattern and the womb of Mary is the womb of rebirth we must all enter. My favorite rendition of "Ave Maria" can be found on YouTube in a live performance of André Rieu and Mirusia. I like this version because it shows audience reaction. The song speaks to people on a deeply personal level. It speaks to the subconscious knowledge that we all must go through this transformation.

When I look at these wonderful works of art and listen to such a beautiful performance of "Ave Maria," I can see how this book falls short of such inspirational works by fellow initiates. I see how they were able to capture the essence and beauty of the experience. This book is my own experience and not meant to inspire but rather an explanation or academic review of this process I went through. I wanted to leave no room for the type of misinterpretation that has been present throughout history surrounding this consciousness initiation. As beautiful as the works are by my fellow initiates they leave too much room for misinterpretation. I'll have more to say about this in the final chapter.

Reddit

Early on in my experiences of consciousness, it occurred to me that I'm not the only one who has gone through something like this. It occurred to me that I must be able to find others online. I began to think about where I might find them. I remembered that Reddit had a bunch of different forums, or subs as they are called on Reddit, and maybe there were subs with people like me. I began to search Reddit and found several subs full of people with consciousness experiences. The catch-all that accepts posts from just about anyone is r/awakened.

There are however secret private subs that also recognize this process as an initiation just as I do. I am a member of a couple of those groups. These subs are very important to me because everyone in them is either initiated or an initiate, in either case it is something that we all handle with care and take it very seriously.

The amount of people who have subscribed to the awakened sub has exploded. When I first came across it in 2018 there were about 40k subscribers; two years later there are about 140k.

I began posting some of my experiences in the awakened sub concerning the beings that had initiated me into this consciousness; thinking that everyone would understand and have similar experiences, but it became clear that nobody else had the same experience as me. This actually makes sense because as I learned in *Light on the Path*, everyone's journey down the path is different. In these subs on Reddit, I have found that the consensus among people who have found this consciousness is that this process is incredibly emotionally painful, and that there are these synchronicities involved. I was surprised that so few actually saw any beings as I did, but I chalk this up to the fact that this is what I needed. I never would have looked at any of this stuff had it not smacked me in the face as it did; nor would I ever have believed anyone who was telling me these things.

I began to explore other subs on Reddit. This brings me to the sleep paralysis and paranormal subs. In examining my own experiences, which involve what we currently describe as sleep paralysis and the paranormal whenever these beings are around, I thought it would be interesting to take a close look at the posts in these subs. I have noticed patterns in what people experience during sleep paralysis, as well as what people experience in the paranormal sub. I began to understand how much my own experiences were similar to experiences others described in these subs. When people describe experiences in the sleep paralysis sub, they talk about this in terms of vivid hallucinations that seem real. Medicine explains it this way because they don't really understand what's happening. The experiences are so incredibly vivid because they are in fact real. They may or may not be happening on the physical plane but that doesn't make it any less real because all of these planes of existence are in fact real. Science simply can't explain it yet, so they dismiss this as some malfunction of the brain.

The things I have been through are too specific for me to dismiss as mere random hallucinations because there was nothing random about them. There's too much substance there. Any one of my experiences on its own could be easily dismissed in this way; but taken in their totality, they become difficult to dismiss. I also couldn't dismiss the fact that I would be introduced to authors and concepts while asleep that I could then find in the physical world during my waking life. Not to mention being told something that was going to come to pass and seeing that play out in my waking life. Taken in their totality against the backdrop of all the world's religions and mythology viewed through the prism of human psychology, there is so much that begins to make a lot of sense. In dismissing this as mere hallucinations or delusions, you're essentially saying that everyone on Reddit is hallucinating the same things over and over, not only today, but throughout human history.

The mare of folklore that visits people in their sleep and sits on their chest causing them to be unable to breathe is an ancient example that we can see on Reddit. In Greek mythology, there is the goddess Nyx, or Night, and her offspring visit people at night. You can see these same experiences being played out on Reddit in the paranormal and sleep paralysis subs. I even came across folklore that involved elves living in the forest during the Middle Ages. The lore described "elf oppression." It concerned them making you feel depressed and watching you while you sleep. Once again, you can see this same experience on Reddit.

In researching people's experiences in these subs, you can begin to see these patterns. Often people describe not being able to see the being's face, blue skin, laughing elves, the feeling of being watched, being watched by a small being, an old lady, shadow people, getting dragged from the bed, the hat man, the slender man… these themes reoccur over and over in the sleep paralysis and paranormal rooms on Reddit. But they can also be seen in folklore and mythology that spans several thousand years.

Two of the more interesting examples are the old woman and the hat man which are prominent experiences in the paranormal and sleep paralysis subs. If you recall the goddess Demeter disguises herself as an old woman as she wanders the earth visiting various mortal cities, looking to do woman's work, transforming children into immortal gods. The "hat man" described by people strongly resembles the Greek god Hermes. He was the only god that could go freely in and out of the underworld and often in mythology he transports people to and from the underworld. Ancient depictions of Hermes show him wearing a helmet with wings on the sides of it; resembling the "hat man."

If you don't believe me when I tell you this, all you have to do is look it up. It's all online. The mythology as well as people's personal experiences listed on Reddit, the same experiences occurring in different people. I've even seen several posts concerning a blue-skinned succubus sucking the energy from people. Ultimately though, this all goes back to the theory of Carl Jung. This phenomenon speaks to us in terms of myth. The myth that plays in the subconscious through tens of centuries. I would further add that the phenomenon builds that myth as well.

In Hinduism, the goddess Kali is usually depicted with blue or black skin and dispenses moksha or the liberation from the cycle of death and rebirth. She's often depicted standing on Shiva. In two of her arms she holds a sword and a severed human head representing the killing of the shadow in the psyche as well as the pain and death associated with transformation. While in her other two hands she gives gifts and blessings.

Pope Sylvester II pushed math and science during his time as pope. He encouraged learning, and on his deathbed it was rumored he confessed that he had been working with a succubus, and he was also rumored to have been an occultist. What wasn't understood about this is that it was actually an initiation experience.

It's easy to imagine a person would witness the blue-skinned being and start to feel depressed; subsequently, they would falsely think that this being is somehow feeding on your negative energy; even that it is keeping you locked in this state; you may imagine this to be a demon in the ignorant sense. Many people have believed this in the past. Clearly, the entire idea of the succubus is a misinterpretation of what is really happening through an anthropomorphic interpretation of the situation.

In the *Homeric Hymn to Demeter* I wrote about in the beginning of the book, there was a word I left in on purpose. As Demophon (which means voice of the people) was progressing under the care of Demeter, his parents looked on him like a "daimon." The word "daimon" has the same derivative as the modern-day word "demon" it is also the same root as "deity," meaning god. So, when people say demon today as it would relate to some evil entity, they really don't understand what they're saying.

Today, doctors associate sleep paralysis with depression, anxiety, PTSD, etc. Coincidently, these are also the symptoms of the onset of this process. As though sleep paralysis is somehow caused by these things alone.

I believe what happens is the onset of this change causes universal forces to become aware of you; so you begin to have these experiences. Further, I think this process, with its pain, may be a type of life review. In Mark Gober's podcast, he interviews people who have clinically died and come back. These same people were case studies in consciousness for the scientists involved. They report having experienced a life review where they are forced to feel the emotions of those around them that they have wronged. Perhaps that is why the transformation experience is so painful. Perhaps it's some sort of life review because it actually does mimic death in that sense. Robert Moore describes the pain and depression as a ballast to keep you grounded through the process, but I think the life review, along with the physiological changes in the brain, may be closer to the truth.

Something else that Robert Moore points out is that people don't understand what sleep is. Sleep is when you "plug in" to the universal consciousness. Without this daily dose of consciousness, we would die. I could now understand this fact in my dreams with Robert Moore teaching me. There is a great deal of historical evidence for this kind of experience that mimics my own.

In Homer's *Odyssey,* he describes dreams as either true or false. Homer describes false dreams as passing through the false gates of ivory; whereas true dreams pass through the gates of polished horn constructed in the underworld. I interpret this to mean that you can take the dreams you have after the transformation as somewhat factual. I can see evidence of this in mythology, mirroring my own experiences, such as the voice I can hear when waking from sleep; which Mabel Collins describes as waking clairvoyance. In Homer's *Iliad,* Agamemnon wakes from sleep with "the divine voice drifting around him." This is also behind the Greek belief that the wind carries the messages of the gods.

In Homer's *Odyssey,* Penelope attempts to understand a dream she had. She states that true dreams pass through the gate of horn and they are to be accomplished for the men who see them. In Greek mythology, there were spirits known as the Oneiroi that were the children of Nyx, the goddess of the night. The Oneiroi pass through one of the two gates as they leave their home in the underworld every night. One such Oneiroi was Phobetor, meaning "to be feared," and was said by Ovid to be the spirit that would shape the dreams of men; accounting for the nightmares that are present in this experience. William Walker Atkinson describes nightmares as the killing out of false ideas in the psyche. The stories of the hero's journey are replete with these descriptions of dreams as they pertain to consciousness. My own experience with Robert Moore began to make more sense in light of this. Something that Robert Moore told me in my dream was that dreams, to those that have not been through this, cannot be interpreted correctly.

One everyday example of dreams can be seen in a hip hop song called "Lucid Dreams" by Juice WRLD. I watched a video where the artist spoke about shadow people, and how many people will perceive an old woman in sleep paralysis, or a shadow person choking them. This song apparently did very well.

There were some ancient cultures that viewed narcolepsy and epilepsy as a divine intervention. I can see the reason for this in my own experiences. I understood I had to go to sleep when I would begin to feel heavy because I was going to have an experience which always coincided with a storm. I think we understood this in antiquity and it could perhaps be the driving force behind the idea of a storm god. The year I went through this was the wettest year ever recorded in the DC area and this is also something people would have noticed in antiquity. This is an example of something Robert Moore told me: knowing something subconsciously without knowing it consciously because we see this in modern stories as well. Whenever the hero in any movie or television show is at a crossroads or is going through some change, there's always a storm outside. We associate a storm with great change when used in the context of a hero on a journey.

People in antiquity would sometimes awaken from these perceived narcolepsy experiences with tales of "visions." There were times in my own experience where I had to go to bed because I knew I was going to fall asleep whether I wanted to or not. How many times have you heard about some artist, scientist, or inventor that, "woke up with this idea in their head." I believe Isaac Newton knew this and that's why such a great deal of his research was along the "spiritual" lines. He had been through this consciousness initiation just like I had. Many would say Newton was a genius. I say he was just more in tune with the universe through this transformation and this is, in fact, what genius is. Albert Einstein's views seem to be in line with this. Einstein, as well as Spinoza, believed that the anthropomorphic conceptualization of a god that doles out rewards and punishments was naive. Einstein wrote:

> *A person who is religiously enlightened appears to me to be one who has, to the best of his ability, liberated himself from the fetters of his selfish desires and is preoccupied with thoughts, feelings and aspirations to which he clings because of their super-personal value. It seems to me that what is important is the force of this superpersonal content ... regardless of whether any attempt is made to unite this content with a divine being, for otherwise it would not be possible to count Buddha and Spinoza as religious personalities. Accordingly, a religious person is devout in the sense that he has no doubt of the significance and loftiness of those superpersonal objects and goals which neither require nor are capable of rational foundation They exist with the same necessity and matter-of-factness as he himself. In this sense religion is the age-old endeavor of mankind to become clearly and completely conscious of these values and goals and constantly to strengthen and extend their effect. If one conceives of religion and science according to these definitions then a conflict between them appears impossible.*

Science, Philosophy and Religion, A Symposium, The Conference on Science, Philosophy and Religion in Their Relation to the Democratic Way of Life, Inc., New York, 1941.

***

A human being is part of the whole called by us "Universe," a part limited in time and space. He experiences himself, his thoughts and feelings as something separate from the rest - a kind of optical delusion of his consciousness. This delusion is a kind of prison for us, restricting us to our personal desires and to affection for a few persons nearest to us. Our task must be to free ourselves from this prison by widening our circle of compassion to embrace all living creatures and the whole of nature in its beauty.

Albert Einstein's letter to Robert S. Marcus, 1950

It opens you up to what I have heard people describe as the "scientific knowledge of God." When you break down the word genius, you understand that it is derived from the Latin *genius,* which was an attendant spirit present from one's birth. It's the idea of a genie; or as William Walker Atkinson would say *kindly mental brownies* to assist you. So, even in ancient times there was a recognition that this transformation made someone smarter; what we would call a genius today. This truth can be seen clearly in our society, when you examine the people we would consider the smartest among us… the geniuses. We would see that person would somewhat fit the Jungian definition of the introvert with greater mental control, living the archetypes in their fullness. It really is amazing how engrained this initiation experience is in our existence. So much that we can see evidence of it in the origin of our words.

The Reddit experiences demonstrate the need to reframe all of this as "the phenomenon" rather than simply referring to the experience as UFOs and aliens. The wholistic all-encompassing experience is much more than such a simplistic and anthropomorphic explanation. It encompasses religion, mythology, dreams, consciousness, and the nature of reality in the universe.

I would further propose that we adopt similar terminology for the rest of the experience. Instead of referring to God, because it's such a loaded and charged term, we can simply refer to the "Source." Instead of referring to aliens, others, or visitors we could refer to them as progenitors. These terms are not anthropomorphic and more adequately and semantically describe the truth. Semantics are important because it is through semantics that I have been able to deduce some truths in my own experiences. As an example, I have come to the conclusion that the voice I hear upon waking is in fact the Source. I say this because one night before bed, I was wondering how often the progenitors were watching me. I wondered if they were still watching me because things seemed to be slowing down at that time. I woke the next morning with the voice telling me, "They're always watching you." In this statement the voice sets itself apart from the progenitors, referring to "they" rather than "we." These semantics are on purpose, they are significant, and they are important in understanding the phenomenon.

Chapter Nine
SUBTLE MANIFESTATIONS OF CONSCIOUSNESS

This chapter will have yet more evidence, but I wanted to explain it in terms of the way in which this evidence came to me. I wanted to do this because I want people to understand some of the very subtle ways in which consciousness can lead you. My experiences started out in a very obvious and shocking way; then I started to wake up with the names of authors or some concept being whispered to me, which I still do, but it seems things can be more subtle still. It's almost like getting weened, because some of these more-subtle manifestations can also become fluid where one thing leads to another. I want to give you an idea of the kinds of things that will be available to you post transformation or they may even be available to you now, but you just don't realize what it actually is. Further, these things can be so subtle that you might accidentally miss them if you're not paying attention.

One such example I have already spoken of. The idea that the people and things you collect are symbolic representations of the areas where you lack wholeness in the psyche. Examine the qualities of those people and things and you will begin to see the subtle manifestations of consciousness that draws you towards them.

Atkinson wrote about the ability to think of a topic or problem for which you need some guidance. He explains it is possible to imagine that problem in your head, wrapping that problem up in a box, placing that box on a trap door in the mind, pulling a string to open the doors and sending that box down the chute. He explains that in a few days' time you will receive the answer. I have found this to be true. I'm mentioning this because it greatly assisted me in writing this book, and it was something that would happen even before I went through this process; but I never realized it was significant. I think I'm not alone in that. I think there will be quite a few of you reading these pages that may find this familiar. I have Dean Koontz to thank for it. The day that I awoke with the name Steven Nadler in my head there was another name that was a bit of a mystery to me. Dean Koontz. The Nadler and Spinoza connection I got right away; that was obvious, but Dean Koontz wrote so much that I had no idea what I was supposed to read.

I put Dean Koontz on the back burner until I could find more information. As I was reading through Steven Nadler's book, Spinoza's Heresy, I often paused to ponder some of the concepts and take notes. I did this to the point that the screen on my Kindle would go black as it was entering power-saving mode. I would have to swipe across the screen to wake it back up. Normally, the first thing I would see was an ad of some kind. On one occasion there was an ad for a book by Dean Koontz called Ricochet Joe. That's gotta be it! I thought, as I immediately purchased the book and began reading it. I laughed when the description of the main character fit me pretty well.

The story was about a guy that seeks out and destroys an evil creature that lives inside the human body. He's led all over town by way of blurting out something like "bus stop," he then proceeds to the bus stop. He puts his hands on the bus stop then blurts out "rats" and proceeds down the road to a store window where there are toy rats on display and so on.

I had finished Ricochet Joe and Spinoza's Heresy. I sat one day wondering what was next. My mind was blank. I wasn't thinking of anything as I sat smoking my cigarette staring at nothing in particular off in the distance. Out of the blue I whispered, "Douglas Fairbanks," for no particular reason. Of course as we all know by now there is no such thing as coincidence; there must have been some reason I said that name out of the blue; and I remembered Ricochet Joe doing this. I looked into who Fairbanks was, because I had no idea, and discovered he was a silent film star. The name sounded vaguely familiar. I looked for books he may have written and came across his self-help books. I took the quotes from the books that I knew he felt were key to his own transformation. In reading his books, it was clear he had been through this because so much of his philosophy about life matched my own. The fact that our philosophies matched is also no accident as Robert Moore and Spinoza both say; we are all alike at this level of consciousness.

On another occasion, I was in my typical trance staring off at nothing when I suddenly whispered, "Chichen Itza." It's an ancient Mayan city in Central America famous for its pyramid that is oriented in such a way as to illuminate the serpent on the pyramids staircase during the autumnal equinox. As the sun sets, the serpent appears to be slithering down the staircase toward the ground, disappearing into the labyrinth below ground. I can see parallels with this complex and those of the rest of the world in terms of this initiatory transformation. Not only can this be seen in the pyramid but it's also more glaringly obvious in the Temple of the Warriors which dominates the Chichen Itza site. This Temple of the Warriors, of course, represents the same inner war and warrior represented in the Bhagavad Gita.

Before I go on explaining the significance of the temple, I need to explain the swastika and why it's such an important mythologic symbol. As the earth rotates there is a point in the sky that it appears the night sky is revolving around. This point is the star Polaris. The big dipper is near to Polaris and is seen rotating around it as the earth spins. Ancient cultures would speak of this point around which the universe seemed to rotate as the center of the universe. Some Native American mythology speaks of god picking up an animal and spinning it above his head and all life in the universe spinning out of this action. So, when one looks at the big dipper as it rests on the outskirts of Polaris, it is in different places around Polaris during the four seasons. The graphic mythological symbol of this is the swastika. It also is represented as a circle cut into four equal parts and perhaps as a spiral.

When viewed from above, the Temple of the Warriors appears to have two arms extending from the temple in the form of large covered patios or halls; known as the Plaza of the Thousand Columns. Each column has a depiction of a different warrior; perhaps previous warriors in the cycle of rebirth. The columned patios, or halls, are oriented to the Big Dipper in the swastika as it is oriented in the autumn and winter; indicating the time of year the temple was used. Autumn and winter, which is the same time of year for initiation.

It becomes easy to imagine the ceremonies held there. The serpent descending the steps of the pyramid down into the labyrinth of the underworld beneath the temple complex. Initiates then being led into the labyrinth where they will be spending a lot of time over the next several months. There was likely an autumnal equinox ceremony at the warrior temple because at the top of the temple steps there is a Chacmool.

The Chacmool is often carved to represent four gods that are concerned with the four directions of the earth. The four gods were known as the Chacs. The Chacs are related to the four Bacabs who are associated with the interior of the earth. The four exterior and four interior gods also being representations of the psychology of transformation: the introvert and extrovert with each of the archetypes in their fullness and in shadow. These eight gods are all associated with the goddess Ixchel, who was the goddess of the moon, love, and gestation. I haven't done a lot of research on this but just with the casual bit I have done, I think this may all be a representation of the eight fold psyche. I believe the single Chacmool at the top of the steps at the warrior temple is a representation of wholeness in the psyche. The Chacmool at the top of the temple steps is laying on its back. Perhaps an autumnal equinox ceremony would have consisted of an initiate walking up the steps to see their reflection in a bowl on the belly of this pregnant Chacmool. Seeing yourself in the belly of this pregnant god as a representation of the fact you are about to experience rebirth.

The reason I go into so much detail here is because I now know this to be the truth that underlies all religions living and dead. So, it only makes sense that you would find this truth even in cultures that were isolated from the rest of the world. The truth has always been the truth regardless of where in the world you are.

Today, we like to think of these ancient cultures as primitive, but in researching the Mayans I came across a belief that they used mirrors in their ceremonies at the Temple of the Warriors. The Mayans often used reflective surfaces in clothing and burials. Many scholars believe this was due to a belief that they played a role in the underworld. I would agree with this, but my take is a bit different.

The priests were aware of how this initiation experience ties in with the human psyche. These priests were in fact also psychologists and possessed knowledge of the human psyche that would far exceed the typical psychologist of today. There is so much of this experience that consists of introspection, and mirrors would be a physical manifestation of that fact. If you were to come across someone wearing reflective garments, you would see yourself in them, as a representation of the singular universal consciousness, but more importantly it speaks to the initiation experience itself. They had an awareness that the underworld was representative of the deeper and darker recesses of the human psyche, and that during initiation it is as though there is a giant mirror held up to the psyche. Mabel Collins says the following about the truth of the initiation experience in When the Sun Moves Northward and this is also why I describe the pain as a kind of life review experience at the same time:

> *The great river is open and clear, and it is like an immense mirror. The disciples, as they enter, pass down to its margin and gaze intently into its depths for a while, then give place to others. Many shirk back at the last moment, for in the still water a formidable vision is seen, a strange and terrible picture arises and forms itself for each one. The disciple who can endure this initiation sees his own life, his past history, shown as in a looking-glass, without any blurring or softening or any hiding away. The facts are there in their simplicity, without excuse or disguise.*

Outside Mexico city there are the ruins of an ancient civilization. The ancient city is called Teotihuacan, built around 100 B.C. When the Aztecs found this city it had been an abandoned ruin for about 700 years; but had once been one of the largest cities in the northern hemisphere. The pyramid complex is enormous and constructed to mirror the belt of Orion. The base of the largest pyramid is the same size as the Great Pyramid at Giza. There is a temple at the end of the pyramid complex called the Temple of the Feathered Serpent. I believe it served the same purpose as the Temple of the Warriors at Chichen Itza.

There was a recent excavation of a tunnel that runs underneath the smaller pyramid at the Temple of the Feathered Serpent. Archeologists believe this tunnel was a representation of the underworld. It was probably filled with water and the ceiling was painted black with fool's gold ground into it to create a ceiling that would glisten like the night sky. This tunnel ends in a cross under the heart of the pyramid, representing the center of the universe. It's clear to me that this was a place of initiation.

There were large amounts of mercury found in this tunnel which I believe is indicative of the performance of alchemy. When I say alchemy, what I'm referring to is the process of extracting gold using mercury in an amalgamation process. It was simply a representation of getting gold from a stone; gold being a symbol of immortality. It was the physical process that mirrored what was happening to initiates internally. This is what alchemy always was. The amalgam is cooked and put under pressure with mercury to create gold.

In the last chapter there were quotes I shared from Mabel Collins concerning the symbolism of the cross and the fact that the different climates of the world have no effect on this symbolism. Perhaps nowhere in South America is this more clearly stated than on the sarcophagus of the Mayan King Pakal. Ancient alien theorists incorrectly have called this a depiction of Pakal in a spaceship. It truly depicts Pakal in the fetal position within the womb of his rebirth. He is descending down the tree of our life, descending from the crucifixion, freed from the pairs of opposites in death, down the tree to his new birth.

South America was supposed to be completely isolated from all of these other religions and yet their religions share many of the same striking similarities with those of the rest of the world. I came across a South American myth that concerns a pair of "divine" twin brothers. They descend into the underworld to free their father. Sound familiar? The hero twins played a role in many Native American cultures. It's unfortunate that Cortez and subsequent settlers brought the native American cultures to such an abrupt end; burning all manuscripts, dismantling temples, all because he didn't understand that their religions were exactly the same.

At the Temple to Demeter in Greece, the men of Eleusis had a great battle among themselves at the right time each year. Just as is stated in the *Homeric Hymn to Demeter*. It was something Demeter stated before she departed her temple in Eleusis. They staged great fake battles outside the temple. There are some that believe these mock battles eventually evolved into the Olympics. In Chichen Itza, I believe the ball courts as well as the Temple of the Warriors served this same psychological purpose. All, of course, representing the great inner battle that occurs during this time of year as man struggles to slay the serpent; to kill out the primordial evil within.

The pyramid complexes in Egypt were not all tombs as scholars currently believe. There is the Bent Pyramid, which is bent because it represents initiation as a shortcut to the top. A forcing of intense, life-altering, and terrifying experiences to bring about this new consciousness. Forcing initiates to navigate a dark underground labyrinth with trap doors and dead ends; perhaps even flooding at times. Experiences that would break you completely in order to constitute a new wholeness within the psyche. I know it may sound a bit out there but I believe the Great Pyramid was never intended to be a tomb. It was intended as a place of initiation and it was also a technological marvel. There is zero evidence that this structure was ever a tomb. I would even venture to bet that anywhere we find these types of impossible megalithic structures we will see evidence of the initiation process. When we visit these sites we are struck by the precision and want to assume ancient cultures never could have done this. But this is not so. These structures were absolutely built by human hands. Today we look at sights like the pyramids, Cuzco, and Tiwanaku; we can't even wrap our minds around why anyone would have built such things if it couldn't be done easily. I see the psychological reason for it. When I look at these impossibly large boulders that are fitted together so tightly that even today you can't slide a sheet of paper between them; I see what others don't. I see patience, attention to detail, persistence, creative human ingenuity, mindfulness, and an insistence on these qualities to an extreme degree. These also happen to be the qualities that will get you to the initiation. It is these same qualities that draw us to incredible works of art. Hand carved marble statues, paintings with incredible detail. We love that we can see these qualities manifest in physical form. Many people are at a loss as to why they are drawn to these things. It's not that you are drawn to the works themselves but rather the qualities you lack that would allow you to produce such things.

As we have seen around the world, there was a great deal of effort put into this idea of the underworld, in making the initiation a magical experience. In the Great Pyramid, the Egyptians chose granite for its interior spaces. This granite was never covered in plaster and hieroglyphics as one would expect; it was left exposed and this could not have been an accident. Granite was chosen for its piezoelectric qualities. Granite has crystals embedded within it. When granite is under pressure these crystals will illuminate. Perhaps they would flood the tunnels in the base of the pyramid and this would cause air pressure to build within the granite chambers. It must have been something to experience this in antiquity.

To enter this pyramid as an initiate; feeling the pressure inside changing as the pyramid breathes and begins to come to life. Initiates may have even been ritually wrapped up as mummies and carried through the pyramid's interior spaces; before being placed inside the sarcophagus to represent their death. As the initiate being carried through, it would almost seem as though you are floating through the living, breathing universe as you are transported through the structure.

This was the point of the pyramid but it's not clear if it ever worked. I believe it did for a time until cracks in the structure rendered it inoperable. There is evidence there were repairs to some cracks in order to maintain this airtight integrity. Because of these later repairs to the interior spaces, the current scholarly interpretation of this structure as the tomb for the pharaoh doesn't hold water. If it was only a tomb there would have been no reason to preserve its airtight integrity by patching cracks. In fact, if it were just a tomb there would have been no reason to enter the structure after it were sealed. But they clearly did.

There is a tunnel that was dug in the pyramid leading to the king's chamber that archeologists believe was dug by grave robbers; but I have a different take on that. I tend to believe it wasn't grave robbers because the tunnelers knew exactly where they were going as they dug. I believe there was a group of initiates inside that became trapped when the ropes controlling the giant granite plugs broke. The tunnel was dug to rescue them, further damaging the airtight integrity of the structure. I saw all of this in a dream one night, so I tend to believe it may be true; although, I'm unsure how they got the electrical qualities in the granite to work. Perhaps an engineer could look at this and figure it out. The ancient Egyptians were aware of the electrical qualities of granite under pressure. There is an excellent article detailing that knowledge on AncientOrigins.net titled *Lighting Up Saqqara: An Electrifying Alternative Theory for the Oversized Serapeum Sarcophagi.*

###***Modern Myth****

I had a dream about the element mercury reacting with a substance. My thought was that there had to be more to mercury then I currently understood. I was then led to a book by a famous and rather mysterious French alchemist named Fulcanelli. He wrote a book called *The Mystery of the Cathedrals* that was published in Paris in 1926. The preface to the first edition of the book is written by one of his students and claims that Fulconelli has described the key to alchemy in a description of one of the colors in the book. I believe stating that was accidental on his part because in reading the book he states that he was hung up on this single aspect for 20 years. This doesn't mean it's the key to alchemy; it just means it was his key. Someone else may get hung up on some other concept.

In the book, Fulconelli describes the alchemical symbols built into Notre Dame. He describes in great detail the symbols carved in stone in the cathedral's porch. As an aside here I want to point out that as I write this I'm watching live footage on the news in which I can clearly see Notre Dame burning to the ground. In describing the panels on the porch it is obvious they describe the process of transformation in terms of alchemy. Alchemy was practiced behind closed doors just as the Greek Mysteries were. I knew this wasn't what I needed to understand about this dream. I knew there was more I had to understand.

A few days later, I was sitting in my truck smoking a cigarette wondering what was next, once again. And, once again, I stopped thinking of anything really. I was again staring at nothing off in the distance when I whispered, "Bernard Shaw." I didn't know who he was either. When I looked him up, I discovered he described himself as a mystic and was the playwright that brought us *My Fair Lady*. He wrote quite a bit, so I had to narrow the search. I began to search for things he wrote that had to do with mythology, and came across a movie he wrote the screenplay for called *Pygmalion,* which is a character in *Metamorphosis* by the Roman poet Ovid.

The mythic Pygmalion is a sculptor who creates a statue of a woman from ivory. He fell in love with her and wished that Aphrodite would bring him a bride that was the likeness of his ivory creation. Aphrodite granted this wish because after asking for this, Pygmalion kissed his statue and brought it to life. The Greek equivalent to the character Pygmalion lived on the island of Crete and was named Daedalus, who was a skilled craftsman and metal worker. Daedalus would pour quicksilver (mercury) in the mouths of the automatons he created to animate them. He also created a labyrinth, for King Minos of Crete, to hold the half man-half beast Minotaur.

In Bernard Shaw's adaptation of this mythology, he more plainly and blatantly portrays the hidden truth behind these myths; the process of initiation. *Pygmalion* is the same story as *My Fair Lady,* however, Bernard Shaw personally wrote the screenplay for the movie *Pygmalion* so it does vary a bit from *My Fair Lady*. The plot is as follows:

Shaw, opens the movie *Pygmalion* on the streets of London with a bit of mystic truth that is never explained anywhere in the movie. The impoverished Eliza, who is the subject of the movie, is selling flowers on the streets. She is incapable of speaking proper English. She begins heading for cover as it starts to rain. A less significant character named Freddy is dispatched to go fetch a cab for his mother and sister as they wait under cover from the storm. Eliza is heading for the same cover from the rain when she runs into Freddy spilling the flowers she was selling into the street. She doesn't know him but blurts out, "Watch out, Freddy!"

As she gathers the flowers and heads for cover, Freddy's mother asks Eliza how she knew her son's name, but Eliza has no real logical explanation. Shaw of course put this in the story on purpose as a hint that this mysticism is what this story is about. In the plot to this story, Shaw disguises the subject of consciousness with the concept of linguistics. Standing near to the action is Professor Higgins, who is a linguistics expert. He begins to write down Eliza's words as she speaks. Some of the other people in the covered area, waiting out the rain, are disturbed by Professor Higgins' actions and suspect he's with the police. They become angry with him for picking on this poor destitute girl, but Professor Higgins diffuses the situation as he tells the angry spectators one by one where they are from, and where in the world they have ever lived. The spectators are amazed at his abilities and he simply explains that he's a linguistics expert and he can deduce, by the minute inflections and tones they use, where they are from and where they have lived.

One of the people who just so happens to witness the events is Colonel Pickering, who was someone Professor Higgins had wanted to meet for some time. Colonel Pickering likewise had been a fan of Higgins' work and wanted to meet him as well. Higgins gives his address to Pickering in front of Eliza and asks Pickering to pay him a visit.

The next morning, Eliza pops in on Professor Higgins at his home as he sits talking to Colonel Pickering. Eliza expresses her desire for English lessons as she would like to work in a proper flower shop. Professor Higgins and Colonel Pickering then discuss how they could transform her into a woman so proper that she would be indistinguishable from royalty.

Professor Higgins gets to work on Eliza; she screams and cries out as Professor Higgins' maid bathes her. He gives her a new wardrobe, jewelry, and begins to teach her proper English late into the long nights of initiation. Eliza is kicking and screaming the whole time. She's a wreck.

Finally comes the big test. Higgins takes Eliza to an evening event where royalty will be present. She is asked by a prince to dance. As she does this, she's turning heads in the room. She's stunning in her transformation. The secretary of the prince, who was one of Higgins best linguistics students, sets out to discover who Eliza is and where she's from. He listens to the way she speaks and proclaims he has discovered she is a fraud. He proclaims that she is not an Englishwoman but is from a certain Hungarian, royal bloodline.

When Higgins, Pickering, and Eliza return home that evening, Eliza becomes upset. She asks the professor what is to become of her now. She realizes it's over and she pulled it off but now can't go back to who she was. She's risen far beyond even working in a flower shop. She gets emotional and tells Higgins he should have left her in the gutter where he found her. Higgins is angered by this. Higgins expresses that he never feels anger but somehow she has managed to make him angry. He goes to bed. Eliza leaves the house and wanders the streets that night; now dressed and behaving like a proper woman. She comes to the street where she met Higgins and is stopped by a poverty-stricken flower girl that asks Eliza if she would like to buy some flowers.

She returns to Higgins' home the next day and continues to ask the professor what she should do now. Higgins and Eliza begin to argue. In the argument, Professor Higgins mentions that he's wasted the treasures of his Miltonic mind on her. It's a reference to John Milton who was an English poet, and whose writings mirror the themes in this book. Eliza tells Higgins that she cares deeply for him. Not in a romantic way but in the way of friendship; which is a symptom of the transformation I mentioned earlier in the book. Eliza here is referring to the platonic love described by Plato in the *Symposium*.

Eliza tells Higgins she doesn't need him, she's going to become a teacher and teach others everything she's learned. Higgins then says he knew he would make a woman out of her one day. He proclaims, "Five minutes ago you were like a millstone around my neck. Now you're a tower of strength: a consort battleship." She then leaves Higgins' house.

It's a beautiful adaptation of the initiatory process in myth, and masterfully written. It's worth your time to watch. I will mention that the ending of the movie was not the work of Shaw. I read accounts that he was upset that Eliza returns to Professor Higgins home after proclaiming that she was going to become a teacher and storming out. After Eliza leaves is where Shaw ended the story. Others working on the film made it into a love story in having Eliza return after her transformation was complete. I read an account that Shaw was furious about this ending and shouted, "No, she doesn't come back!"

Another great film by Bernard Shaw is *Major Barbara* where Shaw speculates on the future of humanity and the "salvation of souls." In the beginning of the movie the camera pans down a note from Shaw to the viewers:

Friend,

What you are about to see is not an idle tale of people who never existed and things that could never have happened. It is a PARABLE.

Do not be alarmed: you will not be bored by it. It is, I hope, both true and inspired.

Some of the people in it are real people whom I have met and talked to.

One of the others may be YOU.

There will be a bit of you in all of them. We are all members of one another.

If you do not enjoy every word of it we shall both be equally disappointed.

Well, friend: have I ever disappointed you? Have I not been always your faithful servant?
   –Bernard Shaw

I was very interested in this note because of the reference to all of us being members of one another speaking to the oneness of the universe. In the beginning of the movie, the themes discussed in this book were immediately apparent. One of the main characters, who is a professor of Greek, discusses the similarities of all the world's religions.

Later, Barbara, a major in the Salvation Army, is on a stage preaching to people about not finding God in a cathedral; but inside you. She preaches about attaining the feeling of unwavering calm and peace. The movie then goes on to display the various archetypal personalities that exist in humanity. The main character, Barbara, meets her absent, aloof father, a wealthy weapons manufacturer and mystic, for the first time in many years. The reason she hasn't seen him in a long time is that, as William Walker Atkinson points out, the advanced yogi will often fall away from his family. They fall away because they recognize all the members of their own family are no different or closer to them than anyone else. We are all just centers of consciousness. We have no mother or father. No sister or brother. We are all members of one another; as Shaw would say.

Throughout the movie, her father is painted as an awful person for being a manufacturer of the weapons of war. In the end of the movie we are able to see the truth of who her father is. He is a mystic who provides materials that could be used for good or for evil. He produces nitrates that could be used to fertilize crops, but instead people want explosives for killing. He produces steel that could be used for human ingenuity, and constructing a new society; but instead society manufactures guns and killing machines.

The workers at this plant, as a foreshadowing of what lies on the horizon for humanity, live in a community resembling utopia, in an awakened state, on the grounds of the factory. In a dialogue with her fiancé, in the midst of this utopia, Barbara discusses "making war on war; the path to life lies through the factory of death," she says. Barbara talks about getting rid of the bribe of heaven. She says, "Let God's work be done for its own sake, the work that he had to create us to do because it cannot be done except by living men and women."

Barbara decides she's going to work in the family business. In this scene, there is a lot to unpack. It is addressed, in this scene, that the church keeps people locked in a cycle of fear and hope. Barbara wants to see souls saved not from fear and hope but because their needs are met through human ingenuity. "Let them be saved not because their bodies are hungry but rather because their bodies are full and their souls are hungry." Not to mention the "factory of death" being a reference to the pain of transformation and rebirth.

The ancient mythology and psychology is found in other modern stories like *Alice in Wonderland*, and even *Star Wars*. I realized this when in my meditative state I whispered, "Lewis Carroll." In *Alice in Wonderland*, Alice follows the rabbit down a hole sending her on her hero's journey. Alice notices what would be called a synchronicity in Jungian psychology in the form of a rabbit wearing a pocket watch. She then follows this through to its logical end in a journey of transformation. In realizing this, I began to look closer at its author Lewis Carrol; he clearly knew about this transformation.

I read that he was an admirer of John Henry Newman who was a poet, theologian, and Catholic Cardinal. Newman once wrote that there is "something true and Divinely revealed in every religion." In *A Grammar of Assent* he wrote that there was "never a time when revelation was not continuous and systematic," just as it is stated in the Gospel of Thomas.

In my research into the night sky I found two constellations that Carrol used in his book. The rabbit who is always chasing time; I found the rabbit in the constellation Lepus and the clock in the constellation Horologium. It was interesting to me that during the time between the winter solstice and the New Year, Lepus appears to be chasing Horologium below the horizon in the night sky. The story correctly depicts the beginning of transformation as being marked by these types of impossible synchronicities. Robert Moore and Douglas Gillette explain this type of experience in their book *The Magician Within: Accessing the Shaman in the Male Psyche*:

> *In Close Encounters of the Third Kind, Richard Dreyfuss plays the part of an ordinary man. He has his kids, his wife, and his pickup, and he's going along quite contentedly with his life, until he has an encounter with what Jung calls the numinous – in his case a UFO that almost lands on his truck. After that point his life is never the same again. He becomes a quester.*

The same themes are present in *Star Wars*. My favorite scene in *Star Wars*, corny as it may seem, is when Yoda is training Luke Skywalker. For me, this scene is a very emotional one. Luke and Yoda stop to rest at the mouth of a cave. Luke feels drawn to the cave. He asks Yoda what's in the cave. Yoda replies, "Only what you take with you." Luke takes his light saber into the cave even though Yoda tells him he won't need it. This is symbolic of the fear Luke takes with him.

There are even more recent stories like the series *Westworld*. I would highly recommend it because it's so wonderfully written. Some of Anthony Hopkins' monologues are brilliant. There is another promising show called Lovecraft Country that I have not seen yet but I know that H.P. Lovecraft was someone that was trapped in the initiation process for some time.

Elias Hicks

In another demonstration of consciousness at work, I said the name "Braithwaite" one day as I sat in my typical meditative trance. I looked into it and found Anna Braithwaite; who was a British Quaker. She traveled to the United States between 1821 and 1827 in an attempt to denounce the views of Elias Hicks; a Quaker preacher in New York whose views were causing a schism within the church. Hicks preached about the "inner light." In a series of publicly published letters, Braithwaite tries to counter Hicks' arguments. In one of the letters she denounces Hicks' views on the crucifixion of Christ and states that by belief alone one is "saved." I believe Hicks' writings to be compelling evidence of yet another initiation. In his later years, he wrote an autobiography titled *Journal of the Life and Religious Labours of Elias Hicks* which was published in 1832. Of his transformation and initiation he wrote the following:

> *My advantages, in a religious point of view, were greater than before; as I had the benefit of the company of several worthy Friends, who were my neighbors, and by whose example I was frequently incited to seriousness and piety; yet, having entered pretty closely into business, I was thereby much diverted from my religious improvement for several years. But, about the twenty-sixth year of my age, I was again brought, by the operative influence of divine grace, under deep concern of mind; and was led, through adorable mercy,*

to see, that although I had ceased from many sins and vanities of my youth, yet there were many remaining that I was still guilty of, which were not yet atoned for, and for which I now felt the judgments of God to rest upon me. This caused me to cry most earnestly to the Most High for pardon and redemption, and he graciously condescended to hear my cry, and to open a way before me, wherein I must walk, in order to experience reconciliation with him; and as I abode in watchfulness and deep humiliation before him, light broke forth out of obscurity, and my darkness became as the noon-day. I had many deep openings in the visions of light, greatly strengthening and establishing to my exercised mind. My spirit was brought under a close and weighty labor in meetings for discipline, and my understanding much enlarged therein; and I felt a concern to speak to some of the subjects engaging in the meetings attention, which often brought speak able comfort to my mind.

I found it interesting that he seems to reference waking clairvoyance in his book, when he writes about the inward divine voice. I also liked the following he said about death and resurrection; describing it as a pattern, as he too recognized the pattern of the Hero's Journey.

Therefore while men disregard this inward divine principle, of grace and truth, and do not believe in it, as **essential and sufficient to salvation**; *they are in danger of becoming either Atheists, or Deists - these are also in danger of becoming so blinded as to not believe in that necessary and very essential doctrine of perfection, as contained in that clear, rational, and positive injunction of our dear Lord: "Be ye therefore perfect, even as your Father which is in heaven is perfect." And we cannot rationally suppose they can ever be otherwise, while they continue in this situation; as* **nothing but the light** *is sufficient to produce the knowledge, on which this belief is founded. My mind was likewise largely opened to communicate, how we all might, by faithful attention and adherence to the aforesaid divine principle,* **the light within**, *come to know and believe the certainty of those excellent scripture doctrines; of the coming, life, righteous works, sufferings, death, and resurrection of Jesus Christ, our blessed pattern: and that* **it is by obedience to this inward light only**, *that we are prepared for admittance into the heavenly kingdom.*

All of the above could have been things that I missed had I not been paying attention. Beyond this whispering of a name in a trance like state, I also experienced the name or concept randomly entering my head while in this meditative state. It's exactly what happened when I described having the random thoughts about looking into mechanization earlier in the book. At the time, I didn't recognize this as a manifestation of consciousness, but I do now.

Another example of this occurred one morning as I was going through posts on Reddit. Someone had posted a photograph of a triangular frieze above a doorway and asked if anyone knew what it meant. The frieze depicted a seated winged angel with outstretched arms at the center. On either side the angel was surrounded by musical and scientific instruments. I answered the post and I asked what the purpose of the building was that the frieze was located on, and stated that it was a representation of the scientific knowledge of God that was available to initiates of the mysteries in Gnostic Christianity. The poster responded that it was above the door to a library. "Oh well, that makes sense then," I thought.

I sat for a moment thinking about this immediately after the exchange and wondered, *Wait, what is Gnostic, and how do I know this, because it's not something I've ever learned.* I began looking into Gnostic Christianity for the rest of the day and realized I was correct, but it was a bit shocking that I knew something so immediately without ever knowing it. These are just a few examples, but the entire transformation experience is full of this. I'm so much smarter than I ever knew I was.

I feel it's important to pay attention, not only because you may miss something but because you may be given some task to complete.

In my case it was this book. For someone else the task could be something completely different. It may be a manifestation of consciousness that is leading you toward wholeness of the psyche, or transformation.

Chapter Ten

ACCIDENTS, BELIEFS, AND SUPERSTITIONS

Finally, I'm going to get into the so-called "spiritual" aspect of this once again. My goal in this chapter is to give you a clear understanding of how and why the truth of the topic in this book has been twisted, manipulated, and misunderstood throughout history. I want to do this so you can navigate transformation with the proper boundaries, because without them things can begin to degrade rather quickly. What I mean by boundaries is the propensity for gross misinterpretation which causes one to become over or undercooked as Robert Moore writes, but there is also the possibility that the oven is never even turned on. Once things degrade, you may find yourself trapped in this process until you can find your way out. In fact, you may never find your way out. I have read many books by people who become trapped in a living nightmare for 20, 30, even 40 years. I want to help you avoid the pitfalls that can cause stagnation in the process.

All of the world's religions are describing a very natural process that takes place in the psyche of the individual. I don't care what anyone says regarding the misinterpretation of their own religion. I can take any major religion in history and break it down to the truths in this book. A psychological process. What inevitably happens with religion is that it usually starts as a cult that has to veil its teachings and knowledge in esoteric stories; lest they be declared heretics. Gradually, the religion grows as people start to transform but this is where it degrades because it's not easily understood, making the truth vulnerable to accidental misunderstanding, and manipulation. You end up in a situation where the beliefs have spread so far and wide, and they encompass such a large amount of people that there aren't enough ritual elders to go around, and you find that the situation has become the blind leading the blind. The religion, having become misunderstood to the point that it no longer has any meaning to anyone and, is therefore, only used as a tool to manipulate the public. Its stories and myths degrade into a mess of beliefs and priestly superstition. We can see how this has happened to Christianity.

Christianity was even more esoteric than the religions before it. Its stories were esoteric and based on esoteric myths from the past making it impossible to understand. Most Christians tend to interpret the Bible and its stories as literal fact. Interpreting these stories as literal fact will do nothing for you. Not to mention the fact that over time people have slipped their own archetypal shadow projections into the Bible.

I've met people who are LGBTQ that have found this consciousness. This is why Christianity is on the decline. If you look at the books that were a part of the Bible before the King James Version, you can see readily for yourselves that Christianity once looked very different than it does today. It's the archetypal shadows people have added over the years that the public seems to cling to most fervently and therefore no longer has an air of truth that would speak to the subconscious. It becomes an exclusive club of proud ignorance where the shadows of hatred, anger, racism, nationalism, and bigotry come to roost. Today, it only succeeds in attracting the extrovert in that sense, as the extrovert seeks a system of belief that will justify their outwardly destructive nature. Today, they proudly cling to God and guns rather than the true doctrine of unconditional love for your fellow man. Rather than being so selfless that you would give the shirt off your back; they would sooner shoot you in the face before you could take that shirt from them.

I don't know if anyone has plainly said this or not, but Robert Moore certainly alluded to it when he stated that we are all alike on the subconscious level. When internalized, the subconscious will seek to destroy anything that is not in line with it. The conscious person will feel the impression that a certain reaction or emotion is wrong. When this is externalized it creates the "other" that will be on the receiving end of our shadow archetypal energy. The subconscious seeks to destroy things that are different. This is how the hypocrite is born. The extrovert will see qualities they don't like in others even though they possess these qualities themselves. They may even learn to hate that person. But since all of this energy is externalized by the extrovert, their own faults become invisible to themselves; they can't even see themselves. This is where we get the headlines of some evangelical preacher that gets publicly outed when the police are called to a drunken domestic disturbance involving a prostitute or pool boy. There is no more morality, just the extremism of the archetypal shadow poles. What is important to these people is not the morality; we see how readily that was given up. What is important to them is the extremism they live in; fluctuating between the sadist and the masochist.

We know these literal interpretations of religious texts with a propensity toward hate are wrong; everything about it feels wrong. This is how religions die. As an example of how this happens, I was watching a YouTube video one day of a man that had discovered truth. He was yelling in one video about how we have all been lied to; that the reality we all know is not reality at all. This is an example of the danger posed with the "Return." In making this some kind of a conspiracy, you only succeed in stirring people to anger, you create the "other" for the public to cast their archetypal shadows on, and attract people who live in the shadow psyche. Anger will prevent this change from taking place. There is also the danger of not being led through this by a ritual elder who can explain to you how this truth is actually embedded in all religions in plain sight, and that even the leadership in these religions has no idea what the truth is. It's not that anyone is lying to you, it's that they don't know the truth. Religions become overrun with the extroverts causing the truth to be once again forced behind closed doors. I feel the same way about the disclosure issue. Many people would call for heads to roll as a result of all this being kept from the public. Nobody has kept anything from anybody. Just as in the *Wizard of Oz*, Dorothy had the ability to go home at any time. I don't think it's useful to point fingers and I'm not waiting for disclosure on the edge of my seat. Just as in a family line of physical and mental abuse, it ends when someone makes the conscious decision to end it.

Well, why don't they just land on the White House lawn? This is a question I hear a lot. They don't do this for the same reason our leaders don't meet with dictatorial and fascist leaders. Why would you lend legitimacy to a government you view as quite illegitimate. Even here in the US our systems and social structures are built on emotions and concepts of the lower self. We see this every day in our politicians. If a politician needs to equivocate on any topic, it's because they are lying. I won't share too many of my opinions on economics, social structures, and government because they are so radically different from anything we have ever seen that I think it would turn some people off.

The mechanism that forces this behind closed doors is a simple psychological reason. It threatens to overturn traditional power structures. As an example of this, let's say we have a community of people with some traditional leadership power structure. It could be a democracy or a monarchy; it doesn't matter. Within the community there is a small group of people that begin going through transformation. They have a ritual elder that understands the process and assists others through the process. The movement begins to build traction. The leaders recognize this and summon the ritual elder to their power center to aid leaders in their own transformation. The endeavor is unsuccessful. The leaders cling to the idea that they are power centers and need to physically exert that power over others. They cannot shake this idea in their own minds and therefore fail at their attempts to transform. The leaders at this point have a choice to make. They know that the fact the universe will not acknowledge them calls into question the legitimacy of their own right to rule over others. They can set out to destroy the movement; forcing it behind closed doors, or; because they have seen for themselves that there is some truth here, decide to tolerate it as a secret as long as it remains behind closed doors and does not call into question their own right to rule.

This happens in the UFO community as well. I feel it's unhealthy to engage in these conspiratorial endeavors because they detract from the main point of it all. This is a very important point: The conspiracy creates the "other" that will be the victim of our archetypal energies and divides camps, which I believe will only succeed in pushing all of this behind closed doors once again, as we seek to gain power over the "other."

What does the government know? Is there wreckage? Do we have alien bodies? What has been reverse engineered behind closed doors? These are all good questions but none of us can answer them right now, so I personally am not going to worry about it. I don't even care what the government has. At this point I know the truth. There are some who believe the phenomenon is evil or demonic. But to what end? As I have pointed out, this interaction goes back as far as 100,000 years. If this is nefarious in some way, why would this go back that far? 100,000 years is a long way to go for some nefarious reveal. Their message has remained consistent throughout this time.

All indications point to the same experience I had. At the very least the implication of this having persisted for so long implies that there are beings, that travel around in exotic technology, that seem to know there is something of a person that survives death. Why would you waste so much time in our past if this was not the case? If you were looking for slave labor why would you not just permanently abduct people and do your own breeding program? I've heard that there have been injuries and deaths as a result of contact. People point to cattle mutilations as well to perpetuate the nefarious intent theory. Well I hate to break it to you, but we massacre animals on a much larger scale than they ever have. I'm sure Texas has executed more people than have been harmed or killed as a result of contact. This is the shadow psyche at work isn't it? We can't see all the damage we do. What we do to each other pales in comparison to anything they've done to us. This is why I don't care what the government thinks it knows, or what it has; they don't understand any of it anyway.

What investigators call "the nuts and bolts" might be a neat read in some magazine in the waiting room at the doctor's office, but the "why" is far more profound than any of that; the "why" is in fact the nuts and bolts of all of this. Just to put it in context, the why is knowing the true nature of the universe for yourself. You don't need to wait for anyone to show you wreckage. You can know all of this now; for yourself.

We see in the UFO community that there are those concerned with only the "nuts and bolts." The physical evidence, and yet completely dismiss the experiencer end of things. They call it "spiritual woo woo." The Navy has said publicly that these craft are unidentified and they are real. There is now video evidence and pilot testimony out there that has been presented to congress as well. But in true Jungian fashion, the extrovert, living in the shadow archetypal lover, is never satisfied, and so the conspiracy theories continue to fly. The hard truth is that you will never know anything about this by studying the physical evidence. Knowing for yourself is the only way. Nobody can have a press conference and reveal to you a truth that lies buried deep within yourself. And that is the ultimate truth of the phenomenon.

There is no cultural immunity to this gradual degradation of the truth. We can see that it happens in Native American cultures as well. Throughout the world there have always been temple complexes where initiations were performed. Often the mythology of the founding of these structures has to do with a meteor that fell to earth in that spot, or some other paranormal event that occurs on that spot; something that makes this spot the center of the world. This is how I came to understand that Skinwalker Ranch is such a place.

I was listening to an interview with the groundskeeper at Skinwalker Ranch. He talked about seeing a big ball of brilliant white light that came up out of the ground. Such displays would have caught the attention of native people. In examining some of the glyphs carved into the rocks in the area around the ranch, it was clearly known by the native population that this was a place of initiation. There is one glyph in particular that is very telling. It is referred to as the "Santa Claus" glyph because it depicts what appears to be nine reindeer. The glyph is located in the Nine Mile Canyon south of Skinwalker Ranch. The scene truly depicts the nine months of gestation in transformation. It starts with a couple of beings, one is holding the harvest moon in his hand next to him is a large reindeer, the next one is a bit smaller, after that is a small child reindeer. From that point on the reindeer get bigger with more mature horns. Above them are depictions of the new moon and an eclipse of the moon or blood moon. Relating the cycle of birth and death with the monthly phases of the moon. It's a representation of death and rebirth within a single lifetime.

Despite knowing this, the area degraded in the minds of the natives as being something to do with the skin-walker. It became in their minds the stomping ground of an evil shape-shifting creature. Just as the succubus is to us today. This is why Skinwalker Ranch makes no sense to us. We look at it through an anthropomorphic lens clouded by our archetypal shadows. So, we visit the ranch and complain about the crazy things that happen there, and the paranormal events that follow us home from there. I recently saw that the History Channel is putting together a show about Skinwalker Ranch. The intended purpose of this ranch is as a place of initiation. The show will be unproductive. The people involved in this will begin to have a great deal of difficulty. Difficulty that could result in severe injury or death. This is the reason the phenomenon follows you home from the ranch.

If you are there as a seeker, the phenomenon recognizes you as such, and will seek to initiate you. This is where you end up without someone who doesn't understand what is happening. I think the phenomenon is aware of this but it also understands that with a flow of people coming through it's only a matter of time before someone gets it.

Where there are misunderstandings in sacred places there are also misunderstandings in texts. In her book, *The Lost Art of Scripture: Rescuing the Sacred Texts*, Karen Armstrong addresses societal inequities. She is clearly very well-educated about the mythology and history of scripture but I have to disagree with some of her finer points.

She addresses inequity when she describes the story of Adam and Eve. She, at one point, correctly describes scripture as a lesson in psychology but states that the story of Adam and Eve and their knowledge of good and evil was an acknowledgment of the inequities that exist in an agrarian civilization; which depends on the oppression of 90% of the population. This allowed the other 10% to advance science and religion. It was a means to an end. I agree, but I also disagree. I agree that the story of Adam and Eve is a description of the fracturing of the human psyche when it is ruled by desire. So, when it is observed that there are inequities throughout history, it does relate to this story insofar as what those inequities represent; the physical manifestation of the fractured human psyche playing out in the pages of history. There has never had to be inequity. We could have evolved to this point while maintaining equity. None of that inequity had to happen.

Karen Armstrong, in her book, describes ancient scribal schools. In these schools, pupils revered their teachers as living gods. The pupils were subjected to grueling activities such as memorizing old religious texts. It was the job of these scribes to update and revise religious texts as well. She implies that the grueling exercises and strict schooling stifled creativity, but I see this differently. I think this is simply an example of a mystery school. In memorizing texts, the students were being taught to cultivate attention and to disregard hardships; leading to a disciplined mind and, eventually, a knowing of the truth through an initiation into the mysteries.

These types of activities noted by Karen Armstrong have always served another purpose that is in keeping with the title of this chapter, and can be seen concerning the mythology of Apollo in ancient Greece. Apollo was the god of the nine muses. The nine muses were the children of Zeus and Mnemosyne whose name means "memory." The nine muses were concerned with music, poetry, history, dancing, astronomy, etc. Apollo was also the god that would steward young boys into manhood. There was an understanding in Greece that a boy moving from boyhood into manhood had to be well-equipped with a vast amount of knowledge on a variety of topics. It was in this knowledge of astronomy, science, poetry, and history that enabled him to interpret the mysteries correctly later in life. He could then take that core knowledge and merge it with the truth learned in the mysteries, and begin applying it to his own work later in life; leading to advancements in science for the betterment of the human race. Without that core knowledge taught to him correctly he would languish and grossly misinterpret the mysteries as we do today. This is why so many people misinterpret the events at Skinwalker Ranch and anything to do with the phenomenon. It's not that we have allowed education to languish, it's that education is something that, for a long time, was only available to the elite. It needs to be more available. College should be available to everyone. Today there doesn't need to be a huge expense associated with education. We can record professors' lessons and put them on YouTube for everyone. That doesn't cost anything. The lessons are being taught anyway so put them up on YouTube. It's very simple. If one insists upon hoarding knowledge, the question has to be asked, "To who's benefit are we keeping knowledge from one another?"

I've been looking at all of this very closely, I've read quite a bit, spoken to experiencers, and I feel like I have learned quite a bit about it. I can see the common threads. Experiencers tend to be people who have cultivated a wholeness within the psyche to some degree. They tend to be individuals with high functioning brains. They can multitask with ease while keeping a healthy positive outlook. They don't view the world the way others do and it is the high functioning wholeness of the psyche that allows them to do this. Onlookers view these people as having an easy life. They're pushovers because they're kind. They don't have easier lives, but their outlook on life affords them the ability to do things that others have to be dragged into kicking and screaming.

Robert Moore said that it's dangerous to have people who lead others through a process that they cannot control and do not understand. There are some aspects of this transformation that cannot be initiated by us as humans; we just can't do it. These are the dangers of cults because they attempt to do this. *The Vow* is a perfect example of the dangers of cults. There were some good mental techniques and exercises there but there was also something very bad going on there. Because that bad part was so bad, people dismiss the entire philosophy.

All I will ever do is dispense advice. I will never start a cult or an organization of any kind. I will steer seekers toward books they need. Even within Jungian psychology there is a lot of misunderstanding. I stated earlier in the book that Jung did not understand the contents of the archetypal structures and this is true. I've come across Jung followers doing shadow work that they misinterpret as a result. I can tell you when I was doing the bulk of this mental work I had no dreams. When the mental work was finished is when I began to feel depressed and started having vivid dreams and experiences. Some of these followers misinterpret the symbolism they are seeing as a result. They may see a lion or a jaguar in their dreams and interpret this as representing their shadow archetypal structure. But these are symbols of the transformation itself. I was shown dead beetles for instance. The symbolism of these creatures is that of death and resurrection. I worry that when people see these symbols and misinterpret them they start to tweak themselves; doing things that are unnecessary; pushing them out of the process. When you see these types of symbols in dreams this is where you let go. You simply maintain and let go. All of this misunderstanding is what accounts for such varied experience with all of this. In the past few chapters I have hopefully given you enough that you can recognize this death and resurrection mythology and not get it confused with archetypal structures. The fact is that the closer you are to center the more you will have dreams and vivid experiences. The transformation takes place from the center.

I didn't immediately understand what accounts for the varied experiences with this. I had been studying religions all over the world in a way I never had before. Throughout human history, I was seeing all kinds of ritual nonsense like animal sacrifice, altars, psychedelic drug abuse; and even human sacrifice in South America. What is all that? I had been through something which led me to believe that all of those things are nonsense. In fact, I had the feeling that most ritual was just nonsense and you don't need any of it. Why so much varied experience? I began to wonder if perhaps my initiation had not finished. Maybe I was a failed initiate because I didn't understand the need for any of this. Was I misinterpreting this or were they? I got my answers after thinking about it for some time but the answer was fairly complex.

I woke up lying in bed one night after I was pondering all of that, as a very tall, thin, all-white, being in a fitted black uniform came through my bedroom ceiling riding something that looked like a space motorcycle. He actually looked like Jack Skellington from the *Nightmare Before Christmas.* The ceiling and roof were gone and I could see the night sky. I could see a larger craft above the house from which he was descending. As he descended, the device he was riding disappeared beneath my bed as he stretched out his legs and lay next to me. He turned his head and looked at me. His head was large and round. I could see his skin was finely ridged like a vinyl record and he was wearing big, dark, black glasses. I asked him; "Why have you been helping me?" He said, "Because we heard calls for assistance. We are pleased that you have been very insistent, and persistent in this endeavor." I told my brother about this the next day and he told me that he meditated a few nights with the thought of assistance for me; after the first encounter with the blue female in my room. I also remembered that I had meditated and asked for understanding before any of this even started. The following morning, as I woke, I heard that voice that normally would give me the name of some author. It said, "You know these things because you have been through the process."

Following my brothers meditations, he had an experience where he was summoned out of the house much in the same manner I was when I found myself at a gas station in the middle of the night. He ended up on a bicycle path near some construction where there was a sign posted. It read, "SHARED PATH." The night after talking to my brother about this I went to bed with my TV on the NASA channel. I woke up at some point in the night and *Arrival* was playing on the TV. I turned up the volume. It was the point in the movie where all the countries had been working together, but start to go off-line after the visitors tell the human interpreters that they are going to give a weapon or tool to these countries.

The main character is imploring her handlers not to go off-line, and to continue working together. The movie then broke to a commercial. It was a commercial for a Marvel movie. There was a green guy that said, "It's time to claim our rightful place in the universe." I understood then that we are all on the path. Some farther ahead than others, but we are all on it. In looking back on this experience, where I caught this section of the movie on TV in the middle of the night, I can see this need for power over others through the control of technology is the manifestation of the archetypal shadow magician that plays out around us and was pointed out in this particular scene.

A bit later there is a foreign general who views this gift of a weapon as unacceptable and is about to try to destroy the visitors by attacking them. The main character, a scientist, then decides she is going to change this generals mind by displaying for him the archetypal energy of the magician in its fullness. She tells him something she should not have known, something that was known only to him; completely shutting down his archetypal shadow magician energy with the archetype of the magician in its fullness. She speaks to him the dying words of his wife which he had never shared with anyone. This experience becomes a synchronicity for the general and an initiatory phase of his life.

It left me with the impression that perhaps there were people that had not completed the process as I had, they didn't know they hadn't completed it, but they need to know that, and so I began to look into this. It became pretty clear to me that I was not misinterpreting things and that I had actually completed the transformation process.

I began to understand what my life of experience was telling me. My life experiences were initiatory as well. I could see clearly that there were different phases in my life where I experienced things that allowed me to shift direction; integrating the archetypal energies in their fullness. This allowed me to move forward. We collectively also have experiences that can perform the function of integrating archetypal energies. Moore and Gillette write the following about this type of experience in their book *The Magician Within*:

> *If a man comes upon an initiatory phase of his life, perhaps a mid-life crisis, and he doesn't recognize it as potentially initiatory, he can end up less of a man than he was to begin with. The crisis can cripple him. If he gets the right guidance during this crisis, he can become much larger than before. But to accomplish this he must die to certain aspects of himself. If he is unwilling to let those aspects go, he reduces himself-by rigidifying the old myths of his life, and not accepting the new ones offered him by his unconscious.*

I feel like it may be useful here to describe an initiatory phase, because too often I think we fail to recognize them.

They are not always big obvious life changing events. Sometimes they're very subtle. It could be as simple as a small moment of reflection at the end of a long day or something someone says that happens to grab you a certain way. Any moment of reflection is potentially initiatory. It can be a small moment when you begin to understand that you had been doing something the wrong way; and from that moment on you tweak this small thing about yourself. I can say in my own life I recognize how these smaller moments of reflection drove my life more than anything else. It was in recognizing this that I was able to be much harder on myself than anyone else could ever be. I would reflect on small things about myself all the time and I was constantly adjusting myself as a result. I had some ideal in my head of the way I should be along with the qualities I should possess. I now recognize those qualities as the archetypes operating in their fullness. I was constantly checking myself. I was always very honest with myself.

Because of the ability to be honest with myself, I became acquainted with myself. I was able to easily tell if people around me were perceiving me incorrectly or if I really was what I was perceived to be. This is how I was able to objectively view myself. I was beginning to see the things I had clearly done in the psychological material I was reading.

I came across a study that implied this consciousness consists of a primary and secondary awakening or shift in the psyche. I could recognize these shifts in my own experience. The feeling that I had when I was driving and I could suddenly "feel" everything around me; would be an example of the primary shift. The feeling slowly subsided. I kept going and reached a secondary shift; a more stable state that in some religions is known as the blowing out; where the entire personality of the person dissolves. There are perhaps people who think the very temporary state is it; they think that's all there is to it, and they've reached the end, but they haven't. The blowing out, or the secondary more stable shift is the goal. Described by Mabel Collins and William Walker Atkinson as the silence that follows the storm.

I began to understand that there are several things going on here. We have failed initiations which are the result of someone rigidifying the old myth in their lives; doubling down on those old ideas rather than accepting the new lessons place before you. We have almost initiations that didn't quite finish and continue to drag on but, further, I realized that because all of this is so deeply rooted in the human psyche; both political and religious movements use the bells and whistles of transformation combined with fear, hope, and hate to grab people's emotional handles to move them as they see fit. All of this leaves the door wide-open for a gross misinterpretation of everything that's happened to them.

People going through this have vivid dreams, perhaps they hear the inner voice telling them what to do, or they have experiences that seem "paranormal" in nature. The Paranormal Reddit sub is full of these types of experiences. So, when these things do occur without the knowledge of what's going on, you find yourself in a situation where the blind are leading the blind. Nobody knows what's going on, and eventually you end up with a priest throwing holy water around, or you bring in someone to burn sage in your house.

Mabel Collins and William Walker Atkinson don't do much in the way of setting boundaries for the experience except to simply say things like, "gaze always on the light" or, "don't look down." What is essentially happening within the initiation is that there is a very powerful magnifying mirror placed before the psyche. It will reflect back to you every flaw and imperfection magnified larger than life and with terrifying intensity. It is, I believe, for this reason that some individuals stop the process right there. They may falsely believe they are haunted by demons in the traditional ignorant sense. Or they may think that all of this is magic that they themselves manifest and control. They see their own psyche being reflected back to them; leading them to believe that they somehow "control the gods" or "spirits." Due to their misunderstandings and false beliefs, the initiation turns into a carnival funhouse; a maze of mirrors from which they may be unable to escape. They begin to inflate these flaws within themselves and begin to falsely believe that they somehow are in control. Robert Moore describes this as "magician inflation."

A perfect, public, and tragic example of this is Aleister Crowley. He was a famous occultist that engaged in all kinds of vile excesses and weirdness. He wrote books on the subject and was unfortunately very influential. When the initiation fails and gradually fades due to this type of inflation, the initiate is left wanting more. The initiate becomes addicted to their larger-than-life-flaws that they have explored, indulged and enjoyed fully under magnification; rather than killing them out. Drug use will eventually become the only way to keep the process going; morphing into a physical outward manifestation of self-destruction; rather than inwardly as necessary. For this reason, Aleister Crowley died a failed initiate and a heroin addict.

No doubt, he did come very close in the beginning because it is apparent he knew something about it. But he unfortunately didn't know enough. With a character like Crowley as the main temple priest in town it is easy to see that things will begin to degrade rather quickly. This is quite possibly what happened in Teotihuacan. At the Temple of the Feathered Serpent, there is some archeological evidence that the temple was partially destroyed just 100 years after its construction. I get the impression that perhaps there was some Crowley-esque character in there that was violently overthrown. Robert Moore says the following about this type of magician inflation in *Facing the Dragon*:

> *It would be the same thing with the true priest, or true clergyman, anyone who can touch the god energy, the numinous, and because of their spiritual practice and wisdom, not be seduced or destroyed by it. When you touch the numinous without the wisdom to regulate the*

grandiosity, it blows you up like the cartoons of the person who cannot get off the air-hose, so they inflate like a big balloon and float away.

Getting trapped in the initiation process is not uncommon. Crowley was there his entire life and created a religion based on it. Unfortunately, this means his followers take the same bad lifelong trip he did. I believe H.P. Lovecraft is possibly another person who may have gotten trapped in the process. Not everyone that gets trapped in the process has the bad trip. An example of this is Whitley Strieber, who engaged in none of the detestable things Crowley did.

Strieber, instead, sought to understand what was happening to him. He spent more than 30 years doing exactly that, and in his latest book *A New World*; it's clear he has an understanding of what it's all about. He asked Anne, his wife who had passed, to give him direction that would give aim to the rest of his life:

> *This is when she said, "Enlightenment is what happens when there is nothing left of us but love." Live that, and the visitors will cease to be demons in your view and become angels. As is said in the film **Jacobs Ladder**, "The only thing that burns in hell is the part of you that won't let go of your life: your memories, your attachments. They burn them away, but they're not punishing you, they're freeing your soul. If you're frightened of dying and you're holding on, you'll see devils tearing*

your life away. If you've made your peace, then the devils are really angels freeing you from the earth."

Near the end of the book he goes on to say:

When you embrace this ambiguity as yourself, you discover the abiding peace the Hindus call **shanti**. *It makes no sense. It reconciles nothing. And yet everything within you, all the fears, the angers, the hatreds, the lusts, the disappointments, the ambitions, all that lies within the scope of your life, comes to rest, and you know that you have found your heart.*

It is what Anne meant when she said, "Enlightenment is what happens when there is nothing left of us but love."

When all that you have been fighting against and for is stripped away, your nakedness that has so frightened you for so long, is soothed by the gauze of the angels.

It's not easy, though. The first step out of oneself and into communion is a very hard one to take. Open, innocent surrender to the enormous presence that underlies reality is never going to be easy, and it is never going to be certain. But it is also a priceless resource, offering a path into greater knowledge, a new science that is more true because it includes more of what is real, philosophical understanding that feeds the mind with the stuff of truth, and limitless expansion of the scope of mankind.

I make these points to explain the varied experiences involved with all of this; but also to explain the dangers, and help readers to understand what Robert Moore describes as the boundaries of sacred space in his book *Archetype of Initiation*. I don't need to do drugs to quiet my mind and connect and neither did Strieber. It is evident in the way I quiet my mind, listen to nothing and everything, think of nothing and yet be aware of everything; and some name will come to me, or some concept to look into. It's exactly what William Walker Atkinson meant when he stated that he was trying to introduce to his readers a group of kindly mental brownies to work for you. If you do need drugs to do this; you invite trouble. In doing so there is no way of telling what kind of information you may receive. Perhaps this was the warning of Homer who wrote of true dreams passing to you through the gates of polished horn in the underworld; whereas, false dreams pass through the gates of ivory.

Mabel Collins, I believe, put her finger squarely on this point. At one point in her life, Mabel Collins was known as a medium and would conduct seances. She later condemned this type of activity for exactly the above reason. It can be misleading and therefore dangerous. Dangerous because it involves ambition. When one engages in activities for one's self it becomes something completely different than being led there by the forces that be. She understood at some point in her life that she was on the same path as Crowley and corrected herself. She understood that she was having experiences not necessarily because she was a "medium" but perhaps because she was trapped in the process. I feel I always pretty much understood that I didn't control this process in myself. I knew I was being shown what I needed to see. I instead continue to work on concentration, attention, mindfulness, and meditation. I'll let consciousness show me what it will; and I will do what I can with that; without forcing anything; and without selfish intent. Always remember the boundaries.

I would also like to add that I've thought this out very carefully. In keeping with Jung's definition of an introvert and extrovert while also coupling that with Mabel Collins' definition of ambition, it is easy to see how things can go wrong. We can see ritual sacrifice and drug abuse as belonging to the extrovert who is seeking action and sensation exterior to themselves. While the true introvert knows the only way to affect anything exterior to yourself is through the interior. So, we can put these types of exterior actions in the category of ambition. It is in this same way we can see how the teachings in scripture become twisted.

In Islam, we see the idea of Jihad as an all-out physical war with spiritual roots, but it's true interpretation is the same inner battle that is described in the Bhagavad Gita, the Book of Revelation, and can be seen in the Temple of the Warriors in Chichen Itza. We can see how at some point in the past, some person who had been through transformation, might give themselves to a ritual sacrifice in order to attempt to effect some change from the other side for the greater good of his people; knowing that there is no such thing as death. But this could be misunderstood over time resulting in the ritual murder of hundreds in a single day. In their book, *The Magician Within,* Robert Moore and Douglas Gillette have the following to say about these types of superstitions and beliefs.

> *In occult communities, the adepts are usually as undercooked as their counterparts in the established religions. Though purportedly more appreciative of sacred space and time, its boundaries, and the mystique of ritual leadership, the unfortunate fact is that many occult leaders are in a "magician inflation." They naively believe that they have "mastered" the spirits. Their inflation disqualifies them for the serious and risky task of stewarding others through sacred reality.*
>
> *The casualties of minority religions, charismatic Christian movements, even the assertiveness-training workshops are legion. So many have been hurt rather than helped because there is a disastrous dearth of mature ritual elders in our society. People seeking self-transforming, liminal experiences encounter only liminoid ones. And when a would-be adept leads seekers through processes he cannot control, does not understand, and therefore cannot steward, the seekers often end up under- or overcooked. Rather than freeing the*

> *souls caught in various forms of psychopathology, these "spiritual leaders" deprive people of healing (and often their earthly goods as well).*

What is meant in the above by *liminal* and *liminoid* experiences is exactly what I have been talking about in terms of using drugs or alcohol to induce experiences. Liminal experiences are truly self-transforming experiences. Liminoid experiences can feel the same but it's a temporary experience and non-transformative. An example of this liminoid experience is the feeling one may get at a rock concert; or a drug induced experience. It may even be the high we feel in a religious experience. They feel good, but they're not transformative. The reason that many of these liminoid experiences cannot be transformative is because they have roots in euphoric sensation or ambition and are completely dependent on that, therefore these experiences belong to the extrovert. If you do anything in the name of religion that has its roots in extroversion, you will find that you end up empty handed in the end. I recently started watching a series called *Vow*, about a cult, that had some very good mental practices; but they also practiced branding and various forms of sexual abuse. We can't forget that transformation is all about mastery of the inner self. This is not to say that someone can't have a truly transformative experience through drug use, but I think in doing so you are walking the sharpest of razor-thin lines and is completely dependent on the degree to which you are an introvert or extrovert.

All too often when one begins to experience what could be a truly transformative experience, they will seek to deaden that pain with alcohol, drugs, or some other distraction. Distraction is a transmutation of the inner pain into a physical and outward expression which will halt a liminal experience in its tracks. Many outward distractions will have this effect. We see it in the midlife crisis where someone may busy themselves with a new car or house. It's the reason there's so much "stuff" for sale everywhere, the more sparkly and outrageous the distraction, the better. I recently entered a department store and was flabbergasted by all the junk. What immediately occurred to me was the wasted effort and man-hours that were put into creating all this junk that, within a year, will likely find its way to a landfill.

I can see all the signs in our society that a shift is upon us. Depression around the holidays is a known and accepted phenomena in the profession of psychology; they call it seasonal affective disorder. Suicides increase around this time of year. Fertility rates are falling. Divorce rates are skyrocketing. The numbers of people attending church has been steadily collapsing. Mental illness is on the rise. To the untrained eye it would seem things are "going to hell" as I heard someone state the other day. I, however, can see the eternal nature of all of these things and they point to a shift on the horizon. What that shift is remains to be seen. I have to say that I am in the Moore camp on this one.

As I wrote earlier, there are initiatory phases that can occur on a massive scale and we are heading into just such an experience. These initiatory phases are generated by us and they build up over time. In this experience there will be those that double down on their rigid views, and there will be others that grow from it; I believe this is what is causing so much polarization all over the world; too many people are doubling down.

The problem with these types of massive initiatory cycles is that they hold this large magnifying glass up to the psyche; just as they would for the individual. Everything is about balance. When you leave people behind in ignorance and poverty, you create a bubble of development that will eventually be popped by those you left behind. If you can't do it smarter and work together, you don't move forward. This is what is at the heart of every revolution that has ever been fought. It is a part of the natural balance of the evolution of the universe. This is why the worldwide polarization we see today is psychologically dangerous.

I think we are all familiar with the scene in a movie where some character meets their nemesis. One of them takes the high road and refuses to fight. This is actually the ideal situation in conflicts big and small; the reason being a psychological one. When someone refuses to hold that evil archetypal energy for you they force you to then look at yourself. It is a test. It transforms a liminoid experience into a liminal one and becomes truly transformative. It causes the parties to realize they don't need to hate each other and begins a thought process to analyze what all of this hate was really about. As with all of these types of initiatory experiences, there are dangers just as there are with the individual. You can grow and learn or you can double down on your old beliefs. Moore writes the following in *Facing the Dragon*:

> *When someone refuses to carry your projections, it creates a psychological crisis for you. Your displacement mechanisms no longer help you regulate your own grandiosity, so your ego must look for another way to avoid the truth.*
>
> *What can you do about this kind of situation? Are we condemned to keep on acting out like this? Does it have to be this way? No, I don't believe that for a minute, but if I were Jimmy the Greek, and you asked me what the odds were that humans will keep this up until they self- destruct, I would have to say the odds are pretty good.*
>
> *Suppose for example that you had to make that bet. Suppose there was a spaceship that could take you somewhere else, like the star Sirius, and let you escape from this world. Would you take the odds that the human species will keep on going the way it has in the past and keep escalating violence until it destroys human civilization? Or would you gamble that people will suddenly start learning just before it's too late and take*

dramatic action toward awareness and responsible behavior? Personally, I must be a gambler. I think there is at least a chance that we as a species can beat the odds against us, but only if we all do our part in facing the dragon of grandiosity.

I believe the reason I had to write this book is complex and will serve many different purposes. This is for all of us. In the years to come, the phenomenon will be making itself seen and heard on a scale that we have not witnessed before. Encounters with our military will continue and intensify. Because of the nature of military life it makes service members ripe for this type of experience. A lifestyle that almost forces you to turn your gaze inward. This book, and many others by different authors, will serve as resources for people seeking answers, and can serve as a simple starting point.

I also think one of the reasons I wrote this book is to serve as an alarm bell and a way forward, because we have strayed too far from the path. We have these initiatory cycles as a race to get us back on track. Pandemics will have that effect as well. The Black Death plague that swept across Europe killing half the population over a decade beginning in 1347 aligns with the beginning of the Renaissance. It was a plague that the father of the Renaissance, Francesco Petrarca, lived through before his death in 1374. As I watch the news coverage about the coronavirus and the social unrest, I can see clearly how far we have to go. Some coverage is centered on how this will affect the economy, who's going to pay for it? When I see this coverage it disappoints me because what I hear is, "how will this virus effect our shadow magician and how can we keep the shadow magician alive?" I hear the "experts" speak about temporarily suspending economic constructs like mortgage and rent payments or taxes to lessen the economic burden. I hear others talking about payments to people out of work.

I know better. I learned in dropping everything and going out to sea that if there were things I could "temporarily suspend" then they weren't things I needed anyway; at all. My need for them existed only in my own mind. And so must we all do with these lower aspects of ourselves.

Greed manifests itself as our economy, it decides our worth as workers and as human beings. It decides if we are worthy of medical care; if we are worthy to live or if we must die. It decides if we are worthy of an education or only good enough to live in ignorance and abject poverty. It decides if we dispose of toxins in a safe way or if we dump them in rivers and streams. It decides if we manufacture new kinds of energy sources or we continue to rely on fossil fuels. It decides if we explore the universe or we remain here chained to the earth by the shackles of our undisciplined minds. We are slaves to the archaic concepts of our own minds.

As the Bhagavad Gita tells us. These ideas of greed and the shadow psyche are finite things of the moment and we must let them die rather than double down on these antiquated ideas. Of course health care is for everyone… Something very important that I learned and one of the last things that carried me over the top on this is that if aid is needed then aid should be given. If someone is in need, it is not my place to judge or to withhold aid based on my own personal judgment. This is what I meant earlier in the book when I wrote of a return to innocence and being a pushover. If aid is needed, it is not my place to ask why. It is not my place to pass judgment and decide I will withhold aid because I believe this person to be lazy. If aid is needed then aid should be given. Period. Whether it's a beggar asking for change, or a national health care plan; the result should always be an act of love that is unconditional. Anything else flies in the face of the natural laws that govern the universe. This is what we learn in situations like this current pandemic. I hate our current way of life. I hate that I own these properties and have had to evict people. I don't even want to participate in things like that anymore. I really struggle with surviving in this world. What am I going to do for a living? Anything I do seems like a lie; some way to earn money covered in blood. If I had my way, we would give all that up tomorrow. We would go into the previously poor communities, we would focus on education in those communities, fixing their housing, teaching them psychology and other skills; because we can't move forward if we don't have everyone onboard.

It's strange how death is viewed by humans. To think that death is final. To think that you only get one shot at happiness. Yet, in such a mindset we deny each other anything we can. In realizing my own immortality and knowing there is no such thing as death, life suddenly isn't so cheap anymore. To me it never did seem cheap and

I never really understood this mentality we have that there are people who can be viewed as expendable. You would think the opposite would be true. Such has always been the great burden of the initiated. Like Atlas, we carry the weight of the world on our backs attempting to drive the race of man onward and upward with our shepherding tools in hand. Walking a fine line between acceptance, toleration, and ill will; lest the flock turn and declare us heretics, burn us at the steak, or nail us to a cross.

Spinoza wrote the following on the topic:

One who seeks the true causes of miracles, and is eager, like an educated man, to understand natural things, not to wonder at them, like a fool, is generally considered and denounced as an impious heretic by those whom the people honor as interpreters of nature and the Gods. For they know that if ignorance is taken away, then the foolish wonder, the only means they have of arguing and defending their authority is taken away.

Along the same vein, I would like to end this thought with two quotes that I have taken from Robert Moore's book, *Facing the Dragon: Confronting Personal and Spiritual Grandiosity*, where Robert Moore conveys the idea that one cannot simply take a back seat or a passive role in their development.

Working as both a Jungian psychoanalyst and spiritual theologian, my recent research has focused on the powerful, grandiose "god-energies" that burn fiercely in the heart of every human being. When we face these energies consciously in faith and with authentic respect, they reflect in us the numinous, creative, and transformative power of the divine presence. But when the human ego engages in a pretentious "unknowing" of the reality and significance of this presence, the result is existential idolatry and malignant narcissism.

Existential denial of the divine presence creates a demonic alchemy that hijacks the sacred energies of the soul and twists them into destructive powers of hideous strength, powers of aggressive nonbeing that reveal themselves as addiction, racism, sexism, homophobia, all forms of political oppression, ritual violence and war, and the ecological destruction of our planet. These same grandiose energies fuel both corporate greed and religious fundamentalism.

Robert Moore then goes on to quote Carl Jung:

Everything now depends on man: immense power of destruction is given into his hand, and the question is whether he can resist the will to use it, and can temper his will with the spirit of love and wisdom. He will hardly be capable of doing so on his own unaided resources. He needs the help of an "advocate" in heaven.... The only thing that really matters now is whether man can climb up to a higher moral level, to a higher plane of consciousness, in order to be equal to the superhuman powers which the fallen angels have played into his hands.

Hopefully, you can now understand the massive dilemma we find ourselves in here in the United States. I believe what we call the American Experiment is over. Some may disagree depending on who wins the upcoming presidential election but I hope that by this point in the book it would be obvious that it doesn't matter who wins. We live in a country of extroverts and we have for a long time. If you can get someone to vote against their own best interests, which seems to have become much easier in recent years, then you can control them. We have never in our society seen the center of any issue. We have crazy ideas about what is extreme. Someone who votes against their own best interests is an extrovert. They are fluctuating between the two poles, the two extremes of externalized warrior energy; the sadist and the masochist. They are engaging in self-harm or harm to others. They aren't even aware of the self-harm they do because the extrovert cannot see themselves. Health care for all benefits everyone, yet it is viewed as an extremist idea. In calling for health care for all you know it benefits yourself and others. It is neither the sadist nor masochist. It is a universal centrist position. The center looks extreme to the sadist or masochist on either pole because it's a long way from where they are. No matter who wins the election, these problems within the American psyche don't just go away. The latest thinking in the US concerning the pandemic is herd immunity. Hurd immunity is an impossibility because we have seen people reinfected just four months after having contracted it the first time. That will also be the best a vaccine can do. To take this approach ultimately means that you hold the position that no life matters. As an extrovert, you can't isolate or practice social distancing. So, you're saying no lives matter. This is a very dangerous place to be.

To hold this position means that you refuse to participate in creation as Adam does in Genesis. When God created, he brought his creations to Adam to name them. To say that no life matters means you think so little of creation that the only name you have is death. It means that you are fundamentally unfit for survival at this current level. Eve and even Adam himself are called death in this world of nihilistic extroversion.

Any way you toss this, there are many decades of very harsh realities and hard lessons headed our way, but there is a right way and a wrong way to do this. The wrong ways are many, but there is only one right way. In the wrong ways we abdicate our right to participate in creation, in the right way we become creation.

We have to take the high ground with leaders that can speak to the creative subconscious. In past moments of crisis we have always had leaders like this. This crisis cuts much deeper than any crisis we have faced before because it cuts deep through the soul.

I, unlike many people, have seen where the evolution of man goes. We see it in our progenitors. The answer is that we care for each other, but in the meantime we make a very hard push towards mechanizing every process. Such a hard push that we begin rationing. We become creation by envisioning new ways to be human. Mechanization to the point that a machine will cultivate seeds from an apple and give us more apples without any human intervention in between; not even in the repair of the mechanized process. Seeds and blocks of metal go into a factory and at the other end there are cans of soup and raw vegetables. The blocks of metal and seeds will be derived similarly. Mined by mechanized processes. Mined in landfills even. For anyone that doubts this type of mechanization can be accomplished I would encourage you to look at the robots put together by Boston Dynamics, Asimo, Da Vinci, and So Fi, and tell me we can't mechanize any process. Every bit of mechanization doesn't have to walk like a person, but it can.

I want to be clear here because my decision to write this book is not one that I took lightly. I really struggled very deeply with it. I have received blowback from both sides of this issue. From those that know this is the truth and think it should be kept behind closed doors, and those that live in delusion. I know that, initially, this book will not be well received and I'm going to be dismissed as an idiot or worse, an all-out liar or profiteer, but the subject of this book is a very serious one, and this is a discussion that needs to happen; uncomfortable as it may be. In my indecision, I weighed the options very carefully. I decided to meditate on this one night because I couldn't readily find the answer. I was so deeply torn, but I also wasn't sure that just outwardly stating the truth of this was the right way. It was so incredibly troubling that I had tears rolling down my cheeks as I meditated. In my session, I asked for a sign if I was supposed to write this book documenting my own experiences then drifted off to sleep.

I got my answer that night. I awoke with the usual heaviness. I could see clearly I was in my dark bedroom. The only light was from large illuminated spots on my walls and ceiling. Within the glowing spots there was writing of some kind. In the darkened areas of my room I could see astral spiders. Just on a side note: I had never seen astral spiders before but they are quite impressive, a spider the size of a small dog crawling around on your ceiling is really something. With that I knew what I had to do; which should be evident in the fact that you're reading this. The writing was on the wall in a web that was spun by the weavers of destiny.

As I drove to work the next morning thinking about this; I put on random music from YouTube. I started with "Heaven" by Angels and Airwaves as I thought about the events of the previous night. The next song was One Republic's *"Secrets."* I began to cry as I listened to the words because I knew it was for me. I started to think that I may not be allowed to publish this. What if the powers that be at work tell me I can't publish this; I would have to do it anyway, and that could ruin me. I knew if I did, I would have to leave the Navy. I would have to promote the book and it wouldn't be conducive to being an active-duty member of the military. I would have to quit with just four years left until retirement. I would get nothing in terms of benefits for my 16 years of service. Not to mention people would attack me for this; even hate me for it. The next song that played was "Nearer My God to Thee." I had to compose myself in the parking lot before I went in to work.

And so I wrote you this little book out of my unconditional love for mankind; to be etched in the timeline of the human experience as a testament to a brutally painful truth; to the difficult journey we all must take; to the beauty of what we must become; and to the strength and resiliency of the human race.

Its significance may never be realized in my time here, but this is my contribution to mankind. The influence of this book and its ideas will be far-reaching. If you have come across it in a seemingly paranormal way, I want you to understand you have a role to play in the future of the race and you must accept the work placed before you. Whether that works is as a future artist, a physicist, an author, a movie producer, or a world leader, you will, or are going to, fulfill an influential role. Just like Francesco Petrarca, Leonardo Da Vinci, Plutarch, Plato, Marcus Aurelius, and many others, it is up to us to define the movement. To inspire and teach through our works that speak to the subconscious and assist others in constituting wholeness in the psyche.

I opted not to explain everything perhaps as fully as one might hope, but I said in the beginning of this book that I didn't really aim to do that. I have been asked by many people if I do readings and what the future holds since I possess mental abilities above and beyond others; my answer is very simple.

Most people have no idea they can know their own future; it's so easy anyone can do this. It will only work if you are capable of brutal honesty which, by the state of affairs in the world currently, I think we are all capable of that kind of brutal honesty necessary for this exercise. We impose this brutal honesty on each other every day; so I know it will be very easy. All you have to do is stand in front of a mirror, tell me what you see in that figure staring back at you. Your future will be a manifestation of that which resides within yourself.

Many people say this but don't clearly convey what that really means. It means, in my own case, I had to do very little research for this book. The ideas I included in this book were placed in my lap. A path to publishing this book was placed in my lap in the same manner. I had to do very little work to those ends. Writing this book was very easy because it was supposed to happen.

I now know how simple the universe actually is. In all of its seemingly infinite complexity of matter, space, and time there are only two constants. One is a force and the other is a physical manifestation of that force. The force binds everything it manifests. The nature of this force lends itself naturally to stability; and an absence of chaos. It is the absence of chaos that allows order to take hold within the universe. The singular force is quantifiable and can be used as an infinite power source if you can harness it. Once you can harness this force, the possibilities are endless. It is only when a race harnesses this force that they become capable of greatness. Constructing craft that take you anywhere as fast as you want to get there. Only when we know the force and understand its manifestations will we be capable of leaving this place. You don't need to explore the farthest reaches of space to find answers to anything; all of the answers are right here; inside us, as the Emerald Tablet states:

The father of all perfection in the whole world is here. Its force or power is entire if it be converted into earth.

Separate thou the earth from the fire, the subtle from the gross sweetly with great industry. It ascends from the Earth to the heaven & again it descends to the Earth & receives the force of things superior and inferior.

By this means you shall have the glory of the whole world & thereby all obscurity shall fly from you.

Its force is above all force, for it vanquishes every subtle thing & penetrates every solid thing.

So was the world created.

The force is love; and it binds all that it manifests as life. Life and love are the only two constants in this vast expansive universe of ours.

This may sound romantically poetic but I assure you it's so much more than that. After I had come to this conclusion, I encountered a paragraph in one of William Walker Atkinson books where he says the same. It's truth. To experience the universe in this way is to experience a liberation unlike anything you could ever imagine. It's the responsibility of each and every one of us to find it, and it is what is meant in those famous words known to everybody in the UFO community concerning what it's all about: "A new world, if you can take it." It is our task to take it. In *Westworld,* Anthony Hopkins character talks to one of the other characters about how in the beginning of this you discover the universe is not what you hoped it would be; and this is true, in the beginning it's unsettling and uncomfortable. In the end you discover that the universe is not what you hoped it would be because it is so much more than you could have ever imagined.

I've given you enough that you can begin to research further on your own just as I have. That way you don't need to take my word for it. It's all out there, and you can find it for yourselves; just as I have. I have decided to leave the military, as I feel I can be more useful elsewhere. I feel it would be much more useful for me to be out there talking about what I've learned and teaching others. The preponderance of evidence, throughout history, of the things I have written about are self-evident; many of the ideas ancient cultures have adhered to begin to make cohesive sense when viewed through the prism of the transformation I have laid out in this book for you.

The criticism I will receive does not bother me in the slightest, because I know I'm correct. To my critics I would say that you can also do this. If you refuse to do it, then your laziness does not give you the right to criticize. This book is about how you can find this. I'm keeping no secrets. I would challenge critics to do this and prove me wrong. As I have read in many ancient sources, the process from start to finish should take anywhere from five to seven years. But that time frame I think depends on what you've already cultivated. It may take you longer or it may take only a single season.

I would liken transformation to the difference between an adult and a child. There are things you did as a child that you no longer do because you outgrew them. Likewise, as an adult you can push yourself far beyond the maturity you currently possess. We don't do this because we don't see a reason to do so but I am here to tell you there is every reason to do so.

Something I have discovered about all of this is that if you've never seen or had any of these experiences, it's because you haven't cultivated the qualities in yourself to make that happen, or you haven't cultivated them to the extent necessary. You need to be at a point, psychologically, that if someone were to slap you or spit in your face, the only emotion you would feel is pity for your aggressor. Pity because you recognize the situation for what it is; someone with an unclean and undisciplined mind. This, like everything, is an evolution; you have to evolve into it.

Until we adopt this as a race, we will be too busy waging war against each other to ever make it happen on a large scale. Perhaps there will be no grand finale for humanity. Maybe this book is just meant for the few that are advancing. I don't know the answer to that but I do know something big is coming. I told my coworkers that there was something very big on the horizon. I could sense it. I knew it would turn our way of life on its head as a corrective measure and I believe that was the current pandemic and the chaos that will result from that. But it's not just the pandemic, there will be more. I have been asked by people who know my experiences what the pandemic is all about. I know that it's no accident, it is by design and we should not fear it. We should embrace and deal with it from a position of love, inner strength, and wisdom. People ask me what will come out of the pandemic and its consequences. After having seen the movie 2010, I simply reply, "Something wonderful." A quote I incorporated in the beginning of this book. I hope the metaphor isn't lost on you.

Jupiter is a gas giant and science believes that gas giants are stars that never got their engines started. At the end of the movie 2010 the monolith that was encountered becomes just one of many that begin pouring out of the planet as the characters flee its orbit. The monoliths start the engine of Jupiter transforming it into a star. The result on earth is that there is no night. Never again does darkness fall on humanity. Forever after we have the eyes to see and the ears to hear.

I am about to reveal something prophetic here about the future. I want to preface this by letting you know right now that I am no prophet. I do not know the future with any degree of certainty. But I do know myself in the way the Temple of Delphi advised. *Know Thyself*, it said to all who entered. In knowing myself and understanding the psychology of transformation I can tell you that Mabel Collins was correct when she wrote that the initiated will "know the hearts of men."

We have a choice to make my friends. The current climate with the pandemic and political polarization has seen to that. The choice is simple: either we care for each other or we don't. There is only one way forward. The way forward may seem dark and uncertain. Racism, hate, fear, and greed must be put away forever because they can only ever end in chaos, destruction, and instability; history has very decidedly shown us that. Investing in each other must become our new currency and economy. There are today great initiated minds among us right now, my friends; some are very public figures. Now is the time to come out of the shadows. I can tell you that the leader of this country in 2024 must be an initiate because in 2021, 2022, and 2023 things will get much worse. After that we'll need someone with the vision to lead us out of the darkness forever by teaching us new ways to be human.

Throughout the course of human history there have been times of renewal brought about by initiatory practices. There were rites of passage from boyhood and girlhood into manhood and womanhood.

It was understood from that point on you no longer are the little baby sucking on your mother's teat. No longer will you be looked after but rather now you will do the looking after. You will care for the others in your community. You will conduct yourself as a proper responsible member of the community and anything short of that will be intolerable. Since we have no such practices today with too many people who never make that pivot, we are about to go through something that will demonstrate why that pivot is necessary. In our culture today there is this opinion that people have some right to their mental illness like the child that insists on their right to cookies and ice cream for dinner. For some reason this is ok. It's ok to be greedy. It's ok to lie and mislead people. It's ok to hate people based on skin color, gender, sexual preference and so on. It's not ok and you have no right to your mental illness.

Now is such a time for the human race. This pivot is expected. No longer will we run this place and each other like the children in *Lord of the Flies*.

Let me be crystal clear. We are under the control of no master. We got ourselves here. As it says in Genesis, it is up to us to decide how we participate in creation. We have built our own prisons and shackled ourselves inside them all by ourselves. We have imprisoned our own minds. There is no grand evil force at work, forcing us into slavery as some may imagine. The natural balance of the universe has ensured that this is not possible. We did that, and I will be happy to debate anyone who thinks otherwise. I will show you a million ways in which it can't happen. For those that still insist there is some higher evil force, my advice would be to take the stoic approach. There's nothing you can do about it, so don't let it control you and it will then have no power over you. This all boils down to the decisions we as individuals make every day all-day long. Think about those individual, personal decisions 24 hours a day, seven days a week.

For those of you that want to hang on to those shackles of slavery you have constructed in your own mind, I would suggest you keep one hand free so you can hold on to your ass as well because it's going to be a bumpy ride. We will have 2021, 2022, and 2023 to show us that. Things will get much worse in ways we can't conceive of today. At the end of that you will see that hanging on will not be worth the trouble. Then in 2024 we can begin to put the world back in order. Hopefully, it will still exist.

I would like to end this with a political thought. Some may say it's not my place to make such a statement because in so doing I may be alienating a certain portion of my readership but I don't care. I'm not here to win a popularity contest, I am here to tell you the truth. I stated earlier in this book that I am a liberal but this is only partially true. Many people believe within truth there is black and white with miles of grey in between. Something I began to understand in my experiences is that there is no grey. Everything is black and white, and any grey that exists only exists as a manifestation of our collective misunderstanding, born from our unclean and undisciplined minds.

The predicament we find ourselves in today is a result of our failure to properly transition our children from childhood psychology to adulthood psychology. In small tribes and villages it was understood that an adult child would be toxic within the greater community. To have an adult that is filled with anger and rage because they refuse to reign in the lower self would destabilize the greater community.

Today, we nurture this type of dangerous psychology. We give it a voice and lend it legitimacy within our political parties. Greed is rewarded and desirable. Integrity is tossed to the wind in a win-at-all-cost mentality. Fear is stoked rather than crushed. All of this leads always to instability and destruction. In today's society we give cookies and ice cream to the screaming angry child while telling them their tantrum is justified and they have a valid point. It's ridiculous. We tolerate this in children and these people grow up to be no better as adults. We allow this type of mental illness to run rampant. We allow adult children to have children, and believe it is up to them as to how they want to raise their children. Then when that out of control adult child beats you up as a result of their uncontrolled rage, we complain bitterly about what a victim we are. In smaller tribes and communities, the entire population raised the children because it was in everyone's best interest. If there was an out-of-control child in such a community, any adult that was around would snuff that out quickly. Don't get me wrong, there was a lot of love and nurturing happening there as well because that too is just as important to the stability of a healthy society.

Psychology is what lies at the heart of the difference between "liberals" and "conservatives." Liberals are not swayed or influenced by the angry hateful rhetoric because they have developed themselves more on the introverted side of the spectrum, while the angry rhetoric mirrors, and therefore reinforces the extroverted extremist conservative. I'm really generalizing here for the purpose of explanation and I'm only doing so to help you understand where you are on the path. Before you get worked up about my seeming endorsement of a political party, I need to tell you that I am an independent because even liberals are not liberal enough for me. They're both wrong because neither one of them has a platform that would manifest the unconditional care we must all have for one another. Neither party, in my opinion, is capable of envisioning new ways to be human, or what it means to be human. The reason I decided to add this here is because if we don't have a clear understanding of the problem we can't fix it. Let's stop pretending like we aren't responsible for each other's well-being regardless of social status, color, sex, or sexual orientation. We are all born naked, and we die the same way, and contrary to popular opinion—very little that happens between actually matters. If we understood what actually matters, and we filled our lives with that sort of substance, the world would look very different than it does.

We could be dwelling in the stars within a generation if we could get ourselves in order. If you can't even relate to your next door neighbor because of the lower emotions you cultivate within yourself, then do not look to the heavens and gaze upon stars, except to know that you have no right to it. If you cannot be your own savior then you cannot be the savior of anyone else so hang your head low in shame and gaze only upon the dirt because this is your home.

There are already those that tell me this book is pointless and will not make a difference, but I will continue to push this message in the face of adversity because I know it matters. My mother came across a short story many years ago and having spent her life as a nurse, I can see why she loved it so much. It was an adapted short story by Loren Eiseley

There's a child walking along a beach that is littered with thousands of starfish that have washed up on shore. The child is picking up starfish one by one and throwing them back into the ocean. A passerby witnesses the child doing this and decides to instill within him a bit of wisdom. The passerby tells the child that his task is useless. There's no point because there are so many starfish that you can't possibly make a difference and therefore it doesn't matter. The child then picks up another starfish and throws it back into the ocean. The child then tells the passerby, "It mattered to that one."

As I write these last couple of sentences, Imagine Dragons' "It's Time" began playing on my laptop as yet another reminder of the need for this book; and the work yet to be done. No matter how difficult things get, know that you have nothing to fear as long as you keep your eyes always on the light of unconditional love. In the words of a wise friend who never gives up on anyone, even as we all give up on each other so easily, "Don't give up, keep going."

Peace be with you, friends.

Now stands my task accomplished, such a work. As not the wrath of Jove, nor fire, nor sword, nor the devouring ages can destroy. Let, when it will, that day, that has no claim but to my mortal body, end the span of my uncertain years. Yet I'll be born, the finer part of me, above the stars, immortal, and my name shall never die.

–Ovid's Metamorphosis.

SELECTED BIBLIOGRAPHY

Armstrong, Karen (2019). *The Lost Art of Scripture: Rescuing the Sacred Texts.* London, UK: The Bodley Head.

Atkinson, William Walker (1906). *A Series of Lessons in Raja Yoga.* Hollister, MO: YOGeBooks.

Atkinson, William Walker (1912). *Mind-Power: The Secret of Mental Magic.* Chicago, IL: Yogi Publication Society

Atkinson, William Walker, Yogi Ramachakara (1912). *The Life Beyond Death.* Chicago, IL: Yogi Publication Society.

Atkinson, William Walker (1910). *The Crucible of Modern Thought.* Hollister, MO: YOGeBooks.

Atkinson, William Walker (1906). *The Science of Psychic Healing - A Sequel to "Hatha Yoga."* Hollister, MO: YOGeBooks.

Atkinson, William Walker, Yogi Ramacharaka (1903). *The Fourteen Lessons in Yogi Philosophy and Oriental Occultism.* Chicago, IL: Yogi Publication Society.

Atkinson, William Walker, Yogi Ramacharaka (1903). *The Hindu-Yogi Science of Breath.* Chicago, IL: Yogi Publication Society.

Atkinson, William Walker, Yogi Ramacharaka (1930). *Bhagavad Gita.* Chicago IL: The Yogi Publication Society.

Collins, Mabel (1919). *Idyll of the White Lotus.* Los Angeles, CA: Theosophical Publishing House.

Collins, Mabel (1885). *Light On The Path.* Los Angeles, CA: Theosophical Publishing House.

Collins, Mabel (2010). *Our Glorious Future.* Whitefish, MO: Kessinger Publishing, LLC

Collins, Mabel (1903). *The Illumined Way: A guide to neophytes, being a sequel to Light On The Path.* Ann Arbor, MI: University of Michigan Library.

Collins, Mabel (1987). *When the Sun Moves Northward: The Way of Initiation.* Wheaton, IL: Theosophical Publishing House.

DeLonge, Tom with Peter Levenda. (2016). Gods, Man, & War: An Official Sekret Machines Investigation of the UFO Phenomenon. New York, NY: Simon & Schuster.

DeLonge, Tom and Heartly A.J. (2017). *Sekret Machines Chasing Shadows.* New York, NY: Simon & Schuster.

Randolph, Beverly Paschal (1871). *Divine Pymander Hermes Mercurius Trismegistus.* Des Planes, IL: Yogi Publication Society.

Fulcanelli, Daniel (1926). *The Mystery of the Cathedrals.* Paris, France (see also, Fulcanelli: Master Alchemist: *Le Mystere des Cathedrales, Esoteric Intrepretation of the Hermetic Symbols of The Great Work*- English version Paperback – January 15, 1984). Koontz, Dean (2017). *Ricochet Joe*. Amazon Original Stories.

Massey, Gerald (1907). *Ancient Egypt: Light of The World*. London, England: T. Fisher UNWIN Adelphi Terrace.

Moore, Robert L. (2001). *The Archetype of Initiation: Sacred Space, Ritual Process, and Personal Transformation*. Bloomington, IN: Xlibris, Corp.

Moore, Robert L. (2003). *Facing the Dragon: Confronting Personal and Spiritual Grandiosity*. Bloomington, IN: Xlibris, Corp.

Moore, Robert L. (2002). *The Magician and the Analyst: The Archetype of the Magus in Occult Spirituality*. Bloomington, IN: Xlibris, Corp.

Moore, Robert L (2003). *Facing the Dragon: Confronting Personal and Spiritual Grandiosity*. Wilmette, IL: Chiron Publications.

Moore, Robert and Douglas Gillette (1993). T*he Magician Within: Accessing the Shaman in the Male Psyche*. New York: William Morrow and Company, Inc.

Moore, Robert and Douglas Gillette (1991). *King Warrior Magician Lover: Rediscovering the Archetypes of the Mature Masculine*. San Francisco, CA: Harpers San Francisco.

Vallee, Jacques (2014). *The Invisible College: What a Group of Scientists Has Discovered about UFO Influence on the Human Race*. San Antonio, TX: Anomalist Books.

Vallee, Jacques (2008). *Confrontations: A Scientist's Search for Alien Contact*. San Antonio, TX: Anomalist Books.

Kelleher, Colm A., Knapp George (2005). *Hunt for the Skinwalker: Science Confronts the Unexplained at a Remote Ranch in Utah*. New York: Paraview Pocket Books.

Nadler, Steven (2001). *Spinoza's Heresy: Immortality and the Jewish Mind*. Oxford, England: Clarendon Press.

Schuré, Édouard (1907). *Jesus, the Last Great Initiate*. New York, NY: Theosophical Publishing Company.

Three Initiates (1904). *Advanced Course in Yogi Philosophy and Oriental Occultism*. Chicago, IL: The Yogi Publication Society Masonic Temple.

Three Initiates (1908). *The Kybalion*. Chicago, IL: The Yogi Publication Society Masonic Temple.

Made in United States
Troutdale, OR
08/18/2024